Planning Without Prices

Planning Without Prices

The Taking Clause as It Relates to Land Use Regulation without Compensation

Edited by
Bernard H. Siegan
University of San Diego
School of Law

Lexington Books
D. C. Heath and Company
Lexington, Massachusetts
Toronto

Library of Congress Cataloging in Publication Data
Main entry under title:

Planning without prices.

Papers of a conference held in San Diego, Calif., Oct. 4–6, 1975, under the joint sponsorship of the Institute for Humane Studies, Menlo Park, and the University of San Diego School of Law.
    Includes index.
    1. Eminent domain—United States—Congresses. 2. Regional planning—Law and legislation—United States—Congresses. 3. Compensation (Law)—United States—Congresses. I. Siegan, Bernard H. II. Institute for Humane Studies. III. San Diego, Calif. University. School of Law.
KF5599.A75P59   343'.73'025   75–26446
ISBN 0–669–00247–x

Published simultaneously in Canada.

Printed in the United States of America.

International Standard Book Number: 0–669–00247–x

Library of Congress Catalog Card Number: 75–26446

Contents

Planning Without Prices

1 Editor's Introduction: The Anomaly of Regulation under the Taking Clause

Bernard H. Siegan

A conference on "The Taking Issue: An Economic Analysis" was held in San Diego, California, on October 4, 5, and 6, 1975, under the joint sponsorship of the Institute for Humane Studies of Menlo Park, California, and the University of San Diego School of Law. Each of the chapters was presented by its author and discussed along with related issues by an invited audience of about fifty people. I served as chairman of the conference.

The conference explored the economics of the taking clause[1] and the costs and consequences of changing its interpretation to meet current challenges and demands. Before turning over the discussion to the authors of the conference papers, I shall examine the judicial framework that surrounds the clause and otherwise probe some of the legal and economic issues its present construction raises. This introduction will augment the ideas expressed by the other authors and enhance the readers' perception of the role and function of land use regulation. It was written in the summer of 1976 and contains some information not available at the time of the conference.

Holmes v. Brandeis on What Constitutes a Taking

The conference was prompted in large measure by the controversy that had erupted in the early 1970s concerning the taking clause. Certain prominent sources had concluded that the existing interpretation of that provision with respect to regulatory legislation hindered achievement of the environmental needs and well-being of the American people. The call went out for a different judicial construction of the taking clause, that is, that in effect it be disregarded largely in the regulation of land use. Lawyers and others supporting this position targeted the decision in *Pennsylvania Coal Co. v. Mahon*,[2] which they blamed for creating what to them was a major legal problem of the day. They said that instead of following the majority opinion of Justice Holmes, the tenor of the times required reversal and replacement by the dissenting opinion of Justice Brandeis.

1

The most publicized expression of this position came from the members of the Task Force on Land Use and Urban Growth,[3] chaired by Laurance S. Rockefeller, and from the authors of *The Taking Issue*,[4] published by the President's Council on Environmental Quality. These quotes from the book authored by the Task Force will give the readers some understanding of the views contained in both books:

> It is important that state and local legislative bodies adopt stringent planning and regulatory legislation whenever they believe it fair and necessary to achieve land use objectives.[5]
> It is time that the U.S. Supreme Court re-examine its earlier precedents that seem to require a balancing of public benefit against land value loss in every case and declare that when the protection of natural, cultural or aesthetic resources or the assurance of orderly development are involved, a mere loss in land value will never be justification for invalidating the regulation of land use.... Although fifty years have passed...it is not too late to recognize that Justice Brandeis was right.[6]

The writers were correct, of course, in arguing that the taking clause had deterred adoption of laws and regulations controlling the use of land. But legislative deterrence is a major goal of all provisions contained in the Bill of Rights, not exactly a subversive outcome for a free society. The authors of *The Taking Issue* contended further that the clause had been misinterpreted by Justice Holmes, entitling one of their chapters "Pennsylvania Coal Co. v. Mahon: Holmes Rewrites the Constitution."

There are two short responses that can be made to the position that the *Pennsylvania Coal* case be reversed. First, Brandeis did not have the better of the argument; second, decisions on the taking clause since that case have so broadened the meaning of "taking" that reversing it would probably do little more than foster judicial confusion. With the advent of the judicially created concept of "reverse" or "inverse" condemnation, and its firm establishment in the law, the courts have expanded the taking clause into new areas. As a result, the critical issue with respect to regulation appears to be different from that posed by the Task Force. The more pertinent questions now are whether and to what extent the remedy of inverse condemnation is applicable to regulation of land use. Before analyzing this issue, let us consider the differences between Holmes and Brandeis.

Justice Holmes had strong views about the "taking" of private property:

> ...The protection of private property in the Fifth Amendment presupposes that it is wanted for public use, but provides that it shall not be taken for such use without compensation. A similar assumption is made in the decisions upon the Fourteenth Amendment [case cited]. When this seemingly absolute protection is found to be qualified by the police power, the natural tendency of human nature is to extend the qualification more and more until at last private property disappears.

But that cannot be accomplished in this way under the Constitution of the United States.... In general it is not plain that a man's misfortunes or necessities will justify his shifting the damages to his neighbor's shoulders [case cited]. We are in danger of forgetting that a strong public desire to improve the public condition is not enough to warrant achieving the desire by a shorter cut than the constitutional way of paying for the change.[7]

Contrary to what might be expected from such rhetoric, Holmes did not proceed to make compensable diminution in value caused by regulation:

If we were called upon to deal with the plaintiff's [landowner] position alone, we should think it clear that the statute does not disclose a public interest sufficient to warrant so extensive a destruction of the defendant's [company] constitutionally protected rights....[8]

The general rule at least is, that while property may be regulated to a certain extent, if regulation goes too far it will be recognized as a taking. It may be doubted how far exceptional cases, like the blowing up of a house to stop a conflagration, go—and if they go beyond the general rule, whether they do not stand as much upon tradition as upon principle.... As we already have said, this is a question of degree—and therefore cannot be disposed of by general propositions....[9]

Accordingly, elimination of value could not be ignored in determining validity of the regulation, but almost regardless of the amount involved, it was not decisive. Brandeis argued that as long as title remained with the owner or property was not usurped by government, reduction in value was irrelevant: "Restriction upon use does not become inappropriate as a means merely because it deprives an owner of the only use in which his property can be put."[10] He would invalidate only regulations that either did not "protect the public" or were not an "appropriate means" to a valid public purpose.[11] Brandeis viewed the applicable law and facts of the case much differently from his colleagues:

Every restriction upon the use of property imposed in the exercise of the police power deprives the owner of some right theretofore enjoyed, and is, in that sense, an abridgement by the State of rights in property without making compensation. But restriction imposed to protect the public health, safety or morals from dangers threatened is not a taking. The restriction here in question is merely the prohibition of a noxious use. The property so restricted remains in the possession of its owner. The State does not appropriate it or make any use of it. The State merely prevents the owner from making a use which interferes with paramount rights of the public. Whenever the use prohibited ceases to be noxious—as it may because of further change in local or social conditions—the restriction will have to be removed and the owner will again be free to enjoy his property as heretofore.[12]

The Justice's position in the case thus was based on two premises: First, that regulation and taking differ, and second, that a noxious use was involved, which could be legislatively abated without compensation. The second theory seems consistent with case law,[13] but confines the Brandeis dissent to a very narrow area that would provide little support for the vast change in the law advocated by the Rockefeller Task Force.

Brandeis' other theory may please the Task Force, but would render largely ineffective the constitutional safeguard for property ownership. It would allow government to reduce through regulation the prerogatives of ownership until the owner's interest were reduced to the virtual scrap of a naked title. Government could not, however, acquire the remaining scrap without fully compensating the owner for it. Form would have won decisively over substance in an area specifically accorded protection by the Constitution.

Brandeis' willingness to reject evidence of damages suffered by an owner is difficult to square with the traditional judicial objective of providing complainants with a full and complete hearing.[14] Moreover, deciding constitutional issues is usually a matter of identifying and balancing conflicting interests and values. Surely the harm sustained by a person or corporation is a material consideration. The more interests to be weighed, the greater the opportunity for a more satisfactory and acceptable resolution of the conflict.[15]

Nor would the Holmes approach pass muster when examined from the perspective of an owner whose interest the taking clause was intended to protect. It gave no special recognition to the removal of value other than that it be included as one factor in a balancing process which was open to the consideration of innumerable other matters. Holmes effectively rejected an important position in the law of the time that only noxious uses of property were subject to state control. Thus there was far less equivocation with regard to property interests in at least two prior leading cases, *Buchanan v. Warley,*[16] decided in 1917, and *Yick Wo v. Hopkins*[17] in 1886. Professor Norman Karlin notes that these cases placed property rights at a very high level, approaching the preferred position the modern court has given other rights. Both decisions suggest that the only uses of property that could be interfered with were those that plainly produced harmful effects in terms of health, safety, and general welfare. Karlin believes that to avoid any possible mistakes as to what was intended by the term *harmful effects*, the Court in both cases defined the limits through the use of examples which consisted of nuisances. Only they could be restricted by the police power.[18]

There was little reason for Holmes' words to disturb people of his day as they do in our time. Although protection for property was specifically declared in the Constitution, he did not accord property owners the preferred status entrepreneurs generally enjoyed under the judicially created concept of substantive (or economic) due process then in vogue at the Supreme Court. Judged under the logic of substantive due process and the special position it gave the rights supporting a system of private enterprise, the opinion was a step backward.[19] The decision has contributed to a greater but not readily definable amount of protection for property owners over and above the rational relationship test now used by the U.S. Supreme Court to determine validity of economic and social legislation under the due process and equal protection clauses.

The Brandeis view of taking was at best questionable at the time of his opinion and is plainly not the law today. In decisions on inverse condemnation, many courts have gone far beyond the requirements of traditional eminent domain in which there must be an actual physical appropriation of property. They will award compensation not only when there is a physical appropriation, use, or invasion of property, but also when a duly authorized and lawful activity of government causes loss in value without any physical entry. A few courts have ruled that the remedy of inverse condemnation is applicable in the regulation of land use. The law has far passed the point at which Brandeis wrote. These conclusions will be explained in subsequent sections of this chapter.

Private Property, Just Compensation, and Inverse Condemnation

Since the period of the *Pennsylvania Coal* opinion,[20] there has also been considerable movement in the meaning given to the four key terms in the taking clause: *private property, taken, public use,* and *just compensation*. With due allowance for inevitable judicial detours, courts have tended to expand the words *private property* and *just compensation* to extend further protection to property owners. They have enlarged the relief for "taking" through inverse condemnation and reduced it in connection with zoning.

The meaning of the term *public use* has also changed, but not necessarily to the advantage of the property owner. *Public use* is now substantially equivalent to *public purpose*, and the courts are willing to let the legislature have considerable reign in deciding this matter. As a result, it is very difficult to successfully challenge an eminent domain action as not being for a public use. The due process and equal protection clauses, however, could provide protection against discriminatory abuse of this power. In broadening the terms *private property* and particularly *just compensation*, the courts are offsetting harm caused by the loosening of the public use qualification. They are making more plausible Justice Douglas's comment in a leading case on this issue concerning owners who did not want to sell, that their rights are "satisfied when they receive that just compensation which the Fifth Amendment exacts as the price of taking."[21] Shorn of the public use protection, however, the unwilling or reluctant owner still has much cause for complaint.[22] Just compensation in the sense of indemnification obviously is not possible for one who does not desire to sell or who is willing only at a price substantially above market.

Property and Just Compensation

Consider briefly some changes that have occurred in recent decades in the definition of private property and just compensation. (Courts have used these words interchangeably so that cases concerning one term may apply also to the other.) The definition of *property* has been stretched by a majority of state courts passing on the matter to include restrictions imposed on the land subject to condemnation. Beneficiaries of such restrictions may own land or buildings adjacent to or many blocks removed from the site being condemned, and yet they are entitled to compensation under this holding. The California Supreme Court, not usually considered the friend of property owners in zoning cases, adopted this rule in 1973 and reversed a 1930 opinion that had rejected it.[23] Although the costs to the condemnor may be increased appreciably by such a definition, particularly in larger subdivisions covered by an extensive declaration of restrictive covenants, and individual awards may amount to no more than a few hundred dollars, if that, the majority view seeks to eliminate the possibility that anyone with any tangible interest in the property will be denied a share in the condemnation award. Said California's high court:

Under the minority view, compensation is denied to persons whose property may have been damaged as a result of the violation of a valid deed restriction, thereby placing a disproportionate share of the cost of public improvements upon a few individuals. Neither the constitutional guarantee of just compensation nor public policy would permit such a burdensome result.[24]

In *Armstrong v. United States*,[25] the U.S. Supreme Court, also not noted for its advocacy of property owner positions in zoning matters, held that the elimination of suppliers' liens for materials delivered was a taking of the liens. A shipbuilder contracted with the government for the construction of boats and agreed that in the event of his default the government would take title to both the material on hand as well as the uncompleted boats and would finish them at the contractor's expense. The contractor defaulted, and the suppliers asserted that the government's action in assuming ownership destroyed their liens and that this destruction was a taking of property for which they wanted compensation. The U.S. Supreme Court upheld their contention:

Neither the boat's immunity, after being acquired by the Government, from enforcement of the liens nor the use of a contract to take title relieves the Government from its constitutional obligation to pay just compensation for the value of the liens the petitioners lost and of which loss the Government was the direct beneficiary.

The Fifth Amendment's guarantee that private property shall not be taken for a public use without just compensation was designed to bar Government from forcing some people alone to bear public burdens which, in all fairness and justice, should be borne by the public as a whole.[26]

The general rules as to what constitutes just compensation in the ordinary condemnation case have been settled for some time. When changes in the definition have been made as new situations have arisen over the years, the trend has been to strengthen the position of the owner. The loss of real property traditionally has been compensated under the prevailing fair market standard, but the so-called consequential damages which include cost of relocating, loss of good will, and anticipated profits, normally are noncompensable.[27] If only a portion of a tract is condemned, the owner is entitled to recover for damages to the remainder attributable to the taking and government use of the property taken.

These rules probably operate relatively well for most owners of land and residential property, who may at different times lose or gain in comparison to "real" value from a condemnation proceeding,[28] but may be quite harsh to owners of businesses and homes for whom changes in location can be highly disadvantageous and the cost of moving, substantial. Many of these problems have been cured by federal and state legislation providing compensation for those expenses,[29] and this legislative action has likely forestalled alterations in judicial doctrine.

Exceptions have been made to the rule against recovering consequential damages. Courts have allowed evidence of lost business profits to be taken into account in making awards in cases of temporary takings,[30] certain instances of inverse condemnation,[31] and actions involving valuation of the remainder of the property taken to determine whether and how its immediate highest and best use has been affected.[32] In the 1972 *Almota Farmers v. United States*[33] opinion, by a 5-to-4 vote the high Court ruled that just compensation required, in some instances, inclusion of the value of the expectancy of lease renewal, thereby expanding significantly the measure for determining certain awards. The lessee had substantially improved the premises under the lease, which at the time of the action would not expire for 7 1/2 years. The Court rejected confining the compensation of the leaseholder to value for that period only. Instead, the standard adopted was one of full fair market value, that is, what a willing buyer would have paid for the leasehold and improvements, taking into account the possibility that the lease might or might not have been renewed. The majority opinion summed up its view of the case as follows:

"The Constitutional requirement of just compensation derives as much content from the basic equitable principles of fairness [citation], as it does from technical concepts of property law" [citation]. It is, of course, true that Almota should be in no better position than if it had sold its leasehold to a private buyer. But its position should surely be no worse.[34]

The majority opinion in *Almota* reiterated that the government "may not take advantage of any depreciation in property taken that is attributable to the project itself."[35] The reference is apparently to what has become known as "condemnation blight," an issue that has risen also to considerable importance as a result of the massive government demolition and construction programs of recent years. Much time invariably intervenes between the contemplation of a government project and the filing of the condemnation suit to implement it. Public information about the proposal may seriously affect values, both up and down. If a particular building or tract is considered for condemnation, there will be much reluctance to rent, buy, renovate, or build on it; and its value may be substantially reduced before the date suit is filed, which frequently is the time for setting the condemnation award. Nearby buildings or acreage not threatened by condemnation action may rise in value due to the expected replacement of blighted properties with new structures, or because of anticipated future growth of the area. The term *condemnation blight* refers to the reduction in value occurring in anticipation of the filing of the condemnation action, and most courts now consider this resultant devaluation as compensable in whole or in part.[36]

In determining the award when government activity is the cause for an increase or decrease in value, the U.S. Supreme Court has ruled that the government must pay just compensation for those interests "probably within the scope of the project from the time the government was committed to it."[37] The California Supreme Court has allowed for precondemnation appreciation as of the time it was "reasonably probable" that the property would be taken.[38] Both tests are intended to work as a reasonable balance with considerable deference to the interest of the owner. Thus, in the California case cited, the government had not originally intended to condemn the nearby property but was not relieved of obligation for payment of the increased market value by the fact that it had largely accounted for it.[39]

Inverse Condemnation

The judiciary has expanded the term *taking* to safeguard owners damaged by actions of government not relievable under a traditional eminent domain concept. To accomplish this, the courts established the remedy of *inverse* condemnation. Under this concept, compensation has been required, both when there has been actual or physical invasion of property and when impairment or destruction of property interests has occurred by reason of certain government actions.

Inverse condemnation on the federal level can be traced back to *Pumpelly v. Green Bay Co.,*[40] decided in 1871, in which the U.S. Supreme Court concluded that taking included destruction of property. The plaintiff's land had been flooded as a result of a dam erected and maintained in a river under the authority of a state statute. It was argued unsuccessfully that these damages were incidental to the accomplishment of an authorized public purpose. The state contended it could, in the interests of the public, "erect such works as may be deemed expedient for the purpose of improving the navigation and increasing usefulness of a navigable river, without rendering itself liable to individuals owning land bordering on such river, for injuries to their lands resulting from their overflow by reason of such improvements."[41] The reply of the Court was that there was no realistic difference between what had occurred and a physical taking.

In 1916 in *United States v. Cress,*[42] the construction and maintenance by the United States government of locks and dams upon the Cumberland and Kentucky rivers caused overflow on 6.6 acres and depreciated the land to half its value. The government contended that the damage did not amount to a taking because it was only "partial injury." The Court replied:

It is the character of the invasion, not the amount of damage resulting from it, so long as the damage is substantial, that determines the question whether it is a taking[43].... [A]nd where ... land is not constantly but only at intervals overflowed, the fee may be permitted to remain in the owners, subject to an easement in the United States to overflow it with water as often as necessarily may result from the operation of the lock and dam for purposes of navigation.[44]

Many cases followed thereafter which did not make clear when or at which point government-caused physical invasion or harm constituted a taking. A number of post–World War II cases in both the federal and state courts have tended to clarify the law in this regard. In *United States v. Causby,*[45] the majority opinion written by Justice Douglas decided that frequent low overflights by United States military planes amounted to a taking of an easement or air corridor over property, entitling the owner to compensation. Douglas stated:

The airplane is part of the modern environment of life, and the inconveniences which it causes are normally not compensable under the Fifth Amendment. The airspace, apart from the immediate reaches above the land, is part of the public domain. We need not determine at this time what those precise limits are. Flights over private land are not a taking, unless they are so low and so frequent as to be a direct and immediate interference with the enjoyment and use of the land. We need not speculate on that phase of the present case. For the findings of the Court of Claims plainly establish that there was a diminution in value of the property and that the frequent, low-level flights were the direct and immediate cause. We agree with the Court of Claims that a servitude has been imposed upon the land.[46]

Griggs v. Allegheny County[47] clarified the *Causby* opinion with respect to who was liable in these actions. The defendant county owned and operated the Greater Pittsburgh airport. It never acquired an air corridor easement over plaintiff's house near one of the runways. The Federal Civil Aeronautics Authority fixed the pattern of flight outside the runway, which caused planes to fly between 30 and 300 feet above the house. The noise, vibrations, and fear of injury caused the owner to move, and he sued the operator of the airport for damages to his person and property. The Pennsylvania trial court treated the action as one in inverse condemnation, but was overruled by the state's highest court which decided that the commercial airlines were the responsible parties and not the defendant county. The U.S. Supreme Court reversed and held that the county took the air easement as the promoter, owner, and lessor of the airport. It is to be noted that in both *Causby* and *Griggs*, inverse condemnation liability was imposed despite the fact that the regulations governing the flights were valid.

At least six state courts have gone further and said that overflight was not necessary.[48] Sound waves emitted by airplanes could just as much reduce the use and enjoyment of property, and the owners should likewise be compensated. These opinions assert that it is not physical possession which necessarily constitutes the taking, but rather the interference with the individual's use and enjoyment of the property caused by noise, vibrations, and fear of injury. In ruling that the municipal operator of a large public airport is liable for a taking when the noise of low, but not necessarily direct, overflights substantially diminishes property values, the Oregon Supreme Court stated:

In effect, the inquiry should have been whether the government had undertaken a course of conduct on its own land which, in simple fairness to its neighbors, required it to obtain more land so that the substantial burdens of the activity would fall upon public land, rather than upon that of involuntary contributors who happen to lie in the path of progress.[49]

The overflight requirement has been strongly criticized by some commentators,[50] but the federal (and some state) courts have refused to go beyond the *Causby* ruling that requires it.[51] With the marked exception of this overflight requirement (which does not apply when the property is rendered useless), the remedy of inverse condemnation usually has been upheld when physical damages have resulted from governmental actions.[52]

The law has progressed still further. There are presently three broad categories of situations in which courts have recognized that government is liable for inverse condemnation: (1) the one previously discussed, that is, when it has done something that has caused physical invasion of the claimant's property; (2) when there has been no physical intrusion but physical conduct by the government outside the property has diminished the property's value; and (3) when it has acted with fault or in bad faith or unfairly toward the property.[53] In addition, courts have invoked inverse condemnation in some zoning cases, and this will be discussed subsequently in the section Inverse Condemnation and Zoning. About one-half of the states' constitutions require, in their taking clauses, compensation for property "damaged" or "injured," and this added language may provide for greater relief.

Damage Caused by Physical Invasion. Professor Jacob Beuscher has listed these instances of physical invasion requiring compensation: (1) flooding by construction of a dam, highway, or other public improvement; (2) raising the goundwater table by reason of a public improvement; (3) imposition of special burdens like concentrations of gas and smoke, by reason of a public improvement; (4) the backing up of sewers or drains; (5) the erection of a bridge or utility wires across private land; and (6) the washing away of riparian land caused by erection of a bridge or other public improvement.[54] The pollution of a public stream and a private lake by sewage from sewage treatment facilities has been held to be a taking.[55] Even the damaging effects upon abutting property of the runoff from highway salting operations have been so held.[56] Claims of taking are made each spring with some success for damages incurred when water from melted snow, impacted on public highways, floods private fields.[57]

Damage Caused by Physical Conduct but without Physical Intrusion. Decisions that do not require overflight to impose damages for inverse condemnation belong more properly in this category. Similarly, liability has been imposed when governmental construction activities resulted in structural damages to abutting property notwithstanding the absence of any fault on the agency's part.[58]

In interpreting the taking clause, courts have not limited the rights of ownership strictly to the area within the boundaries of the property. Many have established that an owner possesses easements for access, light, air, and view to or from an abutting street,[59] and has a right to privacy in relation to activities carried on in that street.[60] Owners are entitled to compensation when the government interferes with these rights. Examples of such compensable infringements include street closures, change of street capacity, installation of freeways cutting across existing streets, the creation of barriers or cul-de-sacs, and the construction of curbs, dividers, bridges, and viaducts.[61] In these situations the government agency is performing a legally authorized activity outside the property intended to be in the furtherance of the police power and public welfare, and the damages to property values are incidental. Nonetheless, compensation liability has been imposed.

A recent *Stanford Law Review* note discusses the California "next intersection" cases in which the state's supreme court has held that a property owner has an easement of access to the street abutting his land, and from there to a general system of public streets. Compensation has been required when this easement is subjected to "substantial interference." Among the factors relevant to whether a compensable interference has occurred include the plaintiff's use of his property, the added distance of travel to the public highway system, the absence of alternative routes, and the extent to which the property's use has been impaired by the reduced access. The dominant consideration appears to be diminution in value of the affected property, a concern which, as the Stanford writer suggests, should not require creating the fiction of an "easement of access."[62]

Governmental Fault, Bad Faith and Unfairness. A number of decisions indicate the courts will hold the government to a certain standard of fair conduct with respect to private property. The case of *Bydlon v. United States*[63] was brought by owners of resort properties in the roadless upper portion of the Superior National Forest. Access to these resorts was almost entirely limited to air transportation. To preserve the wilderness character of the area in which the resorts were located, a government order was issued prohibiting air flights, except in emergency situations, below 4000 feet. This air ban substantially curtailed plaintiffs' business, and they sued for inverse condemnation; those who had a way of necessity through the airspace won a judgment against the government in the Court of Claims, from which no appeal was taken. The measure of damages was based on the resulting diminution in value of those properties. Under a federal statute, the government was forbidden to condemn plaintiffs' properties without their consent. Thus, the flight policy could lead indirectly to the eventual elimination of these resorts, something which the government was by law unable to accomplish directly. Said the trial commissioner, referring to the impairment of the rights of access by air, "It is no longer the rule that there must be a physical invasion of property to constitute a taking."[64]

In *Arastra Limited Partnership v. City of Palo Alto,*[65] a U.S. District Court ruled that the city had effectively confiscated, and therefore must purchase, 515 acres of land. In 1970 Palo Alto's council decided to buy this land along with other tracts in its foothills section for open space and recreational purposes, and subsequently allocated $4 million for acquisition. It took all other steps toward this end short of payment, rejecting development of the land pending acquisition. Evidently, when the city authorities found that the cost of the property had exceeded their expectations and neither federal nor state government would share the expense, they demurred on purchase and substituted zoning. They zoned the land so restrictively that it could not be economically developed and, although privately owned, it would remain largely as open space. The court did not find the zoning was invalid; just as applied to the property in question, it amounted to inverse condemnation:

When the open space ordinance is examined in this context, it compels the conclusion that the City had the purpose, by way of zoning regulation, to accomplish without expense to the taxpayers all of the benefits it could have received from the acquisition.[66]

The judge ruled that a jury would determine the property's fair market value at the time the open-space ordinance was adopted and Palo Alto would have to pay this amount for acquisition. (The city subsequently, before trial, settled with the plaintiff for $7.5 million.)

In support of its holding, the federal court cited, among others, *Peacock v. County of Sacramento*[67] in which a judgment for the landowner in inverse condemnation was sustained by a California court of appeal. The county board in that case declared its intention to acquire a considerable portion of the plaintiff's land which he sought to develop. Pending the actual acquisition of the land, the county imposed height restrictions and otherwise refused to authorize any development of the property. The court found the county's activities relating to acquisition commenced in 1958 and culminated in late 1963. Notwithstanding these efforts, the project was subsequently abandoned. The trial judge concluded that a reasonable period of time had elapsed for the county to consummate the project, and continuation of it after 1963 constituted "a compensatory restriction upon the use of plaintiffs' lands."[68] It held that the interest taken was the fee, and it did not find that at any time was there bad faith or procrastination on the part of the county officers and supervisors; events beyond their control caused the proposed purchase to fail.

In *Sneed v. County of Riverside*,[69] the defendant imposed height restrictions on the plaintiff's property, the effect of which was to create an airspace easement above it that could be used as an approach to the county airport. Flights operated over the restricted area. The Court of Appeal held that the plaintiff had stated a cause of action in inverse condemnation.

In *Klopping v. Whittier*,[70] the defendant city had filed a condemnation suit to acquire the plaintiff's land to build public parking facilities. Subsequent to the filing of the condemnation action, another suit was filed, challenging the bond financing program for the parking facility. Because of the problems the latter suit created for marketing of the bonds, the city dismissed the condemnation proceedings. However, in the resolution authorizing the dismissal, the city stated that it would renew the condemnation if the bond litigation were successfully completed. About two years after the first condemnation resolution, the property owners brought suit in inverse condemnation for blight caused by the overhanging threat of a future condemnation proceeding. In ruling for the plaintiff the court stated:

[W]hen the condemnor acts unreasonably in issuing precondemnation statements, either by excessively delaying eminent domain action or by other oppressive conduct, our constitutional concern over property rights requires that the owner be compensated. This requirement applies even though the activities which give rise to such damages may be significantly less than those which would constitute a de facto taking of the property so as to measure the fair market value as of a date earlier than that set statutorily....[71]

The court also asserted that, in such situations, the owner could claim these losses either in an inverse condemnation suit or in the eminent domain proceeding, if it were ever filed.

That price-depressing activities of the condemnor associated with the actual or proposed filing of a condemnation suit are subject to compensatory relief may now be the prevailing rule.[72] State courts in Oregon, Pennsylvania, Wisconsin, Connecticut, Michigan, Ohio, New Jersey, Washington, and California (in *Klopping*), a federal court in Michigan, and the U.S. Court of Claims have entered decisions consistent with this approach,[73] whereas state courts in New York, Missouri, Illinois, and Texas have ruled otherwise.[74]

Several other cases involving questionable conduct by the government also merit comment. The plaintiff in the New York appellate division case of *Charles v. Diamond*[75] was given authority by a village board to build three apartment buildings on his land. The State Department of Environmental Conservation, however, informed him that his application to tie into the village sewer system would not be approved until the village corrected the deficiencies of the system. The village had been under a consent order to improve the system for nine years, but had not done so and did not appear likely to be able to do so in the near future. The owner filed suit requesting as alternative damages the amount of $100,000 for appropriation of his property if a sewer connection was not approved. The court held:

[W]e believe that a property owner who has been denied an existing governmental service proves a constitutional taking when he demonstrates that such denial is (1) economically confiscatory in effect, (2) unreasonable in terms of necessity, and (3) indefinite in duration [citations]. Petitioner should be given an opportunity to prove this cause of action in a trial for money damages.[76]

Another New York case, *Keystone Associates v. State of New York*,[77] proceeds in a generally similar direction. In order to preserve an historic old opera building (the "Old Met" in New York City), the State of New York created a corporation with the power to condemn the property. The law provided that a demolition permit could be refused the present owner for 180 days on request of this corporation and upon deposit of $200,000, which was to stand as security for payment of any damages that property owner might suffer should no condemnation subsequently take place. This law was held unconstitutional. After that determination, the property owner filed an action against the state seeking $3,500,000 damages for the temporary appropriation of its property between the period of the enactment of the statute and the date when it was finally issued a demolition permit.

The court noted that it was not necessary that there be a valid statute or lawful action essential to give rise to a de facto appropriation and that the prior litigation concerning constitutionality, in fact, had established that there was some interference with the property rights of the plaintiff. It concluded that "there was in fact an appropriation of property interests necessarily temporary in nature prior to the final determination by the court as to the validity of the special law. A *de facto* appropriation requires compensation to the same extent as a *de jure* appropriation."[78]

Professor Buescher concludes that "American courts have in inverse condemnation cases done something which they have long since done in direct condemnation actions. They have moved from the earlier primitive positions, requiring a physical invasion or taking to a set of holdings which say that loss of intangible property interests may be a basis for a claim of just compensation."[79] The courts thus appear to be applying a fundamental rationale for eminent domain provisions so well stated—if not necessarily always followed—by the California Supreme Court:

"...The decisive consideration is whether the owner of the damaged property if uncompensated would contribute more than his proper share to the public undertaking." In other words, the underlying purpose of our constitutional provision in inverse—as well as ordinary—condemnation is "to distribute throughout the community the loss inflicted upon the individual by the making of public improvements [case cited], to socialize the burden ... to afford relief to the landowner in cases in which it is unfair to ask him to bear a burden that should be assumed by society."[80]

And again:

> ...The constitutional guarantee of compensation extends to both types of cases and not merely where the taking is cheap or easy; indeed the need for compensation is greatest where the loss is greatest....[81]

Zoning: The Major Exception in Interpreting the Taking Clause

The foregoing presentation would suggest that, at least in the areas discussed, the courts generally have been holding firm on or gradually strengthening the taking clause, frequently giving the benefit of the doubt to its intended beneficiaries. An exception to this is the judicial limitation of the "public use" qualification, but other protections provided for in eminent domain tend to confine appreciably the detrimental consequences for most owners affected. Judged solely from the prior discussion, the conclusion that there has been a demise of property rights is highly premature. Courts and even legislatures are providing increasingly greater protection for owners of property interests that the government seeks to acquire through eminent domain. It is also apparent that courts will preserve property interests against a variety of government acts that cause diminution of value, and the amount and kind of protection provided seems to be multiplying. [82] The taking clause is obviously neither myth nor ghost.

There is nevertheless considerable basis for concern about the demise of property rights. Lay people (and many lawyers) reading opinions on eminent domain and inverse condemnation would find unbelievable the tenor and results of cases involving the regulation of land use. The pattern of concern for property rights stops abruptly when regulation is involved. Unless a zoning ordinance removes all economic value from property, there is little certainty as to how it will fare in the courts. It is even possible that the judges may at times uphold regulations that eliminate virtually all commercial values.[83]

The judiciary has clothed the municipalities with powers entitling them to strictly regulate property notwithstanding serious reductions in values. The police power has provided courts with a rationale for carving out a huge area of special dispensation under the taking clause different from and inconsistent with the treatment accorded property owners under other terms of the clause, as previously described. The landowner seeking to preserve the value of his land in a zoning controversy with the local municipality faces these obstacles:

(1) The courts will presume that the ordinance adopted by the locality is a reasonable exercise of police power, and the burden is on the challenger to prove otherwise. "In all kinds of litigation it is plain that where the burden of proof lies may be decisive of the outcome."[84]

(2) The loss in value of the property attributable to the ordinance is but one of a host of factors involved in this legal exercise. In the *Euclid* case,[85] in which the constitutionality of zoning was established, an alleged loss of hundreds of thousands of dollars to the landowner was not sufficient in itself to cause the Court to declare the ordinance invalid.

(3) If the court does strike down the ordinance, the municipality in many states will have an opportunity thereafter to adopt another one that will still have a drastic impact on value.

The comparative unimportance of the money question can be discerned from this compilation of the factors for determining validity of a zoning ordinance used by the Illinois courts, which are considered relatively favorable to the landowner:

1. The existing uses and zoning of nearby property;
2. The extent to which property values are diminished by the particular zoning restriction;
3. The extent to which the destruction of property values of plaintiff promotes the health, safety, morals, or general welfare of the public;
4. The relative gain to the public as compared to the hardship imposed upon the individual property owner;
5. The suitability of the subject property for the zoned purposes; and
6. The length of time the property has been vacant as zoned, considered in the context of land development in the area in the vicinity of the subject property.[86]

The differences in treatment of monetary loss between eminent domain and zoning are alluded to in Chapters 7 and 4, respectively, by both Johnson and Hagman, and are dramatically illustrated in a 1968 New York zoning case.[87] The owners sought to rezone, from residential to commercial, a 14.5-acre tract at a major intersection in the Village of Old Westbury. When 4.5 acres of the original 19 acres had previously been taken for road widening, the owner had received compensation in the sum of $105,800. In the zoning case, the court found that the balance of the land was worth from $200,000 to $225,000 as residential, and $1,500,000 as commercial. The other three corners of the intersection were commercially zoned and used, and a major department store (Bloomingdale's) had shown interest in the fourth corner, the site in question. Yet the court refused to upset the residential zoning of the property, stating that the huge reduction in value caused by the zoning was not a decisive factor.

Given the choice, the owner obviously would have preferred a reclassification rather than receiving compensation for the taking for the road. Nor will she find much consolation in the distinction that there was actual conveyance of ownership in the one situation and not in the other.

Labels can be decisive in these proceedings. An example is provided by the decision of the California Supreme Court (4 to 3) to uphold a 30-foot height limitation imposed on a large portion of the city of San Diego as a result of a public vote.[88] This restriction establishes no less an easement than that created by government-owned airplanes when they fly low over land and for which compensation would likely be required. Nor is such a restriction of minor consequence. High-rises may easily reach 300 to 400 feet in height, and therefore a 30-foot height regulation may restrict some lands to 10 percent of their potential use. There is a difference, to be sure, in that under zoning there is no intrusion into the area above the specified ceiling. That technical distinction would be much less likely to stand if the courts were interpreting other terms of the taking clause.

It has become commonplace to state that there is no set formula for determining when the police power or regulation ends and taking begins. The test is said to be one of reasonableness, and there are innumerable considerations that may enter into an evaluation of reasonableness and perhaps just as many opportunities to engage in weighing the importance of each. In the area of zoning, the interests of property owners have been left to the not always tender mercies of the legislatures and the courts.

As is evident from the broadness of the reasonableness test, courts approach the matter differently. Few would disagree that if the government rezoned a tract of, say, 100 forested acres zoned for high-rise apartments to public park and allowed no other use of this land, it should compensate the owner for the full value of the property. Although title to the land may remain with the owner, the public has, for all practical purposes, assumed ownership. Zoning that effectively classifies property for a public park, school site, highway, or public building will be struck down[89] (or possibly compensation required as in the *Arastra* case previously discussed).

The problem arises over regulation that is not as severe. For example, if these 100 acres were rezoned (or downzoned) to permit construction of only twenty homes, each on a minimum of 5 acres, the value of the property would be considerably reduced; and, in effect, the public would acquire the advantages accruing from very low-density development without having to pay for it. While much has been written on the subject and there are numerous opinions by courts concerning it, no one can predict with certainty the legal consequences of this regulation. It might be considered as a taking in such states as Pennsylvania, New Jersey,

Virginia, and Illinois, particularly if it were located in developing areas. On the other hand, California might be one state where the courts would uphold such a regulation. And it is probable that whichever way it was decided in the lower courts, the U.S. Supreme Court would not consider the case worthy of review.

As the regulation becomes less onerous, that is, density is decreased to where one unit is permitted on 1 or 2 acres, it is more likely to be upheld in those states that would overrule the 5-acre requirement. Each case stands on its own facts, and what would be appropriate in a rural area clearly might be inappropriate in a downtown section.

All these situations and considerations, however, do not obviate the fact that the community is benefiting at the expense of the individual owner. Regulation has clearly become the subterfuge, loophole, or escape hatch in the taking clause. Government is being allowed to transfer resources from the individual to the community without compensation.

The Police Power

Consider the celebrated case involving Ramapo, New York, and its phased growth ordinance to control development over a period of 18 years.[90] The plan called for the installation of specified facilities during this period, and building was not permitted on any parcel of land until it was serviced pursuant to a set formula. This meant that owners of vacant property might be denied use for development purposes for as long as 18 years! It is exceedingly difficult to imagine the kind of emergency conditions that would allow government to appropriate property for so long a period without any compensation. The court reasoned that this restraint was justified to ensure orderly growth and in effect acknowledged that the cost would have to be borne by the owners of undeveloped property:

In sum, where it is clear that the existing physical and financial resources of the community are inadequate to furnish the essential services and facilities which a substantial increase in population requires, there is a rational basis for "phased growth" and hence, the challenged ordinance is not violative of the Federal and State Constitutions.[91]

We can be reasonably certain that Ramapo and most other cities are limited by normal budgetary considerations in acquiring more land and property for schools, parks, and municipal buildings. The appropriation of property for any period of time for these purposes would surely run afoul of the taking clause. Eminent domain procedures would have to be scrupulously observed regardless of need. Nor can it be accepted that acquisition for any of these purposes is less critical to the maintenance of the public welfare than phased growth of the community. The answer to the riddle lies in the application of the police power on a selective and essentially arbitrary basis.

Those seeking to determine the relationship of police power to the taking clause will seldom find satisfaction in the cases. There is often little justification for the flowery rhetoric. An example is provided by one of the most quoted statements on the subject, Justice Douglas's dictum in *Berman v. Parker*[92] which places little restraint on the police power:

Public safety, public health, morality, peace and quiet, law and order—these are some of the more conspicuous examples of the traditional application of the police power to municipal affairs. Yet they merely illustrate the scope of the power and do not delimit it [cases cited]. . . . The concept of the public welfare is broad and inclusive [cases cited]. The values it represents are spiritual as well as physical, aesthetic as well as monetary. It is within the power of the legislature to determine that the community should be beautiful as well as healthy, spacious as well as clean, well-balanced as well as carefully patrolled. . . .[93]

The record of the Justice clearly indicates, however, that he did not believe universally in the wisdom and competence of the legislature. He has contended that speech, press, and religion were beyond the reach of the police power.[94] It is also doubtful that he would invoke police power to eliminate protection against arbitrary searches and seizures, such as, say, the rights of suspicious-looking characters and vehicles to roam the streets at will despite the high crime rates. Although many acts of speech or press create problems for the public health, safety, morals, and welfare, courts would exercise the utmost caution before subordinating them to the interests Justice Douglas suggests are encompassed by police power. A similar conclusion holds when religion, voting, or rights of travel, association, and privacy are involved. The procedure of the courts in these situations is precisely the reverse: it is incumbent upon the state to show that it has a compelling reason for restricting these interests or liberties. The courts will subject legislation or regulations affecting these concerns to strict scrutiny and rigorous review, laying upon government the heavy burden of showing that police power should prevail.

Plainly, the police power is not nearly so far reaching as the Douglas dictum suggests: it recedes and expands, depending upon the other interests involved. When confronted with the rights referred to, the police power tends to evaporate, leaving nary a trace. It becomes robust, however, when land use is concerned. The police power is therefore not a measurable concept on its own; its scope and applicability depend on something else—the concepts and doctrines with which it competes. When the courts say that the police power authorizes a particular zoning regulation, what they effectively mean is that they are unwilling to construe the taking clause or other constitutional provision to nullify the restriction.

In the name of the police power, courts have allowed severe restrictions on the rights of ownership. Examples are presented in all phases of zoning. An owner wants to build a 30-story building but is restricted to 3; instead of a gas station, the land is classified for homes; a tract is limited to a minimum lot size of one house for every 4 acres instead of one unit to 1/2 acre; a research and development plant is allowed but not a manufacturing plant. In the event the police power were not applicable, the same result in these cases could be accomplished by the payment of money to the owner of the property in question. The land classified for the erection of a 30-story building may have a value of $500,000, but its value when limited to 3 stories is $75,000. The application of the police power in this case saves the locality $425,000, all of which is borne by the owner. The situation is no different in the case of the gas station or the subdivision tract or the industrial plant. *The police power is not being used to preserve the public health, safety, morals, or welfare; it is serving solely to save the community's funds.*[95]

A major purpose of the taking clause is to avoid precisely that result. The courts have repeatedly stated in cases of direct as well as inverse condemnation that an objective of each is to allocate and share the costs among beneficiaries of the service or installation, and not allow individual owners to bear that burden alone. There may be instances when, under a compelling state interest standard, the legislation is *truly* necessary to protect the public health, safety, morals, or welfare. In some cases it may not be possible to quantify the harm to the owner or to compensate the owner without incurring transaction costs exceeding the amount of recovery, or to avoid the petty larceny of the police power that Justice Holmes said was inherent in the operation of government.[96] The law never should operate, however, merely to place the cost of measurable community benefits on the shoulders of selected property owners.

Philosophical and Pragmatic Premises for a Taking Clause

Some courts have rejected the dichotomy under the taking clause where zoning is on one side and most everything else is on the other, and have applied inverse condemnation to zoning regulations. Before discussing these cases, it is well to consider the reasoning that supports the existence of a taking clause in federal and state constitutions. The explanations are both philosophical and pragmatic, and I have sought to set them forth under these separate headings, fully aware that precise demarcations do not always exist between the two. The chapters that follow will supply much greater detail for some of the points I will present in capsule form.

Philosophical Reasons

The philosophical underpinnings of our constitutional institutions have not remained static in the last 200 years, but certain essential premises continue intact. These ideas provide at least six major explanations of the necessity for a taking provision.

The Taking Clause and Personal Freedom. The taking clause represents one of the fundamental commitments of a free society that government will let people alone to further their own destinies. It is rooted in the great historical movement away from the authoritarian state where the individual was beholden to designated masters. The predominant concern of our society is the dignity of the person; our state exists to serve the individual, and not the reverse, as was the condition in prior centuries and in many countries today. This requires that people largely be free to pursue their own interests as they deem best, secure in the knowledge that the government will not interfere with those efforts.

For most people, the essence of freedom is that they will be able to retain the fruits of their labor, knowledge, ingenuity, and industry. It makes meaningful that portion of life devoted to physical or mental endeavors. What does it mean to labor, experiment, innovate, or create if the material rewards of those efforts can be arbitrarily taken away by the state? The existence of such governmental powers would destroy the incentive to save, invest, and plan for the future. Far fewer people would be able to achieve self-fulfillment or attain happiness. The nation would suffer in being denied the input and talent of highly productive and creative individuals.

People whose property is not secure from government are extremely limited in their freedom because they have to depend on the state or others for their existence. Protection of property is vital to the preservation of liberties "for the free range of the human spirit becomes shriveled and constrained under economic dependence."[97] The right to property therefore preserves other personal rights and maintains a separation between the state and individual.

If the threat of taking makes investment precarious, the role of government would have to increase to compensate for reduced production by the private sector. More governmental involvement will reduce the freedom of individuals to produce and create. As dependence on government grows, it becomes exceedingly more difficult to participate freely in the political process and criticize officeholders and programs. The historic trend away from repression would be irreparably reversed.

Equality of Burden. There should be an equality of all citizens before the law. No one in society should bear more than his or her fair share of the burdens of government. Professor Ernest Freund, in his definitive work on the police power, considered the need for fair compensation as a:

...logical outgrowth of the principle of equality which demands that no burden be imposed upon a person from which others are free unless there is some causal connection between him or his property and the condition which the burden imposed upon him is intended to relieve; "it prevents the public from loading upon one individual more than his just share of the burdens of government, and says that, when he surrenders to the public, something more and different from that which is exacted from other members of the public, a just and full equivalent shall be returned to him."[98]

Blackstone commented in this manner on the law of eminent domain:

In vain may it be urged, that the good of the individual ought to yield to that of the community; for it would be dangerous to allow any private man, or even any public tribunal, to be the judge of this common good, and to decide whether it be expedient or no. Besides, the public is in nothing more essentially interested than in the protection of every individual's private rights, as modeled by the municipal laws. In this and similar cases the legislature alone can, and indeed frequently does, interpose, and compel the individual to acquiesce. But how does it interpose and compel? Not by absolutely stripping the subject of his property in an arbitrary manner; but by giving him a full indemnification and equivalent for the injury sustained.[99]

The rise of the doctrine of inverse condemnation similarly evidences concern about acts of government that produce harmful impact upon certain persons. Those who happen to be at what turns out to be the wrong place at the wrong time should not have to bear special and increased costs for governmental services and installations created for their benefit as well as that of many others.

Abuses of Power by the State. Were government not restrained from confiscating or diminishing property interests, it could use such power in an arbitrary way to accomplish tyrannical or coercive designs. Politicians could exact graft and contributions and otherwise obtain tribute by the threat of appropriating property interests. While such abuse is a possibility in the making of any legislative and executive decisions, property ownership is a highly prized personal right that should be beyond the bargaining prerogatives of government officials. Some commentators believe the compensation requirement has more to do with political freedom than property protection.[100] Professor Friedrich Hayek presents this view in the following manner:

The principle of "no expropriation without just compensation" has always been recognized wherever the rule of law has prevailed. It is, however, not always recognized that this is an integral and indispensable element of the principle of the supremacy of the law. Justice requires it; but what is more important is that it is our chief assurance that those necessary infringements of the private sphere will be allowed only in instances where the public gain is clearly greater than the harm done by the disappointment of normal individual expectations. The chief purpose of the requirement of full compensation is indeed to act as a curb on such infringements of the private sphere and to provide a means of ascertaining whether the particular purpose is important enough to justify an exception to the principle on which the normal working of society rests.[101]

Separation of State and Individual. The existence of a representative and nontotalitarian society assumes a strict separation between the identity of the individual and that of the state. The state is a separate entity without any right or authority to deprive a person of life, liberty, or property, save when it is so authorized in a constitution (i.e., taxes) and when it is essential to maintain law, order, and personal freedom, adjudicate private disputes, and protect against fraud. Government should otherwise pay for property interests it acquires or removes from its constituents, for under ordinary circumstances its status is no different than that of any stranger. The taking clause is a prohibition against theft by government comparable to numerous other laws that forbid theft by any of its citizens.

Infirmity of the Legislative Process. Legislation is supposed to respond to the "will" of the people. In theory, majorities are supposed to rule, but because they are not necessarily wise, good, or just, our constitutions limit their powers and protect rights of minorities. An added problem is that frequently laws do not represent the desires of the majority. Davis, in Chapter 5, presents some illustrations of the lawmaking process showing that minorities at times can succeed in causing the passage of legislation designed to benefit themselves. Government often is more responsive to vocal minorities than to silent majorities. Further, lawmaking can be quite haphazard. Legislators may not have the time or ability to comprehend fully the scope and meaning of a bill. Provisions may be inserted only to obtain the relatively few votes needed for passage of the overall measure. Laws are enacted accordingly for a wide variety of reasons, ranging from the noblest to the basest, and there is nothing scientific or otherwise "right" or certain about the resultant product.

With respect to many issues resolved by legislatures, the losers have not been as influential, adept, or fortunate as the winners in the legislative deliberations and in convincing the legislators. Society should consequently make certain that laws do not appreciably diminish or wipe out people's acquisitions and investments. It is an unconscionable penalty to pay for having failed to persuade the politicians.

Safeguarding the Interests of the Law-abiding. Society should not penalize or punish people who have committed no wrong. The innocent should not suffer in a manner intended for wrongdoers. These objectives are compromised when government confiscates valuable possessions of individuals or corporations who have not intentionally inflicted any harm. Similarly, liability should not be imposed in the absence of very strong and equitable cause. The credibility of a state's dedication to justice and equity is seriously jeopardized when it does not safeguard the interests, aspirations, and expectations of those who abide by its rules.

Pragmatic Reasons

An analysis founded in terms of economic and social considerations also presents strong arguments in support of a taking clause.

Encouraging Investment. Entrepreneurs invest on the basis of the risks they expect to encounter. The risks usually are of two varieties: economic and political. The higher the risk, the fewer the number of investors and the greater the expected return:

If people generally act like risk averters ... they will prefer smaller steady incomes to erratic incomes even when these average out to a higher figure. Therefore, economic activities that involve much uncertainty and risk ... will be forced by comparative entry and exit of risk takers to pay, over the long run, a positive profit premium to compensate for aversion to risk. The yield on capital invested in such industries will involve, in addition to pure interest corresponding to safe investments, an extra element corresponding to positive profit.[102]

If, to the usual economic risk inherent in any investment, is added the political one that allows government to expropriate at will all or a portion of the value of property, the result will be a lesser number of investors. A recent California case quotes a portion of an article on taking that discloses inadvertently the seriousness of the problem for a private-enterprise society:

[They] bought land which [they] knew might be subjected to restrictions; and the price [they] paid should have been discounted by the possibility that restrictions would be imposed. Since [they] got exactly what [they] meant to buy, it can perhaps be said that society has effected no redistribution so far as [they are] concerned, any more than it does when it refuses to refund the price of [their] losing sweepstakes ticket.[103]

The analogy to sweepstakes is unfortunately all too often appropriate. If the risks are of the kind involved in sweepstakes, the expected rewards will have to be commensurate with them. Purchasing land for development requires the expenditure of huge sums of money, much of which may come in the form of loans from lenders who usually seek a specified return and not a windfall. Lenders will be deterred by the possibility of substantial future diminution in value. It is likely therefore that as political risks increase, more potential investors, lenders, builders, and developers will drop out. Who, then, will build the houses, apartments, supermarkets, and industrial complexes?

Nor is there any way for the market to quantify the risk of future regulations or change in regulations. If there is little restraint on their actions, how can anyone forecast what the politicians who establish and control the regulations will do? The public mood may change over the months or years, or the next election may replace members of the legislative body.

More Competition and Lower Prices. In a consumer-oriented society, government should encourage rather than discourage investment. Greater production in real estate will allow more people to benefit from it in the way of more, different, and better products and lower prices. The biggest beneficiaries are likely to be those at the lower economic levels who depend on a greater supply to increase their opportunity to acquire more goods and services, and for whom almost any increase in price can be most arduous. Prices affect the freedom of individuals in a very significant manner. Paying more for housing leaves less for the acquisition of other goods and services. There is, as a result, an important relationship between a taking clause and the personal freedom of the less materially fortunate in society.

Huge Cost of Taking. It is probable that a broad application of the taking clause, with respect to both appropriation and regulation, will lead to greater governmental expenditures for open space, parks, and recreational sites. The argument is made, therefore, that modern needs demand a strict interpretation. For example, it would cost enormous amounts to purchase some or most of the waterfronts and mountainous areas, canyons, and other lands that environmentalists consider "ecologically sensitive." Were the taking clause not in the way, the state might control the use of these properties to achieve in whole or in part the purposes intended, and not have to compensate the owners. More development could be prohibited and more land kept in a natural state. The public, it is said, would be saved considerable funds.

My judgment would be to the contrary. For the reasons suggested above, it could be an extremely costly undertaking for the prime casualty would be the country's private property system. Such policies will increase substantially the risk and uncertainties of ownership and would consequently inhibit investment, raising prices and limiting competition. Employment and commerce would suffer. Total tax receipts would be less. In view of the adverse consequences to the nation's economic system, it would seem overall less expensive for government to obtain the amenities referred to by purchase rather than by uncompensated appropriation or regulation.

Efficient Allocation of Resources. The market is better suited for determining the optimum use of land than is the political process. Investors, lenders, builders, and developers risk their own funds and tend to be specialists in their field. For both reasons, they will seek to use resources more efficiently and with minimum waste, at least as compared to those in the public sector. The incentives for the public, planners, and politicians (all of whom are instrumental in zoning) are much different. They have little, if any, personal stake in efficiency and may even profit in terms of job promotion, political advancement, or personal satisfaction from wasteful practices and inefficient application of resources in the development of property. Unlike the developers, they do not stand to gain financially if the land serves to satisfy existing consumer demands. They also have much less knowledge in the operation of the industry than those actively engaged in it. The taking clause is a means for curtailing the powers of the public, planners, bureaucrats, and elected officials to control the use of land, and thereby operates in the cause of more efficient allocations.

Monetary Restraint on Acquisition. If there is no monetary restraint on government's ability to acquire land or curb its use, it will have the power to arbitrarily restrict large quantities of it for purposes deemed politically advantageous at the expense of more socially and economically desirable uses. The high court of New York has made the point in the following manner:

[T]he ultimate economic cost of providing the benefit is hidden from those who in a democratic society are given the power of deciding whether or not they wish to obtain the benefit despite the ultimate economic cost, however initially distributed [citation]. In other words, the removal from productive use of private property has an ultimate society cost more easily concealed by imposing the cost on the owner alone. When successfully concealed, the public is not likely to have any objection to the "cost-free" benefit.[104]

Johnson gives considerable attention to this issue in Chapter 2, and I yield further discussion of it to him.

Time Pressures on Development. If there is no restraint on local legislatures, they can alter their policies at will. Under such conditions, owners and developers may rush at times to use their land under the real or imagined belief that their zoning will be changed to one with lesser profit potential. For example, there was a great surge of high-rise condominium construction in San Diego several years ago when it appeared that maximum height limitations would be substantially reduced. The market was flooded with condominium units, many of which were ultimately sold at a loss. The housing market as a whole was adversely affected by a sudden increase in construction not attributable to consumer demand.

Discriminatory Impact. Laws restricting individuals do not necessarily impact these individuals equally. This result stands out prominently in land use regulation. Those in the best financial position to hire lawyers and experts to negotiate with or battle the regulators will not suffer to the same extent from the regulatory process as those without the same resources. The more official discretion permitted, the greater the difference in treatment is likely to be since the regulators will be able to establish more and firmer rules. Therefore limiting the applicability of the taking clause in land use matters will enhance the opportunities for the wealthiest owners and developers and diminish or eliminate them for the less financially fortunate ones. The input of smaller entrepreneurs into the market (and the values they bring) will be reduced or in time possibly terminated.[105]

Irrational Redistribution of Income. The absence of a taking clause or a restricted construction of it would operate to redistribute wealth irrationally because of four reasons.

(1) There is no relationship between the wealth of the owner of land and the desire of the regulating body to confine its use to a classification having limited value. Acreage purchased for speculation, investment, or development would be in the same jeopardy as land owned by a farmer or inherited. Location would be the decisive factor; identity of ownership would be irrelevant.

(2) The wealthier landowners or developers would be in a far better position to withstand regulatory efforts because of much greater ability to hire experts to contest the controls or exercise political influence over the regulators.

(3) Limitations on growth that are likely to accompany or result from greater regulatory powers will have considerably more adverse impact on the poor than on the rich.[106]

(4) The experience of zoning shows that it benefits the more affluent to a much greater extent than the less affluent.[107] Increased power for the regulators would exacerbate the problem.

Inverse Condemnation and Zoning

Given the strong rationale in support of the taking clause, and the evolution of the remedy of inverse condemnation to include harm not resulting from physical invasion, there is good reason for extending it further to include land use regulation or, at the very least, certain aspects of it. Several lower and intermediate courts in California, the U.S. Court of Claims, and at least two and possibly three other federal courts have now taken that course, and it has gained a limited acceptance by the high court of California.

On four occasions in which there were no findings of bad faith or unfair conduct by the locality, California appeal courts (once unanimously and three times by 2-to-1 margins) have applied inverse condemnation to land use regulation or planning. California's high court vacated three of these decisions and has let the fourth stand by denying review to the city. As a result of these cases, inverse condemnation does not lie in California for zoning actions that merely reduce the market value of property but still allow a reasonable and substantial use. It is applicable, however, when the zoning regulations deny any such use. Moreover, to be actionable, there must be actual and specific, not potential, injury to the property owner. The three cases that establish these rules are *Selby Realty v. City of Buenaventura*,[108] *HFH Ltd. v. Superior Court*,[109] and *Eldridge v. City of Palo Alto*.[110]

In 1966, HFH and a leading supermarket chain agreed to buy 5.8 acres of land at a major intersection in Cerritos, California, conditional on the property being rezoned from agriculture to commercial use to permit the development of a shopping center. The city reclassified the property as requested, and the two plaintiffs, relying on the new zoning, purchased the property for $388,000. In 1971, the city conducted new studies of this zoning. Although the other three corners of the intersection were either classified or used for commercial purposes, Cerritos in 1972 downzoned the parcel in question to low-density, single-family residential. The owners filed suit in inverse condemnation, claiming that the downzoning had reduced the land's value from $400,000 to $75,000 and seeking payment of the difference from the city. The trial court dismissed the suit but was reversed by a 2-to-1 decision of an intermediate court that the city would be liable for whatever lowering of value could be proved.

In sustaining the trial court by a 6-to-1 vote, the California Supreme Court refused to approve the imposition of inverse condemnation when a zoning ordinance's "only alleged effect was a diminution in the market value of the property in question."[111] The court limited its opinion to the situation, stating that the case did not present "the question of entitlement to compensation in the event a zoning regulation prohibited substantially *all* use of the land in question." The dissenting opinion argued that:

... not all governmental downzoning must be compensated. However, the compensatory "or damaged" provision of the California Constitution should apply when by public action land has (1) suffered substantial decrease in value, (2) the decrease is of long or potentially infinite duration, and (3) the owner would incur more than his fair share of the financial burden.[112]

In *Selby*[113] the city and county adopted a general plan that showed future routing of streets through the plaintiff's property. When the plaintiff applied for a building permit on the land within the city, the latter would not issue it without a dedication of land for a street shown in its plan. The California Supreme Court said that for various technical reasons the city's refusal to issue a permit did not constitute a "taking" and that the appropriate method by which to consider plaintiff's claim for relief was a proceeding in mandamus to determine the legality of the city's action. With respect to the county which had taken no action concerning the property in question except to adopt the general plan, the high court said that such plans were in nature "tentative and subject to change" and dependent upon unpredictable future events. The court set forth this rule:

The adoption of a general plan is several leagues short of a firm declaration of an intention to condemn property.... In order to state a cause of action for inverse condemnation, there must be an invasion or an appropriation of some valuable property right which the landowner possesses and the invasion or appropriation must directly and specifically affect the landowner to his injury.[114]

The court further said that if the plan were implemented by the county and actually affected "plaintiff's free use of his property," then the validity of the county's action could then be challenged. The appeal court had unanimously ruled to the contrary, holding that the plan had a clear and measurable effect on the owner's property interest, and that, therefore, inverse condemnation was an appropriate remedy.

The Eldridge suit against Palo Alto[115] was brought by the owner of 750 acres then zoned "Open Space (O-S)" in the foothills section of the city. This classification was also the subject of the *Arastra* controversy previously discussed.[116] It allowed only one dwelling unit for every 10 acres and permitted certain agricultural, conservation, and recreational activities. Eldridge contended that his property had a fair market value of $4 million before it was zoned for O-S, and that he had been deprived of that amount by the zoning. He conceded that the O-S zoning ordinance affecting his property was a valid exercise of municipal powers, but argued that this factor did not eliminate his right to compensation. The majority of the appellate court ruled that the suit stated a cause of action for inverse condemnation.[117] This decision was vacated by the California Supreme Court and transferred back to the appeal court for reconsideration in tbe light of the *HFH* ruling.[118] The appeal court, (2 to 1) in a second decision in the case, again ruled that inverse condemnation was applicable, this time on the ground that Palo Alto's ordinance had gone beyond the mere diminution of market values and had instead deprived the owner of any reasonable or beneficial use of his property. In a companion case *(Beyer)* decided in the same opinion, the appeal court found that Palo Alto's open-space ordinance was a valid exercise of the police power and beyond constitutional or other attack, except in proceedings for damages in inverse condemnation. It dismissed Beyer's alternative request for relief that sought a declaration that the ordinance was constitutionally invalid. The California Supreme Court, as indicated, refused to vacate this second *Eldridge* opinion.

The appeal court majority in *Eldridge* said that whether compensation is constitutionally required is a question of degree depending on individual fact situations. When the line had been crossed into the compensable area would be a factual question that would have to be determined separately in each case. Zoning property for open space would clearly require the payment of compensation, as might zoning which allowed some, but not considerably more, use than open space.

Dahl v. City of Palo Alto[119] was an action filed in federal district court against the city by the owner of 291 acres zoned "O-S," to recover damages for the taking of land without just compensation. Plaintiff alleged that the O-S regulation was arbitrary and capricious and did not allow a reasonable use of property. Her complaint also contended that moratoriums on development which preceded the rezoning to O-S constituted a taking in that they were intended to prevent development of the land. The court upheld the complaint against the city's motion to dismiss for failure to state a claim.

Another federal district court in California denied a motion to dismiss in an inverse condemnation suit filed by the owners of 206 acres of unimproved mountain land against the County of Santa Cruz.[120] In a footnote the court observed that "monetary damages are not judicially favored in land regulation cases absent actual physical damage or invasion, regulations which allow no reasonable use of the complainant's property or are exceptionally restrictive, or confiscatory intent or bad faith on the part of the government.... Plaintiffs will therefore have a heavy burden of proving entitlement to monetary relief on the basis of excessive restriction, bad faith or confiscatory intent by the County of

Santa Cruz." In this case the county had rezoned the subject property from one residence per 2½ acres to one residence per 100 acres, and had rejected applications for rezoning, for subdivision into smaller parcels, and for "conceptual approval" of a proposed project.

Two lower California courts have granted relief in inverse condemnation for extremely restrictive zoning. The trial judge in *Friedman et al. v. Fairfax*[121] found that the "declared and subtle policy of the City of Fairfax, aimed at preserving as nearly as possible in its present condition, the plaintiff's country club." The city's zoning ordinance restricted the 23-acre property for that purpose, and the court concluded that a decree invalidating the zoning would not be sufficient since the evidence disclosed the city's determination to retain the same use. The court found that this use was not economically feasible and that the ordinance created "spot zoning." It decided that the adoption of the zoning ordinance amounted to a taking of plaintiff's property for a public use, that the interest taken was a fee, and that the date of the taking was the date of the adoption of the ordinance.

The City of San Diego was defendant in an action filed by the San Diego Gas and Electric Company, challenging its zoning of a portion of plaintiff's land as open space.[122] The trial court held that the plaintiff had been deprived of "any practical, beneficial or economic use of property designated as open space" and was entitled to judgment against the defendant city for money damages in the amount of the fair market value of the property at the date the property was so designated, together with damages to the remaining adjoining parcels it owned.

In a class action filed in a federal court against the Tahoe Regional Planning Commission, the complaint alleged that the land use ordinance affecting the lands in question was so restrictive as to deprive plaintiffs of all benefit or use thereof, and in effect constituted a dedication to the public for use as park, forest, or general recreational area.[123] Relief was sought in the alternative and included a request for an award in inverse condemnation, if the restrictions of the ordinance were found to be valid. The court upheld the complaint in inverse condemnation:

At first blush, this Court entertained the view that the Agencies' land use classifications were either reasonable and valid or unreasonable, arbitrary and invalid, and that, regardless of the final conclusion, there could be no claim for compensation. Further study, however, with the assistance of briefs of counsel, has led to acceptance of an alternative, that is, that public welfare and necessity may reasonably require exceptionally restrictive land use classification for the protection of the public interest in the Lake Tahoe Basin, but that such valid regulations may nevertheless constitute a taking of private property for public use entitling the owner to just compensation.[124]

Subsequently the court reconsidered its position, and in an unpublished order ruled that the plaintiffs were entitled to declaratory and injunctive remedies and not compensatory ones.[125] It appears that the court withheld the availability of the inverse condemnation remedy because of its belief that the defendants lacked the power of eminent domain and hence could not be liable in inverse condemnation. The same court reiterated this position in a subsequent decision.[126]

Regulations causing total loss in value to personal property were held to constitute an inverse condemnation by the U.S. Court of Claims in the case of *Pete v. United States*.[126a] The controversy concerned regulations imposed pursuant to the Wilderness Act of 1964 by the Secretary of Agriculture that prohibited the use and operation of plaintiffs' three barges for commercial purposes within a designated portion of a national forest in Minnesota. The court found that as a result, the commercial value of the vessels was totally destroyed. In awarding damages based on the fair market value of the property, the opinion observed:

When the effect of a governmental regulation on a citizen's property is so pervasive that the property is greatly depreciated in value or that the owner's right to use the property is substantially interfered with, the citizen is entitled to compensation.[126b]

Regulation Eliminates Interests in Property

As the foregoing presentation indicates, the application of inverse condemnation to zoning regulation is no longer a matter solely for discussion among the commentators; a small number of judges have accepted the proposition. It may have more going for it presently than those lonely dissents of history that paved the way to the future. On the other hand, the idea has been rejected by other courts and could be confined at best to very limited use in the future. Even a narrow application, however, will serve as an additional deterrent to municipalities who now confront only the threat of invalidation in zoning matters. Municipalities that act unfairly toward landowners or adopt regulations that remove substantially all value from property should be subject to more than a small slap on the wrist—and that is about all a judgment that zoning is invalid means to most localities, especially the more affluent ones. But a limited invocation of inverse condemnation will not satisfy the intent or objectives of the taking clause. The treatment of property owners under zoning regulation will remain an anomaly in a society dedicated to the preservation and maintenance of individual rights.

The authors of *The Taking Issue* express concern about "the important issues of civil liberty associated with ownership of property."[127] Their approach to preserving an owner's liberties is a rather novel one, however. They contend that a regulation of the use of land "if reasonably related to a valid public purpose, can never constitute a taking"[128] but would be willing to pay compensation (only) when regulation results in an "actual appropriation of land for public use, such as for a park, highway or reservoir."[129] Thus government would be empowered to regulate land use virtually as it pleases until the stage is reached when the owner retains only the last remaining prerogative of ownership. It is only then that the civil liberties issue would arise, although the owner might have sustained considerably more harm under prior restrictions. The time for judicial intervention would have no relation to the damages suffered.

The Taking Issue and the Rockefeller Task Force are willing to tolerate measures extremely harsh to owners on the assumption that the nation will thereby obtain a better environment. In the eternal competition between regulation and liberty, they are clearly on the side of the former when it comes to the use of land. Such faith in government performance is difficult to comprehend in view of (1) the questionable and counterproductive results of government social programs over the years,[130] (2) the experience of communities which have never adopted zoning,[131] (3) the record of California's efforts to control for environmental purposes the use of land along its coast,[132] (4) the impact on land use caused by the new environmentalism,[133] and (5) the record of zoning.[134] While most civil libertarians acknowledge that no liberties are absolute, they strongly oppose invoking limitations in the absence of very strong cause. Using that guide alone, a most persuasive case can be made for expanding rather than minimizing the impact of the taking clause.

Nor does the distinction between regulation and taking stand up in any realistic sense. The *Restatement of the Law of Property* suggests that property consists of intangible interests,[135] a theory consistent with Justice Holmes's famous "bundle of sticks."[136] There is nothing unusual or strange in this perspective:

... [W]hat is really bought and sold in markets is not simply physical objects, but sets of rights in those objects—the right to take physical possession, the right to resell, the right to consume, the right to change the form of the object, the right to transport it, etc. It is not the price of a bushel of wheat as a physical object that is determined by the forces of supply and demand; it is the price of the set of rights which goes with "title" to wheat, i.e., the right to resell it, to grind it into flour, to take physical possession, to transport it, etc. If the bundle of rights which goes with owning wheat is changed, the value of the "wheat" changes. The same comments hold for land, (e.g., does it include mineral rights?, how is it zoned?), for buildings, for capital equipment, for radio frequencies, for money, even for the value of the services which we perform with our minds and muscle. The value of all goods is determined by the rights individuals possess in those goods.[137]

The *Cress*[138] and *Causby*[139] cases, among many others, recognized that an owner can retain many property rights and still sustain serious harm because of the destruction of the others. Regulation operates with the same consequences to the owner.

The late Justice Harlan's dissent in the *Central Eureka Mining Company*[140] case reflects on the prevailing approach:

In these circumstances making the respondents' right to compensation turn on whether the government took the ceremonial step of planting the American flag on the mining premises [citation] is surely to permit technicalities of form to dictate consequences of substance.... [141] But where the government proceeds by indirection, and accomplishes by regulation what is the equivalent of outright physical seizure of private property, courts should guard themselves against permitting formalities to obscure actualities. [142]

The Taking Issue raises another question about regulation of property use. Its authors say that due to the requirement of Holmes's balancing test, land use regulation is subject to a stricter judicial standard than other types of governmental regulations which are only tested to determine whether they bear a reasonable relationship to a valid public purpose. [143] While this may be correct with respect to many economic controls, it is clearly not accurate when it comes to regulation affecting most guarantees in the Bill of Rights. Such a position fails to recognize that the taking clause is part of that document and should be entitled to the stricter standard of review accorded various of its provisions. [144]

When rights or interests are involved that the courts consider preferred, transcendent, or fundamental, the government carries a heavy burden of persuasion that the legislation or regulation is constitutionally valid. "In a long series of cases, the court has held that where fundamental personal liberties are involved, they may not be abridged by the states simply on a showing that a regulatory statute has some rational relationship to the effectuation of a proper state purpose." [145]

The list of preferred interests has been growing in recent years as rights are added and even new ones created. Specific guarantees in the Bill of Rights have been construed to include penumbras "formed by emanations from those guarantees that help give them life and substance." [146] On the basis that the Bill of Rights intended to guarantee basic, deep-rooted, and fundamental values that may not have been specified, some justices have sought to delineate certain activities as within the scope of protection. [147] One noteworthy exception stands out in these efforts to enhance individual rights, and it is the interpretation given "taking" in the regulatory context. This exception exists to the detriment of those in the population intended to be protected by the property safeguard in the Bill of Rights.

The strongest voice to date against general imposition of inverse condemnation to zoning comes from the California Supreme Court in the *HFH* case previously discussed. Probably that opinion's most persuasive argument is that if the plaintiffs were accorded the relief they sought, the court would have to act contrary to the holding of the *Euclid* case, which validated the constitutionality of zoning. In view of the progression of inverse condemnation and the experience of over 50 years of zoning regulation, however, the *Euclid* decision can hardly be considered a beacon of judicial wisdom. Zoning is no longer that auxiliary to nuisance law as conceived by the *Euclid* court. It is being used by local residents and politicians to accomplish whatever purposes they deem desirable at the serious expense of, among others, owners of property.

In the *Euclid* case, the landowner claimed that the zoning ordinance reduced the value of a portion of its land from $10,000 to $2500 per acre. The court upheld the ordinance, and for some that decision settled two questions: (1) a municipality has no obligation to compensate the owners for the difference in value, and (2) the substantial loss was not in itself sufficient to invalidate the ordinance. There is no doubt that the case accepted in principle the latter proposition; however, the same cannot be concluded about the former. While inverse condemnation was not unknown at the time, it certainly had not progressed to the operational level of today. In the federal courts at least, inverse condemnation did not become readily usable until the *Causby* case, decided 20 years after *Euclid*; and even in that action, Justice Black sharply dissented from the idea of creating a constitutional remedy for the harm complained about.

There are other aspects of the *Euclid* case that warrant reconsideration of its outcome. First, the courts, as previously discussed, since the date of that decision have shown ever greater concern for the rights of property owners in eminent domain and inverse condemnation proceedings. Second, the subsequent experience of zoning has revealed much about it that the courts could not possibly have comprehended in its early stages. Zoning has given enormous discretion to politicians, citizens, and courts over the use and enjoyment of private property to such a degree that for many owners the taking clause has for all practical purposes become meaningless.

In addition, the *Euclid* remedy of invalidating ordinances found to be unconstitutional has these serious shortcomings:

(1) Owners have to pay legal and court costs and fees involved in vacating the existing classification and rezoning the property to a judicially acceptable classification, and will continue paying taxes and possibly interest on a mortgage while the proceedings are pending, which may be many months and probably years.

(2) If a proposed development is delayed, it may in time become unfeasible because market and mortgage conditions change. Thus, there have now been three credit crunches since World War II, and each has had the effect of discouraging some proposed projects.

(3) Because of owners' problems in undertaking and succeeding in litigation, municipalities have to a large extent become the final arbiters in

land use. It is far less onerous for a locality to carry the case to the highest court and thereby maximize the plaintiff's burden. The penalties it faces are that the land will be zoned not to its liking, and it will have to pay legal and expert fees.

In *HFH*, the California high court opinion construed the term *damage*, which appears in the taking clause of the California Constitution, to mean not a diminution of market value, but actual physical damage. It states that whether the governmental action is wrongful or not is irrelevant if actionable harm has occurred. The decision raises these other issues in regard to the applicability of inverse condemnation in zoning matters:

(1) The court distinguished between diminution in value due to physical damage and that due to regulation. From the perspective of the owner whose rights are supposed to be protected, it makes no difference what action of government caused the loss. Other courts have ignored this distinction in inverse condemnation cases, and the subsequently decided *Eldridge* case has eroded it in California. Prior opinions in that state in "next intersection" cases had stretched the physical invasion requirements to fictional status.[148]

(2) The court quotes from a 1923 Wisconsin case that states: "[I]ncidental damages to property resulting from governmental activity or laws passed in the promotion of public welfare are not considered a taking of the property for which compensation must be made." That approach likewise has been changed in inverse condemnation. The damages recognized under that doctrine are often incidental to some authorized public purpose engaged in by a lawfully acting governmental agency. The *Pumpelly* and *Causby* cases should have settled this point.

The California court seems to have confused cause and effect. It apparently still subscribes to the "dispassionate" theory of zoning wherein lawmakers are concerned only with the "public interest." Fifty years of zoning experience reveals that virtually the opposite occurs in connection with the more significant matters. Zoning responds to the self-interest of those able to influence the local legislators, and it is frequently incidental whether the public interest has been served. I do not know the details of the *HFH* case. Typically such rezonings occur to satisfy the special interests of nearby home or possibly landowners. As voters, residents are likely to have much more influence with the lawmakers than several nonresident owners are. Such a contest over self-interest can hardly be termed an exercise in promoting the public welfare.

(3) The California court talks about the reciprocal benefits and burdens of zoning, contending that zoning led to the development of homes in the area surrounding the subject property and that these homes created the need for the shopping center. Zoning is what gave value to the land, says the opinion, and now the owners were trying to "avoid the enforce-

ment of residential zoning on their property while benefiting from its enforceability as to other property''.[149] The majority does not understand urban development. It is probable that, even if there never were a zoning ordinance in existence, the corner tract owned by plaintiffs would have been developed for commercial uses and the surrounding area for homes or apartments. The experience of cities without zoning clearly discloses such land organization at major intersections. It is even possible that zoning reduced density in the area adjoining the HFH property, lowering to some extent its value. In the absence of zoning, the surrounding land might have been developed for multifamily or higher-density single-family units.

(4) The court believes that land prices are discounted in accordance with the likelihood of future zoning changes. This is highly doubtful. Alterations in zoning are made by local legislators, and there is usually no way of evaluating years in advance when or if they will occur. It seems almost inconceivable that a parcel at a corner of a major intersection would be downzoned to single-family use. How does one discount the probability of changes in the political climate or of the council's makeup, except as a general risk? Decisions such as *HFH* could cause a developer to overstate the risk of loss, and they might thereby inhibit development substantially.

(5) In asserting that buyers of real estate assume the risk of future changes in zoning, the court denigrates property rights. It establishes a standard which no court would countenance for other rights protected in the Bill of Rights. Liberties should remain stable in spite of changes in the will, whim, or mood of the legislature. Moreover, there are others besides speculators and investors (assuming there is a difference between the two) involved in property ownership. Some people acquire land for farming or inherit property. These groups will find it extremely difficult to sell for development purposes if the buyer has to assume great risks of future changes in zoning. Difficulty in selling translates into lower prices, a penalty for which neither the farmer nor heir has bargained.

The Taking Clause and Better Housing Conditions

Johnson's position that planning without the restraint of prices creates serious problems for society is supported in many court decisions which express concern over the limitation on housing construction and mobility brought about by restrictive zoning practices. Unfortunately, the opinions usually are not reasoned from the same perspective as Johnson's, and certain of the solutions prescribed either will not alleviate or will compound existing land use problems. These courts have not recognized the likely superiority of prices as a planning mechanism, and they are substituting their own version of planning and regulation for those that have failed. Landowners frequently benefit indirectly from these opinions which are intended primarily to aid housing consumers. The cases in question have been referred to as the "exclusion cases," and they follow three separate courses, each illustrated by a leading case from a different state: *Southern Burlington County NAACP v. Township of Mt. Laurel* in New Jersey,[150] *Berenson v. Town of New Castle* in New York,[151] and *The Appeal of Kit-Mar Builders Inc.* in Pennsylvania.[152]

In the *Kit-Mar* line of cases, the Pennsylvania Supreme Court struck down zoning ordinances in part because they caused a taking of property. But the more important impetus for these decisions came from the exclusionary impact of such restrictions on would-be migrants to the suburbs. Large lots may reduce density and congestion, lessen the cost of utilities, and offer virtually greenbelt living, but only at a substantial cost to the well-being of those who want to reside in the localities but cannot afford these amenities. To protect the interests of such persons, the Pennsylvania high court in the *Kit-Mar* case in 1970 nullified 2- and 3-acre minimum lot sizes in favor of 1-acre usage, and New Jersey courts subsequently overturned smaller minimum lot size requirements.

In all the cases cited above, the high courts concur with Johnson's conclusion about the consequences of existing regulation. The majority and one of the concurring opinions in the *Mt. Laurel* case can be considered primers for demonstrating how local legislators serve the interest they represent at the expense of others. Together, both opinions relate what can happen in a state when little restraint is applied to zoning. Prior cases reveal the problems that had been created. Until recent years, the high court of New Jersey was a strong proponent of a kind of restrictive zoning that many who now identify themselves as environmentalists insist we must have lest the quality of life deteriorate. In 1952 in the *Township of Wayne*[153] case, the Chief Justice observed the following in the course of his opinion:

Has a municipality the right to impose minimum floor area requirements in the exercise of its zoning power? Much of the proof adduced by the defendant Township was devoted to showing that the mental and emotional health of its inhabitants depended upon the proper size of their homes. We may take notice without formal proof that there are minimums in housing below which one may not go without risk of impairing the health of those who dwell therein. ... But quite apart from these considerations of public health which cannot be overlooked, minimum floor-area standards are justified on the ground that they promote the general welfare of the community.... The size of the dwelling in any community inevitably affects the character of the community and does much to determine whether or not it is a desirable place in which to live....[154]

A concurring opinion embellished these sentiments:

The provisions with respect to two-story dwellings were influenced in considerable by aesthetic considerations which I believe to be entirely proper [citations]. In the Point Pleasant case I recently expressed the view, to which I adhere fully, "that it is in the public interest that our communities, so far as feasible, should be made pleasant and inviting and that primary considerations of attractiveness and beauty might well be frankly acknowledged as appropriate, under certain circumstances, in the promotion of the general welfare of our people."[155]

Ten years later in a decision affirming a zoning ordinance excluding all mobile homes, the majority opinion of the New Jersey Supreme Court sustained the desires of local residents:

Trailer camps, because of their particular nature and relation to the public health, safety, morals and general welfare, present a municipality with a host of problems, and these problems persist wherever such camps are located.... Clearly trailer camps bring problems of congestion with all their attendant difficulties.[156]

Such a legal climate obviously has not been helpful to the development of housing for the less affluent. The conclusion of a study made of the four most important counties in northern New Jersey—Morris, Somerset, Middlesex, and Monmouth—is probably applicable to most of the state and describes the dire picture confronting persons of average or less-than-average income who want to move to the newer communities:

The present policy is to prohibit all mobile homes and practically to prohibit multiple dwellings (especially for normal size families). As for single-family housing, the policy (except in part of Middlesex County) is to make very little provision for small houses on small lots, about 1/4 of the available vacant residential land is zoned to permit only large single-family houses and large lots.[157]

In eight counties 60 percent of the vacant, residentially zoned, developable land was classified for a minimum lot size of 1 acre or more. An additional 22 percent was zoned for a minimum of 1/2 to 1 acre.[158]

Responding to this experience, the New Jersey Supreme Court reversed its prior course and came full circle with its holding in 1975 in the *Mt. Laurel* case, that every "developing" municipality in that state with "sizeable land areas"

...must, by its land-use regulations, presumptively make realistically possible an appropriate variety and choice of housing. More specifically, presumptively it cannot foreclose the opportunity of the classes of people mentioned for low and moderate income housing and in its regulations must affirmatively afford that opportunity, at least to the extent of the municipality's fair share of the present and prospective regional need therefor. These obligations must be met unless the particular municipality can sustain the heavy burden of demonstrating peculiar circumstances which dictate that it should not be required so to do.[159]

The opinion used three terms which subsequently have been the subject of considerable litigation: *developing communities, sizable land areas*, and *fair share*. It appears to have established for those communities affected a quota system of zoning for low- and moderate-income housing. This was the interpretation given the *Mt. Laurel* decision in an opinion delivered in 1976 by Superior Court Judge David Furman of Middlesex County in a suit filed against twenty-three municipalities of that county by the Urban League of Greater New Brunswick and various private individuals as a class action.[160] Judge Furman struck down as unconstitutional the zoning ordinances of eleven of the municipalities, dismissed without condition the case against one municipality, and granted eleven other dismissals conditional upon their passing specially negotiated amendments to their zoning ordinances acceptable to the plaintiffs and approved by the court.

These amendments included deletion of limitations in six of the localities on the required number of bedrooms or of rooms in multifamily housing, deletion of special procedures for obtaining zoning for multifamily housing in six localities, reduction of parking space requirements in two localities, and reduction of minimum floor area requirements or minimum lot sizes in six localities. One community agreed to increase the maximum density allowable for multifamily housing; two others to increase height limitations; one to delete a multifamily housing ceiling of 15 percent of total units; and six others to rezone certain tracts of land from either industry or single-family to multifamily residential.

Furman ordered the eleven municipalities whose ordinances he declared unconstitutional to revise their zoning to permit the development of 18,697 low- and moderate-income housing units by 1985. He proportioned this amount among the municipalities to create a balance of 15 percent low and 19 percent moderate income, equal to the county averages. Assuming a possible average density of 10 per acre, it is apparent that a considerable amount of land would have to be zoned for the designated housing.

The New York high court, in the *Berenson* case decided in late 1975, adopted a policy for zoning that seems to be headed toward that of New Jersey. It goes much further in controlling zoning than the Pennsylvania court's practice of merely overturning the ordinance in issue. In *Berenson*, owners of a vacant tract sought to erect a large condominium development on their property which was zoned for 1-acre residences. They brought a declaratory judgment action against the locality, attacking the validity of the zoning ordinance in its entirety on the ground that the ordinance excluded multifamily residential housing from the list of permitted uses. In sending the case back for trial, the Court of Appeals set forth new rules for determining the validity of zoning. According to this court, the primary goal of a zoning ordinance "must be to provide for the development of a balanced, cohesive community which will make efficient use of the town's available land."[161] The test to determine whether this has been accomplished is twofold: first, whether a properly balanced and well-ordered plan has been provided for the community; second, whether adequate consideration had been given to regional needs and requirements. The court acknowledged that in enforcing such standards, it was performing the work of a regional planner. Until the legislature acted in this regard, however, the court said it had no other alternative.

The *Berenson* opinion suggests that its authors believe that geographic areas should contain specified kinds or amounts of various housing. Such an approach can lead to the establishment of quotas, and if that occurs, the New York jurists like their brethren in New Jersey will have entered the field of planning without prices, subject to those severe constraints and handicaps discussed in the chapters that follow. These courts will have given themselves the unenviable task of making decisions that our society has generally left to the marketplace. How does one go about determining housing needs or requirements, for either the present or the future? How many low- and moderate-income units are needed to satisfy community or regional housing needs? How much land should be used or reserved for certain kinds of housing? What constitutes a "balanced" community? The *Mt. Laurel* decision is still warm, and already the community is embroiled in controversy about carrying it out. The New Jersey Public Advocate filed a complaint in May 1976 against that community contending that it had failed to comply with the Supreme Court ruling.[162] The advocate protested that *Mt. Laurel* had rezoned for an unreasonably small number of low- and moderate-income units, and was proposing to adopt ordinances that provided little suitable land for erecting them and required excessively expensive building specifications.

The New Jersey high court is also subject to the criticism that it has created unrealizable expectations. Consider the outcome of the Middlesex County litigation.[163] By causing eleven municipalities to reduce their zoning standards, Judge Furman's ruling will lead to the production of more conventional housing. The impact on the other eleven towns of the requirements for zoning for low- and moderate-income housing units may be much different, however.

Building for these income levels requires government subsidies which presently do not appear likely to materialize anywhere near the numbers proposed. Success also requires attracting competent developers, managers, and desirable occupants, all of which, prior experience indicates, may be in short supply for such developments.[164] It is doubtful that only zoning has been holding back minorities and people of less income and that they would otherwise flock to the suburbs.[165] Land costs are high, public transportation limited, and living more expensive and frequently less comfortable in suburbia for poorer people. It is possible to raise the subsidies to levels where such reluctance could be overcome; but this could become exceedingly expensive, and abandonment might in time become a very serious problem.

From what I can determine, the average cost of producing in 1976 a housing unit of about 800 to 1000 square feet (minimal size for family occupancy) in the highest cost areas of the nation was approximately $25,000 to $30,000 (including land cost). At this rate, the total cost to comply with Judge Furman's ruling for about 18,700 units at 100 percent subsidy would be at least $470 million for the nine years from 1976 to 1985. The annual cost of such a subsidy under current programs varies from 13 to 15 percent of the cost of providing the unit.[166] This amounts to a large burden for taxpayers to sustain, satisfying alleged housing needs in one county of New Jersey which, incidentally, has only 9 percent of the state's population.

The political feasibility of the court's objectives is therefore highly doubtful, and as a result the *Mt. Laurel* decision may prove to be counterproductive. At a density of 10 units per acre, Furman's decision would require 1870 acres to be designated for low- and moderate-income housing. When land is zoned for uses not in demand, or is tied up pending resolution of zoning conflicts, less will be available for what is needed, and other lot prices will rise accordingly. Those not able to afford the increased cost will be excluded.

Housing quotas within a locality can be accommodated by building completely subsidized projects or by dispersing a small percentage of units for low- and moderate-income levels, say 15 to 20 percent, in conventional housing developments. Some communities have required such integration in certain types of developments and thereby may have further encumbered housing construction.[167] Even when density or building code bonuses are offered, many builders resist these quotas. They consider them as adding to the risk and cost, lowering the rentability or salability of the conventional units, and raising operating expenses. Investors consequently will hesitate to undertake projects with required quotas or seek bigger returns (if that is possible) to compensate for the added risk. Neither alternative is desirable in this day of low housing production and high inflation.

The New Jersey, Pennsylvania, and New York courts are reacting pragmatically to the abuses of zoning regulations. The New Jersey judges seek to correct existing conditions by causing the construction of more housing for people of average and less income, and are moulding the law to accomplish what they consider in the public interest. One criticism of their conduct is that they are not fulfilling the judicial function of applying the law, but are instead creating it. It is perhaps too late in time to insist that courts observe restraint and avoid undertaking tasks assigned to other institutions in our society. Courts determined to act pragmatically, however, can accomplish more for housing by allowing the market to operate and not inhibiting it with new controls. The legal device to achieve this objective is the taking clause; a broader application of it to regulation would eliminate much of those restrictions which presently curb the production of housing. Nor would this judicial course do violence to the notion of judicial restraint for the reasons set forth previously.

In his concurring opinion in the *Mt. Laurel* case, Justice Pashman detailed the regulatory devices by which exclusion has been accomplished. He categorized them into six groups: minimum house size requirements, minimum lot size and frontage requirements, prohibition of multifamily housing, restrictions on number of bedrooms in apartments to limit school children, prohibition of mobile homes and overzoning for nonresidential uses. Most of these regulations also have the effect of reducing the value of privately owned land, and therefore might well fall to the prohibitions of a broadly interpreted taking clause. Or if compensation were required for the owner, it is not likely that the locality would be eager to pay for the amenities these restrictions may provide. In the absence of such restrictions, a larger supply of housing would result. This would lead to lower prices and more variety, and provide greater mobility in the market for shelter, which would be especially advantageous for those of lesser incomes who have to rely largely on the filtering process to acquire better homes and apartments.[168] Employment and business would likewise benefit. Those seeking to use the judiciary to obtain better living conditions should be aware of their affinity with the cause of property owners under the taking provision.

The Taking Clause and Optimum Land Use

When considering land use regulation, neither the legislatures nor the courts have accorded the taking clause the special recognition given other provisions in the Bill of Rights. Most writers and commentators do not seem disturbed. When the Rockefeller Task Force said that the country's mood had changed and demanded severe limitations on the application of that clause,[169] there was some anger, but not near the outrage that would have occurred were almost any other part of the Bill of Rights involved. There are at least two reasons for this. First, the aspect of the clause that bothers the Task Force has already been decimated through the years as courts have increasingly approved harsh zoning regulations. Second, the clause relates to property, which many writers and commentators do not associate with personal liberties. This group seems willing to condemn zoning only when it excludes minorities or the poor or perhaps prevents communal living, and prefers to use the more "socially" oriented constitutional provisions in the attack. Civil rights groups grounded their challenge in *Valtierra*[170] on the equal protection clause, and the ACLU contested Belle Terre's zoning under that provision and the right to travel.[171]

The New Jersey Supreme Court based its *Mt. Laurel* ruling on the substantive due process and equal protection of the laws requirements of the New Jersey Constitution. It decided that these provisions require that the police power be exercised only to promote the public health, safety, morals, or general welfare. The court found that the Mt. Laurel ordinance did not afford a reasonable opportunity for the development of low- and moderate-income housing, and therefore did not promote the public welfare. The affected municipalities were told that they must henceforth regulate the land to enable all sectors in society, rich and poor alike, to live in the more desirable areas, preserving at the same time important environmental values.

The court thus satisfied those who want controls placed on property owners and the white affluent suburbs, both leading villains in egalitarian morality tales of the day. As has been indicated, it is questionable whether the pragmatic results of this decision will achieve expectations. Nor is the morality story accurate or appropriate. It would be misleading to denote heroes and villains in a situation where the law is supporting the normal desires of people to secure what they believe are optimum living conditions. The fault lies with the adoption of well-intended laws that experience shows can be readily subverted to the accomplishment of undesirable purposes. The New Jersey judges continue on the same erroneous course.

Assume the existence of the small township of Paradise, located in a developing area adjoining the ocean where the terrain and climate are idyllic. Suppose for purposes of the illustration that the poor are as anxious and willing to live in this town as the rich. In the absence of any quota requirements, the township's land will be very expensive and will house almost exclusively the wealthy. Probably there would be more people and a greater variety of structures and incomes if there were no zoning. But in no event would a system dependent chiefly on market forces allow for the development of low-cost housing within such a town. The proponents of quotas argue that they are necessary to prevent exactly this result. The land belongs to all the people, they say, and regulation is essential to prevent the most pleasing portions of the earth from being monopolized by the rich.

It is much simpler to voice this rhetoric than to achieve its goal. Surely if the rich are not entitled to preponderant use of this area, neither is any other group. All income groups should somehow be equally represented. And if we carry this idea to its logical conclusion, so should minorities and possibly even large families and occupational groups (particularly those who work in the community or possibly nearby). Then there is the question of who makes the decision as to which groups are represented, where, and to what extent. It will have to be done either by some governmental commission or by judges—and that fact in itself creates a major problem. Requiring that 15 or 20 percent of the housing or population of Paradise be limited to low- and moderate-income families means roughly that somewhere near this number of richer families will have to be excluded. (Regardless of how small the area devoted to the less expensive housing is, it would still require use of land that would otherwise be developed for more costly construction.) The desire to help poorer people can be achieved only at the expense of families whose failing is that they have more wealth.

Moreover, since the inexpensive housing would have to be subsidized, more people would qualify for it than the quotas would permit. Estimates have been made that 25 million American households—40 percent of the total population—were eligible for the major housing subsidies under the federal programs in existence in the early 1970s.[172] Obviously only a fraction of that number ever obtained it. In many instances there were long waiting lists for subsidized projects, and some applicants used special pressures to qualify. The question arises as to how selections for the subsidies should be made. What rules of morality, ethics, or philosophy should be used to establish priorities? Can any objective criteria ever be devised to determine which human beings are entitled to or merit or deserve to live in the most desirable areas? Even if we assume that such standards are somehow attainable, among the least qualified to determine them would be a publicly appointed body whose members are selected most frequently on the basis of their political acumen rather than any other form of wisdom.[173] Comparable criticism can also be leveled at the judiciary. Since payment of subsidies would have to be involved, those denied entry into the highly desirable areas, both rich and poor, would be sacrificing to some extent for the benefit of those selected. Taxes would be higher or other social programs limited, or there would be more pressures on interest rates as the government borrowed money to finance developments. A study released in 1972 showed that in most of the subsidized housing programs used in Boston, between one-fourth and one-half of the total federal subsidy did not reach the residents but went for federal and local administrative expenses and for tax benefits to investors.[174]

Why, then, is a quota system morally or socially preferable to the selections of the impersonal and more efficient and less expensive marketplace? Egalitarians may still support these quotas as contributing to greater equality in society. This position would have to ignore the substantial powers given commissions, courts, and people of political influence in determining the makeup of the quotas and those who will be benefited. In many instances persons granted these powers will be able to use them to advance their own financial interests. Administrators in the programs will acquire considerable discretionary powers and probably increased earnings. Builders and developers who specialize in the programs also can be expected to profit most handsomely. Perhaps the least desirable result for a representative society is the authority that certain individuals will have thereafter over the lives of others. Whatever lessening of housing inequalities the quotas will cause would accordingly be negated by increases in other inequalities.

For those who insist on optimum use of land within Paradise, I again refer to the use of the taking clause to eliminate political barriers curbing the development of housing. If the taking clause were interpreted in a manner that would invalidate zoning, the result probably would be greater density in single-family housing in the town, and this would enable more people to benefit from this land (at the cost of minimal additional congestion and somewhat less open space). The likelihood is that there would be some or greater development of apartments, townhouses, and condominiums. The income range of residents would consequently be broader. Being a highly desirable community in which to live and without barriers to development, it would not take long for the land to be developed; people would be moving in from other homes, starting a chain of moves which would enable more low-, moderate-, and average-income families within the general area to obtain better housing.[175]

Law and Economics

There may be no better illustration of the relationship between law and economics than is provided by judicial interpretation of the taking clause. Over 95 percent of municipalities with populations of 5000 or over are zoned,[176] and what they do in relation to land use has great impact on the building industry, one of the largest in the nation, as well as on those dependent on it for their well-being, which includes a large percentage of the population. It would seem incumbent on the judiciary in land use cases to consider as at least one critical factor, the economic costs and consequences of the regulation, which is the subject of the litigation before them. This has not been the approach of the U.S. Supreme Court in the recent crop of zoning cases it has decided. In none of these cases has there been other than cursory economic analysis. Instead, we have been told on occasion of the meritorious service zoning is performing, without any mention of the enormous cost entailed. Zoning adulation appears to cut across ideological grounds. Justice Powell, concurring in the *Young* case,[177] quoted from Justice Marshall's dissent in *Boraas*:

... it also is undeniable that zoning, when used to preserve the character of specific areas of a city, is perhaps "the most essential function performed by local government, for it is one of the primary means by which we protect that sometimes difficult to define concept of quality of life."[178]

Justice Douglas' majority opinion in the *Boraas* case, also contained comments most favorable to the regulation.[179]

Possibly the Justices are unaware that zoning is far from an accepted good in American society and for a great many is an undesirable form of land use control. Justices in state high courts have excoriated certain zoning practices.[180] Some cities, notably Houston, Texas, and a larger number of counties either have never adopted zoning or have repealed it.[181] Most elections on zoning (referendums or straw votes) appear to have gone against it.[182] Due chiefly to inadequacies and failures, zoning has changed substantially over the years since its adoption by New York City in 1916, so that the resemblance is little more than in name only. The political process has not been comfortable with any brand of zoning for very long throughout its existence. I am confident that Justice Sutherland, author of the *Euclid* opinion, would find hard to believe the amount and severity of regulation that has resulted over the years to a system he considered as not much more than an adjunct to nuisance law.

Assuredly, the Burger Court is concerned about the prerogatives of ownership. Its decision in *Hudgens v. NLRB*[183] should leave little doubt about that. In the case, strikers picketed in front of their employer's store in a shopping center, and when the center's manager threatened them with arrest for criminal trespass, they terminated their activities and left. Their union subsequently filed with the NLRB an unfair labor practice charge against the owner of the shopping center. The board entered an order in favor of the union, concluding that the constitutional rights of free speech guaranteed the union's right to picket the employer's store in the center. In a 6-to-2 opinion, the high Court disagreed and held that the strikers did not have any such constitutional right. Five of the Justices, in two separate opinions, joined to overrule a 1968 decision of the Court which would have supported the union's position.[184] The majority made it clear that the typical shopping center has all the characteristics of private property, and the public has those privileges within it as accorded by the owner.

The relevancy of the opinion to what occurs under zoning should not be lost. If the present Court is willing, as it did in the *Hudgens* case, to hold the line on speech rights in confrontation with property rights, what consideration should it accord to the garden variety of zoning laws, downzoning, or growth controls which infringe on ownership? An Oregon Supreme Court justice once observed that in constitutional terms, zoning protections are not in the same league as speech and press.[185]

Nor can it be said that the Burger Court is reluctant to engage in economic analysis in adjudicating regulatory legislation. In the case in which the Court struck down the Virginia law banning the advertising of prescription drugs,[186] Justice Blackmun's majority opinion climaxes with an exposition of the operation of advertising in our society and asserts that the commercial speech involved performed microeconomic functions worthy of protection under the First Amendment. The Justice observed that "the particular consumer's interest in the free flow of commercial information . . . may be as keen, if not keener by far, than his interest in the day's most urgent political debate."[187]

Deciding the constitutionality of zoning laws usually involves resort to a reasonableness standard, and there is virtually no limit to the considerations pertinent to making this judgment. It is essentially a weighing process involving a comparative evaluation of competing values and interests. Economics has a role in this analysis.

The importance of economic issues in zoning cases is shown by the situation in *City of Eastlake v. Forest City Enterprises*,[188] decided within weeks of the Virginia advertising case but lacking a discussion of economics. The plaintiff owned an 8-acre tract zoned for light industrial use. He applied to the city planning commission for a zoning reclassification to permit construction of a high-rise apartment building. The commission approved the request and recommended the change to the city council, which then had final authority in the matter. Before the council could act, the voters of Eastlake amended the city charter to require that any changes in zoning agreed to by the council must be approved by a 55 percent vote in a referendum, the costs of which were to be borne by the owner. The charter amendment was apparently directed at multifamily housing in general and the proposed high-rise in particular. The city council passed the requested change in zoning for the 8 acres, but it was not approved in a referendum by the requisite 55 percent margin, killing the proposed rezoning.

The Ohio Supreme Court, by a 5-to-2 vote, held that the popular referendum requirement was an unlawful delegation of legislative authority from the council to the voters and for this and other reasons violated the due process guarantees of the federal Constitution.[189] The U.S. Supreme Court reversed on a 6-to-3 vote, ruling that no constitutional violation had occurred. The lawsuit did not consider the taking question or any issues about the legality of the existing zoning classification.

It is apparent from the split in voting of the federal and state justices that learned minds can readily differ on the legal issues. The same cannot be as easily concluded about the economic effects of the opinion. If such referenda become popular, these are likely ramifications (assuming, of course, that the courts do not enter wholesale into the zoning business):

(1) This decision will give members of the public who bother to vote decisive powers over zoning changes, and more applications for amendments are likely to fail. Fewer developers will be willing to spend the added time and money to obtain zoning amendments, and that translates into less production of housing and other improved real estate. There will be higher prices, less competition, and reduced variety in real estate.

(2) The demand for land will be less, adversely influencing its price. More of it will remain idle. On the other hand, the prices and rents of existing structures will rise, possibly skyrocketing in time if the voters continue to reject changes in their communities.

(3) Decisions on the allocation of resources relating to land use will be increasingly transferred from those assigned this task in a private enterprise society, that is, participants in the private market, to a combination of planners, politicians, and certain voters. Each of the latter groups has minimum technical and entrepreneurial expertise in construction and development, and little incentive to satisfy pressing economic demands.

(4) There will be reduced economic activity in the construction and related industries to the disadvantage of employers and workers. Because of the multiplier effect of all economic activity, business conditions in other areas will also suffer.

(5) The essence of a private-enterprise system is individual initiative. It is a system premised on the belief that the common good is best served when the energy, creativity, and imagination of producers are allowed relatively free reign. On this basis, private enterprise in land use and development will be severely limited in those places that require referenda for approval of zoning changes. While buildings will be built and land developed by private investors, they will be carrying out, to a much greater extent than heretofore, rules and designs established not in response to consumer desires but by local politicians for whom the demands of local voters are decisive.

The *City of Eastlake* case is very damaging to the role of private enterprise in a major industry. Government will be making many more decisions ordinarily left to the marketplace. This result could never have been the intent of the designers of our form of government, and is clearly contrary to the meaning and significance of the taking clause which, though not directly at issue in the case, is the ultimate source of the zoning power.

Notes

1. "... nor shall private property be taken for public use without just compensation." U.S. Const. Amend. V. The U.S. Supreme Court has held that these requirements are "incorporated" in the Fourteenth Amendment to the federal Constitution. Missouri Pacific Railway Co. v. Nebraska, 164 U.S. 403, 417 (1896).

2. 260 U.S. 393 (1922).

3. W. Reilly (ed.), The Use of Land: A Citizen's Policy Guide to Urban Growth, A Task Force Report sponsored by the Rockefeller Brothers Fund, (New York: Thomas Y. Crowell Company, 1973).

4. F. Bosselman, D. Callies, and J. Banta, The Taking Issue (Washington: Government Printing Office, 1973).

5. *See* note 3 *supra* at 173.

6. *Id*. at 175.

7. Pennsylvania Coal Co. v. Mahon, 260 U.S. 393, 415 (1922).

8. *Id*. at 414.

9. *Id*. at 415.

10. *Id*. at 418.

11. *Id*. at 417.

12. *Id*.

13. Hadacheck v. Sebastian, Chief of Police of the City of Los Angeles, 239 U.S. 394 (1915); Mugler v. Kansas, 123 U.S. 623 (1887).

14. *See* F. Bosselman and C. Sieman, "Improving Due Process in Local Zoning Decisions," *Environmental Reporter*, Aug. 1976, at 14: "[I]n order to be fair under due process standards, the decisionmaking process must insure that decisions are made comprehensively with a sincere effort to consider as many relevant facts and issues as reasonably possible." *Id*. at 15. *See also* F. I. Michelman, *The Supreme Court and Litigation Access Fees: The Right to Protect One's Rights—Part I*, 1973 Duke L. J. 1153.

15. *See* K. L. Karst, "Legislative Facts in Constitutional Litigation," in P. B. Kurland (ed.), The Supreme Court Review (Chicago: University of Chicago Press, 1960), p. 75.

16. 245 U.S. 60 (1917).

17. 118 U.S. 356 (1886).

18. N. Karlin, *Land Use Controls: The Power to Exclude*, 5 Envt'l L. 529 (1975). *Cf*. Ambler Realty Co. v. City of Euclid, 297 F. 307 (N.D. Ohio), the lower court opinion in that famous case in which Judge Westenhaver expressed a similar position on the priority of property rights. In reversing, the U.S. Supreme Court never responded to this or any of the lower court's arguments. Village of Euclid v. Ambler Realty Co., 272 U.S. 365 (1926).

19. This subject is discussed in R. G. McKloskey, "Economic Due

Process and the Supreme Court: An Exhumation and Reburial,'' in P. B. Kurland (ed.), The Supreme Court Review (Chicago: University of Chicago Press, 1962), p. 34; R. E. Rodes, Jr., *Due Process and Social Legislation in the Supreme Court—A Post Mortem,* 33 Notre Dame Law. 5 (1957); R. L. Stern, *The Problems of Yesteryear—Commerce and Due Process*, 4 Vand. L. Rev. 446 (1951). Some state courts still seem to be applying a standard of review in the areas of economic regulation close to that of substantive due process. Maryland Board of Pharmacy v. Sav-a-lot, Inc., 270 Md. 103, 117–120, 311 A.2d 359 (1973); Pennsylvania State Board of Pharmacy v. Pastor, 441 Pa. 186, 272 A.2d 487 (1971).

20. Pennsylvania Coal v. Mahon, note 2 *supra.*

21. Berman v. Parker, 348 U.S. 26, 36 (1954).

22. As possibly do scholars of constitutional law. See the dissenting opinion of Justice Rosellini in Miller v. City of Tacoma, 61 Wash.2d 374, 378 P.2d 464 (1963).

23. Southern California Edison Co. v. Bourgerie, 9 Cal.3d 169, 507 P.2d 964, 107 Cal. Rptr. 76 (1973).

24. *Id.* at 175.

25. Armstrong v. United States, 364 U.S. 40 (1960).

26. *Id.* at 49.

27. *See generally* 6 Nichols, The Law of Eminent Domain, § 13.3 rev. 3d ed. (New York: Matthew Bender & Co., 1975).

28. I know of instances where investors have purchased property in the face of a likely condemnation and have profited handsomely. Apparently the condemnation market can also be profitable to those with inside information as to future projects. Many politicians in Chicago were criticized for making substantial profits as a result of such practices.

29. *See* 3 Nichols, The Law of Eminent Domain, § 8.10 (rev. 3d ed. 1975); *see also* Community Redev. Agency v. Abrams, 15 Cal.3d 813, 543 P.2d 905, 126 Cal. Rptr. 473 (1976).

30. Kimball Laundry Co. v. United States, 338 U.S. 1 (1949); United States v. General Motors Corp., 323 U.S. 373 (1945).

31. Natural Soda Pro. Co. v. City of Los Angeles, 23 Cal.2d 193, 143 P.2d 12 (1943); Inyo Chemical Co. v. City of Los Angeles, 5 Cal.2d 525, 55 P.2d 850 (1936); Irustuck v. City of Fairfax, 212 Cal. App.2d 345, 28 Cal. Rptr. 357 (1963).

32. Ventura County Flood Control Dist. v. Security First Nat. Bank, 15 Cal. App.3d 996, 93 Cal. Rptr. 653 (1971) and cases cited therein; People ex rel. Dept. of Public Works v. Giumarra Vineyards Corp., 245 Cal. App.2d 309, 53 Cal. Rptr. 902 (1966).

33. Almota Farmers Elevator and Warehouse Co. v. United States, 409 U.S. 470 (1973).

34. *Id*. at 478.

35. *Id*. citing United States v. Virginia Electric & Power Co., 365 U.S. at 635–36.

36. G. Kanner, From Here to Obscurity: Pennsylvania Coal Co. v. Mahon and Beyond, 32–33, 1976 (unpublished manuscript prepared for a conference Oct. 1976 sponsored by the Institute for Humane Studies (Menlo Park, California.). *See also* G. Kanner, *Condemnation Blight: Just How Just Is Just Compensation?*, 48 Notre Dame Law. 765 (1973); D.Hagman, Urban Planning and Land Development Control Law (St. Paul: West Publishing Co., 1971), pp. 334–36; United States v. Miller, 317 U.S. 369 (1943).

37. United States v. Reynolds, 397 U.S. 14, 16–18 (1970); *see* United States v. Miller, 317 U.S. 369, 377 (1943).

38. Merced Irrigation Dist. v. Woolstenhulme, 4 Cal.3d 478, 483 P.2d 1, 93 Cal. Rptr. 833 (1971).

39. *Id.*; *see also* United States v. Miller, 317 U.S. 369 (1943).

40. 80 U.S. 166 (1871). *Cf.* United States v. Lynah, 188 U.S. 445 (1903); Belford v. United States, 192 U.S. 217 (1904); Monogahela Nav. Co. v. United States; 148 U.S. 312 (1892); Portsmouth Harbor Land and Hotel Co. v. United States, 260 U.S. 327 (1922); Richards v. Washington Terminal Co., 233 U.S. 546 (1914).

41. 80 U.S. 166, at 174.

42. 243 U.S. 316 (1916).

43. *Id*. at 328.

44. *Id*. at 329.

45. 328 U.S. 256 (1946).

46. *Id*. at 266.

47. 369 U.S. 84 (1962).

48. Martin v. Port of Seattle, 64 Wash. 309, 391 P.2d 540 (1964), *cert. denied*, 279 U.S. 989; Thornberg v. Port of Portland, 233 Or. 178, 376 P.2d 100 (1962); City of Jacksonville v. Schumann, 167 So.2d 95 (Fla. Dist. Ct. App. 1964); Aaron v. City of Los Angeles, 40 Cal. App.3d 471, 115 Cal. Rptr. 162 (2d Dist. 1974); City of Atlanta v. Donald, 111 Ga. App. 339, 141 S.E.2d 560 (Ct. App. 1965), *rev'd* for insufficiency of complaint, 221 Ga. 135, 143 S.E.2d 737 (1965); Johnson v. City of Greeneville, 222 Tenn. 260, 435 S.W.2d 476 (1968).

49. Thornberg v. Port of Portland, 235 Or. 178, 194, 376 P.2d 100, 107 (1962).

50. W. F. Baxter and L. R. Altree, *Legal Aspects of Airport Noise*, 15 J. L. & Econ. 1, 35–40 (1972); W. B. Stoebuck, *Condemnation by Nuisance: The Airport Cases in Retrospect and Prospect*, 71 Dick. L. Rev. 207 (1967).

51. Batten v. United States, 306 F.2d 580 (10th Cir. 1962) U.S. *cert. denied* 371 U.S. 955 (1963); *see also* Fergurson v. City of Keene, 108 N.H. 409, 238 A.2d 1 (1968).

52. *See* text accompanying notes 54 through 57 *infra*.

53. *Cf.* A. Van Alstyne, *Modernizing Inverse Condemnation: A Legislative Prospectus,* 8 Santa Clara L. 1, 5–7 sets forth five categories of cases to guide legislative drafters in California.

54. J. H. Beuscher, "Notes on the Integration of Police Power and Eminent Domain by the Courts: Inverse Condemnation" (1964) in J. H. Beuscher and R. R. Wright, Land Use Cases and Materials (St. Paul: West Publishing Co., 1969), p. 727.

55. *See Measure and Elements of Damages for Pollution of a Stream,* Annot., 49 A.L.R. 2d 253 (1956).

56. Foss v. Maine Turnpike Authority, 309 A.2d 339 (Me. 1973); 64 A.L.R. 3d 1230 (1975).

57. J. H. Beuscher, note 54 *supra* at 727.

58. Holtz v. Superior Court of the City and County of San Francisco, 3 Cal.3d 296, 475 P.2d 441, 90 Cal. Rptr. 345 (1970); Holtz v. San Francisco Bay Area Rapid Transit District, 17 Cal.3d 648, 552 P.2d 430, 131 Cal. Rptr. 646 (1976); Reardon v. San Francisco, 66 Cal. 492, 6 P. 317 (1885).

59. Utah State Road Commission v. Miya, 526 P.2d 926, 928–29 (Utah 1974); 2A Nichols, The Law of Eminent Domain, §6.445 (1) (rev. 3d ed. 1975); 2 Nichols, The Law of Eminent Domain, §6.32 (rev. 3d ed. 1975); Metropolitan Atlanta Rapid Trans. Authority v. Datry, 220 S.E.2d 905 (Ga. 1975); Donovan v. Pennsylvania, 199 U.S. 279, 300 (1905); Sauer v. City of New York, 206 U.S. 536 (1907). *See* United States v. River Rouge Imp. Co., 269 U.S. 411 418–19 (1926) concerning rights of access to a navigable stream of riparian property owner.

60. Utah State Road Commission v. Miya, 526 P.2d 926, 929 (Utah 1974). *See* 4A Nichols, The Law of Eminent Domain, § 14.2432 (1) (rev. 3d ed. 1975).

61. D. Hagman, note 36 *supra* at 318–20; J. H. Beuscher, note 54 *supra* at 727; notes 59 *supra* and 62 *infra. See* A. Van Alstyne, *Just Compensation of Intangible Detriment: Criteria for Legislative Modifications in California,* 16 U.C.L.A. L. Rev., 491 (1969).

62. Note, *Inverse Condemnation: The Case for Diminution in Property Value as Compensable Damage,* 28 Stanford L. Rev. 779 785–86, n. 39 (1976).

63. 175 F. Supp. 891 (Ct. Cl. 1959).

64. *Id.* at 899.

65. 401 F. Supp. 962 (N.D. Cal. 1975).

66. *Id.* at 980.

67. 271 Cal. App.2d 845, 77 Cal. Rptr. 391 (1969).

68. *Id*. at 854, 77 Cal. Rptr. at 398.

69. 218 Cal. Rptr. 2d 205, 32 Cal. Rptr. 318 (1963).

70. 8 Cal.2d 39, 500 P.2d 1345, 104 Cal. Rptr. 1 (1972).

71. *Id*. at 51, 500 P.2d at 1355, 104 Cal. Rptr. at 11.

72. *See* G. Kanner, *Development in Eminent Domain: A Candle in the Dark Corner of the Law*, 52 J. Urb. L., 861, 891–95 (1975); see text accompanying note 36 supra. For a recent case on the subject, *see* Lincoln Loan Co. v. State, State Highway Commission, 274 Or. 49, 545 P.2d 105 (1976).

73. Lincoln Loan Co. v. State, State Highway Commission, 274 Or. 49, 545 P.2d 105 (1976); Conroy-Prugh Glass Co. v. Commonwealth, Dept. of Trans., 456 Pa. 384, 321 A.2d 598 (1974); Klopping v. City of Whittier, *supra* note 69; Luber v. Milwaukee County, 47 Wis.2d 271, 177 N.W. 2d 380 (1970); Textron, Inc. v. Wood, 167 Conn. 334, 355 A.2d 307 (1974); *In Re* Elmwood Park Project Section 1, Group B, 376 Mich. 311, 136 N.W.2d 896 (1965); City of Cleveland v. Carcione, 118 Ohio App. 525, 190 N.E.2d 52 (1963); Washington Market Ent., Inc. v. City of Trenton, 68 N.J. 107, 343 A.2d 408 (1975); Lang v. State, 86 Wash.2d 585, 547 P.2d 282 (1976); Foster v. City of Detroit, Michigan, 254 F. Supp. 655 (E.D. Mich. 1966), *aff'd*, 405 F.2d 138 (6th Cir. 1968); Drakes Bay Land Co. v. United States, 424 F.2d 574 (Ct. Cl. 1970).

74. City of Buffalo v. J. W. Clement Co., 28 N.Y.2d 241, 269 N.E.2d 895, 321 N.Y.S.2d 345 (1971); Chicago v. Loitz, 11 Ill. App.3d 42, 295 N.E.2d 478 (1973); City of Houston v. Biggers, 380 S.W.2d 700 (Tex. Civ. App. 1964), U.S. *cert. denied* in 380 U.S. 962 (1965).

75. 47 App. Div.2d 426, 366 N.Y.S.2d 921 (1975).

76. *Id*. at 430, 366 N.Y.S.2d at 926.

77. 82 Misc.2d 620, 371 N.Y.S.2d 814 (Ct. Cl. 1975), *aff'd* 33 N.Y.2d 848, 307 N.E.2d 254, 352 N.Y.S.2d 194 (1972).

78. *Id*. at 178, 333 N.Y.S.2d at 29. The extent of harm may be determinative in New York. The state's high court rejected inverse condemnation in a case where an attempt was made by New York City to rezone for a public park land classified for high-rise construction which was being used then as a park for the exclusive benefit of tenants in adjoining buildings. The owners were to be compensated by a transfer of development rights. The amendment was declared void a little over a year after its adoption. While the opinion acknowledged that there was still a "significant diminution" in value, it stated a taking had not occurred because there was no physical invasion or any assumption by the city of control or management. The court asserted "the parks served the same function as before the amendment, except that they were now also open to the public." Fred F. French Inv. Co., Inc. v. City of New York, 39 N.Y.2d 587,

385 N.Y.S.2d 5(Ct. App. 1976). *See also* Horizon Adirondack Corp. v. State of New York, 388 N.Y.S.2d 235 (Ct. Claims 1976).

79. *See* note 54 at 728.

80. Holtz v. Superior Ct., 3 Cal.3d 296, 303, 475 P.2d 441, 445, 90 Cal. Rptr. 345, 349 (1970).

81. Klopping v. City of Whittier, 8 Cal.3d 39,43, 500 P.2d 1345, 1349, 104 Cal. Rptr. 1, 5 (1972).

82. Professor Stoebuck has concluded that "property" in eminent domain means every species of interest in land and things of a kind that an owner might transfer to another. W. B. Stoebuck, *A General Theory of Eminent Domain*, 47 Wash. L. Rev. 553, 606 (1972).

83. *See*, e.g., Just v. Marinette County, 56 Wis.2d 7, 201 N.W.2d 761 (1972) and Consolidated Rock Products Co. v. Los Angeles, 57 Cal.2d 515, 370 P.2d 342, 20 Cal. Rptr. 628 (1962).

84. Speiser v. Randall, 357 U.S. 513 (1958) (Brennen, J., in delivering the majority opinion); *cf.* Goldblatt v. Town of Hempstead, 369 U.S. 590 (1962). The presumption has been reversed in some of the exclusion cases referred to in the section The Taking Clause and Better Housing Conditions. In Virginia and Michigan, the plaintiff's burden is less, but the initial presumption has not been shifted. City of Richmond v. Randall, 215 Va. 506, 211 S.E.2d 56(1975); Sabo v. Township of Monroe, 394 Mich 531, 232 N.W.2d 584 (1975).

85. Village of Euclid v. Ambler Realty Co., 272 U.S. 365 (1926).

86. La Salle National Bank of Chicago v. County of Cook, 12 Ill.2d 40, 46–47, 145 N.E.2d 65, 69 (1957).

87. Gardner v. Downer, 61 Misc.2d 131, 305 N.Y.S.2d 252 (Sup. Ct. 1967).

88. San Diego Bldg. Contractors Assn. v. City Council, 13 Cal.3d 205, 529 P.2d 570, 118 Cal. Rptr. 146 (1974).

89. City of Plainfield v. Borough of Middlesex, 69 N.J. Super. 136, 173 A.2d 785 (L. Div. 1961).

90. Golden v. Planning Bd. of Town of Ramapo, 30 N.Y.2d 359, 285 N.E.2d 291, 334 N.Y.S.2d 138 (1972).

91. *Id.* at 383, 285 N.E.2d at 304, 334 N.Y.S.2d at 156.

92. 348 U.S. 26 (1954).

93. *Id.* at 32–33. Although widely quoted in zoning cases, this dictum actually applied to a situation involving only the public-use qualification of the taking clause. *Berman* was not a zoning case.

94. *See, e.g.,* Douglas dissenting in Beauharnais v. Illinois, 343 U.S. 250 (1952) and concurring in Speiser v. Randall, 357 U.S. 513 (1958). *See also* L. F. Manning, *The Douglas Concept of God and Government*, 39 Wash. L. Rev. 47 (1964).

95. There is the question of whether a municipality may under the

"public use" qualification of the taking clause acquire a fee or a lesser interest in land for the purpose suggested. The American Law Institute's Model Land Development Code apparently assumes the existence of this power by allowing local or state government to buy land to further planning objectives and regulatory powers. American Law Institute, A Model Land Development Code, Art. 5 and 6 (1975); *see also* Puerto Rico v. Eastern Sugar Associates, 156 F.2d 316 (1st Cir. Ct. App. 1946) upholding condemnation under a land distribution law; Berman v. Parker, 348 U.S. 26 (1954); 2 Nichols, The Law of Eminent Domain, §7.516 (rev. 3d ed. 1975); D. Hagman, note 36 *supra* at 330–31. Nor does the logic of the situation change if there is a lack of authority for public purchase of land to control use.

96. M. Howe (ed.), Holmes-Laski Letters (Cambridge, Ma.: Harvard University Press, 1953), vol. 1, p. 457. *But cf.* J. Kephart, in *Appeal of White*, 287 Pa. 259, 267, 134 A. 409, 412 (1926): "What reasonable relation has the setback line, or space in front of houses in ordinary residence districts, to the health, safety, or morals of the community? It certainly would not disturb the comfort of the ordinary person; it is not offensive to the eye, nor a source of sickness; it does not materially increase or decrease fire hazards. To bring this, and other like regulations under the police power, would be to sweep away constitutional guarantees on the ownership of property. It is regulation run mad."

97. F. Frankfurter, Mr. Justice Holmes and the Supreme Court, 2d ed. (Cambridge, Ma.: Harvard University Press, 1961), p. 74.

98. P. Freund, The Police Power (Chicago: Callaghan & Co., 1904), p. 542.

99. W. Blackstone, Commentaries, Vol. 1, 1904, p. 542.

100. J. L. Sax, *Takings and the Police Power*, 74 Yale L. J. 36, 53–60 (1964).

101. F. Hayek, The Constitution of Liberty (Chicago: University of Chicago Press, 1960), pp. 217–18.

102. P. A. Samuelson, Economics: An Introductory Analysis, 7th ed. (New York: McGraw-Hill, 1967), p. 604.

103. H. F. H., Ltd. v. Superior Court, 15 Cal.3d 508, 521, 542 P.2d 237, 246, 125 Cal. Rptr. 365, 374 (1975) [Quoted from F. I. Michelmen, *Property, Utility and Fairness: Comments on the Ethical Foundations of 'Just Compensation' Law*, 80 Harv. L. Rev. 1165 (1967)].

104. Fred F. French Inv. Co., Inc. v. City of New York, 39 N.Y.2d 587, 385 N.Y.S.2d 5, 11 (Ct. App. 1976).

105. Comparable concerns relating to the vindication of basic rights have been voiced in the context of procedural due process. F. Bosselman and C. Siemon, note 14 *supra* at 15, citing among others Boddie v. Connecticut, 401 U.S. 371 (1971) and Rutherford v. United States, 399 F.

Supp. 1208 (1975). *Boddie* struck down certain state procedures for commencement of a divorce case including filing fees averaging $60. *But see* United States v. Kras, 409 U.S. 434 (1973) and Ortwein v. Schwab, 410 U.S. 656 (1973), both of which confine very narrowly the holding in *Boddie*.

106. B. H. Siegan, Other People's Property (Lexington, Ma: D. C. Heath & Co., 1976), pp. 39–43, 128–29.

107. *Id.* at 39–41; *see Mt. Laurel* case, *infra* note 134.

108. 10 Cal.3d 110, 514 P.2d 111, 109 Cal. Rptr. 799 (1973).

109. 15 Cal.3d 508, 542 P.2d 237, 125 Cal. Rptr. 365 (1975).

110. 57 Cal. App.3d 613, 129 Cal. Rptr. 575 (1976).

111. 15 Cal.3d at 514, 542 P.2d at 241, 125 Cal. Rptr. at 369.

112. *Id.* at 526, 542 P.2d at 250, 125 Cal. Rptr. at 378 (Clark, J., dissenting).

113. *See* note 108 *supra*.

114. *Id.* at 119, 514 P.2d at 117, 109 Cal. Rptr. at 805.

115. Eldridge v. City of Palo Alto, 51 Cal. App.3d 726, 124 Cal. Rptr. 547 (1975), vacated; reconsidered in 57 Cal. App.3d 613, 129 Cal. Rptr. 575 (1976).

116. Arastra Limited Partnership v. City of Palo Alto, *supra* note 65.

117. *See* note 115 *supra*.

118. Cal. Supreme Ct. Minutes, Jan. 21, 1976. Official Advance Sheets of the Supreme Ct. No. 5, Feb. 17, 1976 at 1.

119. 372 F. Supp. 647 (N.D. Cal. 1974).

120. Sanfilippo v. County of Santa Cruz, 415 F. Supp. 1340 (N.D. Cal. 1976).

121. Superior Ct. of California, County of Marin, No. 66506, Notice of Intended Decision, filed July 15, 1975.

122. Superior Ct. of California, County of San Diego, No. 357022, Findings of Fact and Conclusions of Law, filed April 9, 1976.

123. Brown v. Tahoe Regional Planning Agency, 385 F. Supp. 1128 (D. Nev. 1973).

124. *Id.* at 1132.

125. Order of Court dated Jan. 10, 1975.

126. Western International Hotels v. Tahoe Regional Planning Agency, 387 F. Supp. 429, 437 (D. Nev. 1975).

126a. Pete v. United States, 531 F. 2d 1018 (Ct. Claims 1976).

126b. *Id.* at 1034.

127. The Taking Issue, note 4 *supra* at 253.

128. *Id.* at 238.

129. *Id.* at 254.

130. *See e.g.,* R. Coase, "Economics and Public Policy," in J. F. Weston (ed.), Large Corporations in a Changing Society (New York:

N.Y.U. Press, 1974), p. 169; C. Reich, *The Law of the Planned Society*, 75 Yale L. J. 799 (1969); F. J. Popper, *Land Use Reform—Illusion or Reality?* Planning 14 (A.S.P.O. Sept. 1974); T. Lowi, The End of Liberalism (New York: Norton, 1969); and T. Lowi, The Politics of Disorder (New York: Basic Books, 1971).

131. *See* B. H. Siegan, Land Use without Zoning (Lexington, Ma: D. C. Heath & Co., 1973).

132. Institute for Contemporary Studies, The California Coastal Plan: A Critique (San Francisco: 1975); R. Ellickson, *Ticket to Thermidor: A Commentary on the Proposed California Coastal Plan,* 49 S. Cal. L. Rev. 715 (1976).

133. *See generally* B. H. Siegan, *Controlling Other People's Property through Covenants, Zoning, State and Federal Regulation,* 5 Envt'l L. 385 (1975); Institute for Contemporary Studies, "No Land's an Island" (San Francisco: Institute for Contemporary Studies. *See* Institute of Economic Affairs, "Government and the Land" (London: Institute of Economic Affairs, 1974).

134. There are few better recitals of the evils and errors of zoning than in the majority opinion of Justice Hall and concurring opinion of Justice Pashman in Southern Burlington County N.A.A.C.P. v. Township of Mt. Laurel, 67 N.J. 151, 336 A.2d 713 (1975).

135. 1 ALI Restatement of the Law of Property, §5 (1936).

136. *See* discussion in The Taking Issue, note 4 *supra* at 240–46.

137. M. C. Jensen and W. H. Meckling, "Can the Corporation Survive?" University of Rochester Graduate School of Management Center for Research in Government Policy and Business, Public Policy Working Paper Series (PPS–76–4, May 1976). Reprinted with permission.

138. United States v. Cress, 243 U.S. 316 (1916).

139. United States v. Causby, 328 U.S. 256 (1946).

140. United States v. Central Eureka Mining Co., 357 U.S. 155 (1958).

141. *Id.* at 181.

142. *Id.* at 184.

143. The Taking Issue, note 4 *supra* at 238, 245.

144. Only one case has come to my attention since publication of The Taking Issue in which this position was specifically raised and rejected by a court: Sanfilippo v. County of Santa Cruz, 415 F. Supp. 1340, 1344 (N.D. Cal. 1976).

The Taking Issue, after describing controls and attitudes prior to and after the American Revolution, concludes that there is no evidence that the founding fathers "ever conceived the taking clause could establish any sort of restriction on the power to regulate the use of land," pp. 82–104. With this kind of standard, the protection of expression contained in the First Amendment would have far less importance than it is given in modern court decisions. Many leaders of colonial times and subsequent to the Revolution were not opposed to punishing people for making political statements that today would pass largely unnoticed. R. Bork, *Neutral Principles and Some First Amendment Problems*, 47 Indiana L. Rev. 1, 22 (1971); T. I. Emerson, *Toward a General Theory of the First Amendment*, 72 Yale L. J. 877, 888 (1963); W. Berns, "Freedom of the Press and the Alien Sedition Laws: A Reappraisal," in P. B. Kurland (ed.), Supreme Court Review, (Chicago: University of Chicago Press, 1970), p. 109.

145. Griswold v. Connecticut, 381 U.S. 479, 497 (1965) (Goldberg, J., concurring).

146. *Id.* at 484 (Douglas, J., in delivering the majority opinion).

147. See the majority opinion of Justice Blackmun and concurring opinion of Justice Douglas in Doe v. Boulton, 410 U.S. 179 (1973).

148. See text accompanying note 62 *supra*.

149. HFH, Ltd. v. Superior Court, note 103 *supra* at 521, 542 P.2d at 246, 125 Cal. Rptr. at 374.

150. 67 N.J. 151, 336 A.2d 713 (1975).

151. 38 N.Y. 102, 341 N.E.2d 236, 378 N.Y.S. 672 (Ct. App. 1975). *See also* Associated Home Builders of Greater Eastbay, Inc. v. City of Livermore, et al. (Decided by Cal. Supreme Court Dec. 17, 1976).

152. 439 Pa. 466, 268 A.2d 765 (1970). *See also* Board of County Supervisors of Fairfax County v. Carper, 200 Va. 653, 107 S.E.2d 390 (1959).

153. Lionshead Lake v. Township of Wayne, 10 N.J. 165, 89 A.2d 693 (1952).

154. *Id.* at 173, 89 A.2d at 697.

155. *Id.* at 176, 89 A.2d at 699 (Jacobs, J., concurring).

156. Vickers v. Township Committee of Gloucester Township, 37 N.J. 232, 246, 181 A.2d 129, 136 (1962).

157. N. Williams and T. Norman, *Exclusionary Land Use Controls: The Case of Northeastern New Jersey*, 4 Land Use Controls Q. 1 (1970).

158. *Id.*

159. Southern Burlington County N.A.A.C.P. v. Township of Mt. Laurel, 67 N.J. 151, 187, 336 A.2d 713, 724 (1975).

160. Urban League of Greater New Brunswick v. Mayor and Council of Borough of Carteret, 142 N.J. Super. 11, 359 A.2d 526 (Super. Ct. 1976).

161. 38 N.Y. at 109, 341 N.E. 2d at 241, 378 N.Y.S.2d at 680.

162. 28 Land Use Law and Zoning Digest, No. 5 at 3 (1976).

163. Urban League of Greater New Brunswick v. Mayor and Council of Borough of Carteret, note 160 *supra*.

164. An extensive critique of sections 101, 235, and 236 of the Federal

Housing Programs in effect in the early 1970s was made by a three-judge panel of the United States Circuit Court of Appeals for the District of Columbia in Commonwealth of Pennsylvania v. Lynn, 501 F.2d 848 (D.C. Cir. 1973). The court upheld the Nixon administration's decision to suspend these programs as a reasonable exercise of administrative discretion.

165. *See, e.g.,* B.J. Frieden, Improved Federal Housing Subsidies: Summary Report (Prepared for Subcommittee on Housing, Committee on Banking and Currency, U.S. House of Representatives, June 1971), p. 4; "New Land Aids Family Relocation," *Chicago Tribune*, 16 March 1971; Office of Policy Development and Urban Research, U.S. Dept. of Housing and Urban Development, Housing Allowances: The 1976 Report to Congress (1976).

166. "Analyst Finds Conventional Public Housing Most Efficient Option," *San Diego Union*, 11 July 1976, p. F–11.

167. Requiring developers to construct and maintain specified percentages of low- and moderate-income housing within new developments may run afoul of a taking clause. Virginia's Supreme Court in Board of Supervisors v. De Groff Enterprises, Inc., 214 Va. 235, 198 S.E.2d 600 (1973), struck down a form of balanced-housing ordinance adopted by Fairfax County. The court held the ordinance defective because it was "socioeconomic zoning" and attempted to control compensation from the use of land. Fairfax's ordinance required a developer of multifamily housing projects of more than 50 units and less than 6 stories to set aside 6 percent of the units for low-income families and 9 percent for moderate-income families. Although acknowledging the need for more housing for lower-income persons, the court still found that the ordinance was not authorized under the zoning enabling act and was contrary to the taking provision of the Virginia Constitution. The ordinance provided for controlled sale or rental prices for the units to be occupied by low- and moderate-income families, and the court decided that "such a scheme" would establish prices not determined by the market and was therefore contrary to the state's taking clause.

168. J.B. Lansing, C.W. Clifton, and J.N. Morgan, New Homes and Poor People (Ann Arbor, Mich.: University of Michigan Press, 1969).

169. Task Force Report sponsored by the Rockefeller Brothers Fund, note 3 *supra.*

170. James v. Valtierra, 402 U.S. 137 (1971).

171. Village of Belle Terre v. Boraas, 416 U.S. 1 (1973).

172. President of the United States, 3rd Annual Report on Housing Goals, 23 (Washington: Government Printing Office, 1971); *see* J. Tobin, *On Limiting the Domain of Inequality*, 13 J. L. & Econ., 263, 275 (1970).

173. Commissions and bureaucracies may cause grotesque alloca-

tions. One recent British survey showed that the richest third of those families living in public housing had higher total earnings than do the poorest third of families buying their own homes. D. Moller, "Ill Fares the Welfare State," *Encounter*, 58, 60 (Sept. 1976).

174. Frieden, *supra* note 165 at 2.

175. *See* note 168 *supra*.

176. U.S. National Commission on Urban Problems, Building the American City, 208–09 (1969).

177. Young v. American Mini Theaters, Inc., 44 *U.S.L.W.* 4999 (U.S., June 24, 1976).

178. *Id.* at 5008.

179. *See* note 171 *supra* at 9.

180. *See, e.g.,* Southern Burlington County N.A.A.C.P. v. Township of Mt. Laurel, note 159 *supra*.

181. *See generally* B. H. Siegan, Land Use without Zoning, note 131 *supra*.

182. B. H. Siegan, Other People's Property, *supra* note 106, pp. 52–54.

183. 44 U.S.L.W. 4281 (U.S. March 3, 1976).

184. Amalgamated Food Employees Union Local 590 v. Logan Valley Plaza, Inc., 391 U.S. 308 (1968). Justice Black dissented in this case, asserting that the taking clause "means to me that there is no right to picket on the private premises of another to try to convert the owner or others to the views of the pickets. It also means, I think, that if this Court is going to arrogate itself the power to act as the Government's agent to take a part of Weis' property to give to the pickets for their use, the Court should also award just compensation for the property taken." At p. 330.

185. Denecke, J., concurring in Lenrich Associates v. Heyda, 264 Or. 122, 129, 504 P.2d 112, 116 (1972).

186. Virginia State Board of Pharmacy v. Virginia Citizens Consumer Council, 96 Sup. Ct. 1817 (1976).

187. *Id.* at 1826.

188. 96 Sup. Ct. 2358 (1976).

189. Forest City Enterprises, Inc. v. City of Eastlake, 41 Ohio St.2d 187, 324 N.E. 740 (1975).

2

Planning Without Prices: A Discussion of Land Use Regulation without Compensation

M. Bruce Johnson

Introduction

The goal of economic analysis is to produce understanding which, if reflected in public policy, will bring about closer correspondence and agreement between human wants and the satisfaction of those wants. In a world characterized by a wide variety of individual tastes, by the niggardliness of nature, and by the imperfections of our institutions, several complications arise: first, human wants far outstrip our ability to satisfy them within our current endowment of resources and technology; second, there is no apparent basis for hope that unanimity can be reached on the importance or ranking of human wants; and third, the institutional (i.e., property rights) structure we choose will influence dramatically which— and whose—human wants are satisfied.

In this context *Planning Without Prices* addresses the difficult question commonly referred to as *the taking issue*. The debate takes its name from the taking clause of the Fifth Amendment which holds: "private property may not be taken for public use without just compensation." Stated simply, the debate centers on the distinction between the government's exercise of eminent domain, where private property is taken by purchase, and the government's exercise of police power, where private property is regulated without compensation to the owner for loss or damages. The issue is what criteria should determine the disposition of a particular case: eminent domain with compensation or regulation without compensation.

To the extent that events are influenced by academic discourse, the outcome of the debate will determine in large measure the disposition and future of a variety of contemporary issues and institutions: environmental protection, private property, the growth of government, the allocation of

The author wishes to thank Robert Deacon, Harold Demsetz, H.E. Frech, III, Norman Karlin, and Perry Shapiro for useful comments on portions of an early draft of the paper. He is also indebted to Edward M. Wolkowitz of Southwestern University Law School for providing valuable assistance. All the above gentlemen are innocent of responsibility for errors in the chapter.

63

resources, the responsiveness of government to its citizens, and the distribution of income and wealth.

In order to impose some structure on the discussion and arguments, this chapter is developed within the theoretical framework of a price system. Note that the adherence to such a framework has no idealogical or normative implications; every society—however organized—utilizes some form of price system to signal to its decisionmakers the value (opportunity costs) of its resources. Although the information provided by prices may be generated in decentralized markets characterized by private property or may, alternatively, be determined by central authority, prices—real or shadow, explicit or implicit—are required. The definition and structure of property rights—the uses to which resources may be put and the conditions under which the rights to use the resources may be traded—determine the configuration of prices and, hence, influence the final mix of goods and services and its distribution among the citizens.

Several generations of economists have studied the performance characteristics of a conceptualized price system based on private property with decentralized decision making through voluntary transactions. The optimality properties that have been attributed to this sytem depend, in part, on the absence of externalities or spillovers. Although other stringent conditions are also required to ensure the optimality of a decentralized competitive system, the extent and importance of externalities are the preeminent issues in the debate over private versus public land use control. Simply stated, the proponents of public control of land use decisions allege that decisions by individuals in a private property regime ignore both the costs and the benefits imposed and conferred on others. Hence, it is frequently argued that public control of land use decisions is necessary to internalize these externalities.

Yet, one can stipulate the existence of externalities without accepting the premise that public control of land use decisions is superior—not to mention optimal—to a decentralized market system of land use decisions. First, this chapter notes that, under standard definitions, externalities are ubiquitous and pervasively associated with virtually every decision taken or contemplated by people. Thus, the issue turns on the empirical importance of each externality in the huge array we confront. What practical criteria can, or should, be used to decide when—and how—to internalize an externality? Should the internalization take place via redefinition and reassignment of private property rights, or should the decision be imposed by central authority? If the latter option is chosen, how will the pertinent information be gathered by the central authority and what incentives and forces will operate on the central decision authority? Can the government be expected to base its decisions on relevant information if such data are, in fact, available?

One important theme in this chapter suggests that environmentalists' solution to the taking issue (government police power regulation of private property without compensation) will short-circuit the economic price system that provides valuable data and information to decision makers. Since the relevant public agencies provide their outputs to society without user charges, the agencies are, by definition, free of the direct discipline of the demand side of the market; to the extent that citizens' desires for environmental goods are somehow filtered through the political process, the incentive to overstate valuations of the goods is strong if the goods are delivered free to the citizen while the costs are thought to be borne by others.

Yet, the most severe distortion of efficient resource allocation is perhaps on the cost side; the use of police power to regulate land without compensation also releases the government from the discipline of the budget process. The resources under the control of the central authority will be perceived to be costless. The opportunity costs will be ignored, and land use regulation without compensation will lead to overproduction of environmental amenities as the agency expands output to the point where the bureaucrats' subjective valuation of the last unit is equal to its perceived zero cost. Free from the discipline of consumer demand via markets and the constraint of costs via compensation and budgets, central control of land use decisions degenerates to planning without prices.

Property Rights

The taking clause of the Fifth Amendment either serves as the last line of defense in the protection of private property or poses a major impediment to the regulation of land use for environmental purposes—depending on one's philosophical predilection and, perhaps, on one's position in the income and power distribution. It is important to agree at the outset that the debate is over property rights, not over physical property itself.[1] Questions pertain to the interests of the property owner: fees simple, future estates, leaseholds, easements, riparian rights, restrictive covenants, etc.[2] The disciplines of law and economics converge in this issue now that the economics has increasingly come to be recognized as a study of property rights.[3]

The question of economics, or of how prices should be determined, is the question of how property rights should be defined and exchanged, and on what terms.[4] An entitlement is protected by a property rule to the extent that someone who wishes to remove the entitlement from its holder must buy it from him in a voluntary transaction in which the value of the entitlement is agreed upon by the seller.... It lets each of the parties say how much the entitlement is worth to him, and gives the seller a veto if the buyer does not offer enough. Property rules involve a collective decision as to who is to be given an initial entitlement but not as to the value of the entitlement.[5]

The assignment of property rights over the ownership, use, and transfer of resources is not unique to Western society or the United States. (Either by design or by default, every society must assign property rights if it is to function. If the wheat is to be cultivated on the land, the grain ground into flour, and the flour baked into bread, some agent—either individual or collective—must have the authority to implement the decisions to use the resources.[6])

In our society property rights to use and trade resources, with limitations, historically have been assigned to individual and voluntary associations of individuals. And so it is natural to think in terms of a tradition of private property in this country. However, the opposite, polar case of common property ownership has also been used; examples are the now familiar cases of the airshed and the ocean fishing grounds where each member of society has an undivided interest in the entire property in question. In spite of the empirically established inefficiency of common property, the difficulties attributed to the private property sysfem have led some to advocate a deliberate shift to some version or another of common property as an alternative to the decentralized market. The familiar slogan "The land belongs to all of us" neglects to inform how "we" will decide to use "our" land.[7]

Much of the recent discussion of land use has focused on the alleged shortcomings of the institution of private property, but little attention has been given to the viability and efficiency problems of the common property alternatives. A convincing case can be made that many of the problems attributed to a private property system in fact result from common property aberrations that, in turn, result from an incomplete specification of property rights. Moreover, a change to unregulated common property will be less efficient, in virtually every relevant characteristic, then the private property system it replaces.[8]

The practical alternative to private property is more likely the de facto assumption of property rights by an agency of the state—regulated common property. Thus the issue becomes clearer: when should the state buy land and when should it regulate private land? When should compensation be paid for the losses caused by regulation of private land? Can these questions be answered without an economic theory of the state—in particular, an economic theory of regulation and bureaucracy?

The problem is an element of a larger issue: how does society coordinate the activities of its many and varied individual members? It is commonly held that if society is to function, its individual participants must operate within a legal, economic, and institutional environment that has some substantial degree of predictability, efficiency, and fairness. Because these several characteristics are substitutes to some degree, it is not surprising to note that modern societies have evolved, whether by choice or by accident, by accepting tradeoffs among the three competing characteristics.

The Police Power

Over time, the state has expanded its ability to interfere with a wide variety of private activities under its police power.[9] Presumably the state interferes because someone desires to alter either the end results of private activities or the private process itself. The police power is extraordinarily broad as judged by the scope of contemporary state action, although it has resisted precise definition.[10] In *Mid-Way Cabinet etc., Mfg. v. County of San Joaquin*, the court states:

Theoretically, not superimposed upon but coexisting alongside the power of eminent domain is the police power, unwritten except in case law. It has been variously defined—never to the concordant satisfaction of all courts or legal scholars—and frequently it has been inconsistently applied by different courts; . . . sometimes, to our belief, by the same court, the police power is described more readily than it can be defined. It has been said to be no more "than the powers of government inherent in every sovereignty. . .the power to govern men and things within the limits of its dominion."[11]

The power of eminent domain is also inherent in sovereignty. The state has the authority by which private property may be transferred to the government over the private owner's immediate, personal protest.[12] But eminent domain is a legislative function that constitutionally requires "just compensation" to the private owner.[13] "Twenty-six state constitutions allow compensation for property 'damaged' as well as that 'taken.'"[14] Since compensation is paid when the court rules that a taking has occurred, the critical decision is: What constitutes (or who defines) a "taking"? On the one hand, the environmentalists suggest a narrow interpretation so as to minimize the compensation required to finance the environmental land use regulation they advocate.[15] On the other hand, concerns for efficiency in resource allocation and for individual liberty have prompted others to argue for criteria that expand the use of compensation and limit the regulation of land under the police powers.[16]

No precise formula or test has been embraced by the courts in their efforts to determine the dividing line between the exercise of police power and eminent domain. According to Prof. Arvo Van Alstyne:

In part, the existing uncertainties can be traced to the propensity of courts to avoid the difficult analytical task of articulating a substantive decision between the competing claims of private right and community order by relying on procedural rules. Most prominently invoked in this connection are the rules placing a heavy burden upon the challenger to prove that a restriction is arbitrary and confiscatory and the presumption (often conjoined with a reference to the burden of proof) that questions are predicated upon rational grounds. Traditional opinions reflecting constitutional attacks on the stated ground that a challenger has failed to discharge his burden of proof, and thus had not refuted the presumption of validity, seldom provide reliable guides to the relevant substantive standards against which the challenger's case was ostensibly measured.[17]

This passage highlights the regulation/taking dichotomy and the current state of the debate. Of the two Fifth Amendment clauses pertaining to property rights—the due process clause and the taking clause—only the former is concerned with police power. The taking clause is entirely separate and distinct, and under it compensation is required.[18]

Due Process

The due process clause states that no person may be deprived of life, liberty, or property without due process of law. Nevertheless, within the due process clause the courts have permitted the police power to intercede and regulate even though such actions resulted in substantial deprivation and loss to individuals.[19] The stated function of the police power is to promote the "health, safety, morals, and general welfare" of the public.[20] Traditionally, the police power had been used to control activities that were judged to be harmful to others (e.g., nuisance situations),[21] and legislative attempts to expand the scope of the police power were often met by opposition from the courts.[22] Under the former doctrine of substantive due process, the Court undertook an independent determination of whether the activities proscribed by the legislatures were in fact harmful or whether the extent of the regulation was justified in view of the harm involved.[23] Thus, the Court independently balanced aggregate benefits and costs.

In spite of the traditional interpretation summarized above, interplay between police power and the due process clause has not been static. The absence of a precise definition of the police power has made it difficult for a particular regulation to be pronounced not in the interest of health, safety, morals, or general welfare of the public. This ambiguity is present in the case of nuisance abatement as well.[24] Perhaps because of the imprecise criteria surrounding the police power, legislative use of the power has expanded; for example, in *Euclid v. Ambler* the Court proceeded to extend the scope of the police power from nuisance abatement to nuisance prevention.[25]

In a more important development, the interpretation of the due process clause changed. The Court began to defer increasingly to legislative judgment concerning which regulations were in the public interest.[26] Consequently, with "submissive" due process emerging,[27] police power functions filled the void left by judicial abdication.[28] As a result, valid exercises of the police power have come to encompass such diverse activities as prohibiting front-yard clothes lines[29] or defining how many people may live in a house as a family unit.[30]

Taking: Degree or Kind?

The fundamental economic distinction between police power regulation and the taking clause is the cost to the state; under the former no compensation is required while under the latter compensation is mandatory. But there is considerable difficulty in determining whether a particular case should be considered a "regulation" or a "taking." In *Mugler v. Kansas*[31] and *Powell v. Penn.*[32] the Court attempted to show that the distinction was qualitative; taking was one "kind" of governmental activity and regulation another. When the Court announced its "physical invasion" test[33] in order to facilitate the application of the interpretation, an unusual incentive structure was established: When the government has a particular action in mind and is faced with the choice between regulating (at zero cost) or taking with compensation (at positive cost), it is obvious which alternative a rational legislature or agency will choose.

Bosselman et al. have argued that Justice Holmes rejected the difference in kind analysis in favor of a quantitative approach in *Penn. Coal Co. v. Mahon.*[34] Thus, in Justice Holmes' view, the difference between regulation and taking was a difference of *degree, not kind.*[35] But there is another interpretation of the case: Karlin[36] cites Holmes' reference to the "seemingly absolute protection" of the due process clause of the Fourteenth Amendment; Karlin argues that First and Fourteenth Amendment rights are closely interrelated and that police power extensions undermine due process guarantees. Under either interpretation, *Penn. Coal* serves as an impediment to expanded regulation of land without compensation.

If Holmes intended to limit or deter government regulatory activity by forcing the government to bear the costs of its actions, the goal was not achieved. Under submissive due process, courts began to permit an increasingly wide variety of legislative regulatory behavior. The net effect was a judicial deference to the legislative function so great that when regulations were involved, the court rarely addressed the question of whether the damage the regulations inflicted on individuals ever reached the magnitude of a taking. And so complete deprivation could be sustained as a legitimate regulation.[37]

Even when a taking is admitted and compensation paid, one might question the reasonableness of a legislative decision to take one individual's property and, as in the case of urban renewal, transfer title and rights to other individuals. As Martin Anderson has observed:

This whole line of argument rests on the assumption that the private use of land is in the "public interest." This may be true in a general sense, but if we accept their principle, it means that the government theoretically could seize anyone's property if the official thought it would be in the "public interest."[38]

Nevertheless, in *Berman v. Parker*, the Court foreclosed the line of argument by stating:

We do not sit to determine whether a particular housing project is or is not desirable. The concept of the public welfare is broad and inclusive.... It is within the power of the legislature to determine that the community should be beautiful as well as healthy, spacious as well as clean, well-balanced as well as carefully patrolled....

Once the question of the public purpose has been decided, the amount and character of land to be taken for the project and the need for a particular tract to complete the integrated plan rests in the discretion of the legislative branch.[39]

In effect, the "reasonableness" of the legislature's actions falls under the due process clause; and, under recent interpretation of that clause, anything the legislature does is reasonable unless someone can show the contrary. The burden of proof has shifted from the legislature to the individual.

The critical question is then posed: At what point does regulation of private property under the police power become a "taking" of private property and, as such, require compensation? When does a government action belong under the due process clause and when under the eminent domain clause?

The polar positions on the issue can be summarized as follows: first, we have proponents[40] of expanding the state's police power arguing that a taking interpretation should be restricted to those cases where the state actually takes title or physical possession of a parcel of property;[41] all other cases would fall under police power regulations and would not require any compensation for diminished value to the property owner.[42] At the other extreme we have the private property enthusiasts who would in large measure restrict or deny the state both police power and eminent domain. Their position does not imply that pollution, spillovers, and externalities are to be ignored but rather that a different, better definition of private property rights would obtain the desired results without the use of arbitrary authority by the state. In other words, they reject the process by which the alleged evils are cured as opposed to accepting the evils themselves. Lawrence S. Moss argues:

[P]roperty anarchism. . .had its roots in America and flourished almost exclusively on this soil.. . .

[T]he beginning of an articulate-private-property-anarchist tradition in the United States is marked by the appearance, in 1847, of Josiah Warren's *Equitable Commerce*. Warren's treatise represents the first systematic attempt to provide an extended discussion of the principal institutions about which a stateless society must be organized if it is to produce an order consistent with "equity" or social justice [footnotes omitted].[43]

The preeminent spokesperson for modern private property view is Murray Rothbard:

[C]ases of "external diseconomy" all turn out to be instances of failure of *government*—the enforcing agency—adequately to enforce individual property rights. The "blame," therefore, rests not on the institution of private property, but on the failure of the government to enforce this property right against various subtle forms of invasion—the failure, e.g., to maintain a free society.

One instance of this failure is the case of . . . air pollution.. . . [T]he remedy, in a free society, is not the creation of an administrative State bureau to prescribe regulations for smoke control. The remedy is *judicial* action to punish and pro-scribe pollution damage to the person and property of others.[44]

In sum, participants in the debate agree that the Fifth Amendment prohibition against uncompensated taking and the traditional regulatory activities without compensation under the police powers should both remain in force; the debate is over where to draw the line.[45] The state can regulate land use without compensation in some cases but must compensate in others. Thus far, legal and economic scholars have been unable to construct a convincing rationale that (even on the theoretical level) would permit a clear, operational, and predictable set of criteria for compensating or not compensating.

Varieties of Regulation

In order to discuss the rational economic basis for state regulation of land, it is instructive to examine the record of past behavior of the state. A representative, but not exhaustive, list of the past uses of police power by the state would include the authority to settle disputes; to levy and collect taxes; to conduct police and military action; to regulate agriculture, industry, religion, and education; and to operate activities such as the post office, roads, warehouses, dams, communication, and transportation. The state also regulates and licenses trades, foods, and drugs; suppresses vice; enforces Sunday closing; regulates traffic; censors the media; requires vaccinations; forbids some monopolies; creates and enforces other monopolies; promulgates zoning; eliminates brickyards in favor of residences; removes cedar trees to protect apple trees; and, in some cases, prohibits all development. What, if anything, do these activities have in common?

The rationalization of the state's interference with voluntary private action includes three reasons: to redistribute income or wealth, to prevent or eliminate monopolies, and to correct spillover effects or externalities.[46] These motives are invariably advanced within a utilitarian ethic in which the satisfaction of individual wants is paramount and social policies are judged solely in terms of their outcomes. Hence, the value judgment that central control (e.g., Maoism, fascism, central planning, etc.) is "preferable" is dismissed here as a justification for state intervention.

On a case-by-case basis, it is difficult to justify past regulation by the intent to redistribute income. Although regulation in some cases may be rationalized publicly by the motive to redistribute income, wealth, or privilege from one set of individuals to another in society, it does not appear that this is a convincing reason for land use regulation. Indeed, in the case of land use regulation in particular and environmental action in general, the redistribution appears to be from lower- to upper-income groups.[47]

The stated purpose of police power regulation is to protect and promote the health, safety, morals, and general welfare of the public. The word *public* would appear to be the controlling factor here. If the purpose in regulating the use of a particular parcel of land is alleged to be in the public's interest, then it would seem to be a violation of the intent if a specific subset of the public received all the benefits of such regulation while another group carried all the costs. Indeed, virtually all the argument and rhetoric of the environmentalist movement that supports regulation without compensation rather than taking with compensation is based on the argument that *everyone* (i.e., the public) will benefit from the proposed regulation.[48] A priori that can hardly be true since the property owner who suffers a loss due to the regulation is not made better off, and he is, by definition, a member of the public.[49]

Pareto Optimality

Strictly speaking, regulation in the public interest should be restricted to those cases where a given action hurts no individual member of society and either benefits or leaves the remainder no worse off. Regulation that meets this criterion is said to be *Pareto-preferred*. By definition, an allocation of goods is Pareto-preferred if, in comparison to a base-case allocation (the status quo), all members of the economy are at least well off and one or more are actually better off.[50] If the Pareto rule is not invoked, regulation will benefit some and hurt others; it can be carried out only if the arbitrary judgment is made that it is acceptable (1) to sacrifice some individuals' well-being in the interest of others, and (2) that, on balance, the gain in welfare to the winners can be summed with the loss in welfare to the losers and if the net effect is positive, the action is legitimate. This involves extraordinarily strong and arbitrary assumptions: that welfare is measurable for individuals, that welfare is measurable across individuals (that interpersonal comparisons can be made), and that the relevant index for decision making is the aggregate *sum* of individual welfare over the society.

If redistribution of income or wealth is the rationale for regulation, then we should observe that regulation would systematically redistribute from the "rich" to the "poor." Since that is obviously not the case in either the intent or the practice of land use controls, this motive can be dismissed from consideration without further elaboration.[51]

The presence of monopolies has also been suggested as the rationale for regulatory activities. In the case of land, private monopolies are conspicuously absent. Except in the trivial sense that any owner of a particular parcel has, by virtue of his property right, an exclusive claim to the use and disposition of that parcel, the proposition is empty. Land in the United States is held in widely dispersed ownership. In any event, the goal of regulation is not to alter the ownership of the regulated parcels; instead, regulation directs the use of a parcel irrespective of its ownership although it has implications for changes in ownership.

Externalities, then, remain the sole defensible rationale for land use regulation. Alternatively described as spillover or neighborhood effects,[52] this concept refers to the case where activity on a given parcel of land has effects on other individuals and collections of individuals and their activities—effects that are not considered in the internal decision making of the original property owner. In the classic textbook case, a factory emits a smoke pollutant that ultimately raises costs for the widow who takes in washing for a living; an airport generates noise that annoys the residents and decreases the value of surrounding property.

Note that externalities can be positive as well as negative. The development of an industrial research and development park may cause the creation of a skilled-labor pool that will lower the costs of acquiring skilled personnel by new firms. A home of aesthetic design surrounded by lovely gardens confers benefits on the surrounding neighbors.

Externalities

A property right, whether owned privately or by the state, carries with it the right to harm or benefit the owner and others.[53] What is meant by "benefit" and "harm"? Traditionally, economists have restricted these concepts to externalities that manifest themselves either through the price system (pecuniary externalities) or outside the price system (technological externalities).

The classic definition of externalities is attributed to A. P. Pigou:

[O]ne person A, in the course of rendering some service . . . to a second person B, incidentally also renders services or disservices to other persons (not producers of like services), of such a sort that payment cannot be exacted from the benefited parties or compensation enforced on behalf of the injured parties.[54]

Note the specific exception of producers of like services since the effects in this case are manifested through the price system. This early attempt to define and identify third-party effects of first- and second-party action led to the conclusion that it was appropriate for the government to impose a tax (subsidy) in order to converge private and social costs (benefits) and, hence, to internalize the externalities and increase social welfare. It was subsequently recognized that the imposition of taxes and subsidies might not be optimal. On this point, we have the contribution of Ronald Coase:[55] in the absence of transaction costs, markets will internalize the externalities and will lead to the appropriate resource allocation for society without government regulation, taxes, or subsidies. The allocation of resources will be invariant to the initial distribution of property rights; the distribution of wealth, however, will not. Harold Demsetz has argued further that even with transactions costs, competitive markets will internalize those externalities that are from society's point of view worth internalizing.[56]

We should note that whether the Pigouvian or Coasian prescriptions are followed, the appropriate allocation of resources may not involve the complete elimination of the spillover in question (e.g., pollution). According to E. J. Mishan:

The essence of a common conception of an external effect, one that is consistent with the usage in this paper, turns on its *incidental* character. The effect of others' welfare, though direct—and not an indirect effect, which is what is involved in any alteration of the set of product and factor prices consequent upon any change in tastes or in supply conditions—is always an *unintentional* product of some otherwise legitimate employment. It therefore does not cease to exist when the external economy or diseconomy is property priced so as to insure that an optimal output is attained. And it does not necessarily exist when the production function of a firm or the consumption function of a person is altered by the activities of others.[57]

A few quotations from the contributors to the debate on the taking issue will illustrate the point that their concerns can be included in the category of externalities. For example,

[I]n the real world everything in the environment is connected to everything else.[58]

[I]n an increasingly crowded and polluted environment can we afford to continue circulating the myth that tells us that the taking clause protects this right of unrestricted use regardless of its impact on society? Obviously not....[59]

It is not novel to say that, in this ever more complicated and crowded world, governmental activities and regulations, often adversely affecting the interests of private owners, are becoming increasingly pervasive.[60]

[H]armful externalities decrease the utility and thus the value of neighboring property.... [T]his factor will be called *nuisance costs*.[61]

An externality is an indirect side effect or spillover impact which results from a decision. Not typically considered a direct benefit or cost, externalities either inflict harm on someone without compensating him for it, or confer gain on someone without demanding payment. In accurately analyzing public expenditure decision, all externalities, good and bad, must be taken into account.[62]

Perhaps the most useful and comprehensive definition of an externality is to be found in work by James M. Buchanan and William Craig Stubblebine:

An externality is defined as *potentially relevant* when the activity, to the extent that it is actually performed, generates *any* desire on the part of the externally benefited (damaged) party (A) to modify the behavior of the party empowered to take action (B) through trade, persuasion, compromise, agreement, convention, collection action, etc. An externality which, to the extent that it is performed, exerts no such influence is defined as *irrelevant*.[63]

Thus, an externality is said to exist when any activity (consumption or production) by the first party leaves some other party worse off. The phrase *worse off* includes psychological as well as physical effects since the only test of the relative worsening of the second party's position is whether he would have the desire to modify the activity of the first party through trade, persuasion, compromise, agreement, convention, collective action, etc. Buchanan and Stubblebine also tie in the Pareto criteria:

An externality is defined to be Pareto-relevant when the extent of the activity may be modified in such a way that the externally affected party, A, can be made better off without the acting party, B, being made worse off.[64]

The authors also define an activity as "any distinguishable human action that may be measured, such as eating bread, drinking milk, spewing smoke into the air, dumping litter on the highways, giving to the poor, etc."[65]

Psychological Effects

These definitions focus on the external effect on the second party, not on the nature of the action itself. In that spirit, if the pertinent issue is whether a second party is better or worse off, the restriction of an activity to be a "human action that is measurable" is arbitrarily restrictive. More generally, a second party may feel better or worse off because of the existence of a condition in the world that does not involve measurable human action. For example, an individual may feel worse off vis-à-vis some contemplated alternative when he views the existing distribution of talent in society.

There is no sound a priori analysis to exclude psychological effects. For example, if we invoke the Pareto criteria, which permit any reorganization of society as long as it benefits some but does not harm any individuals, should not psychological effects be included as well? Suppose parties A and B voluntarily agree to exchange certain amounts of one commodity for another. A third party, individual C, who is not directly involved in the transaction may feel worse off because the transaction has taken place. This qualifies as an external effect not taken into account by the principal parties to the transaction. To be more concrete, the transaction might involve the exchange of a packet of marijuana for sexual favors.

On a less dramatic level we can imagine a transaction between the owner of a stand of redwood trees and a timber company. The third party outside of the transaction might be an individual living on the opposite coast of the country who, although he will never visit the forest or see the trees, feels worse off because he knows the trees will be harvested.

Should the welfare of these remote, but interested, third parties be taken into account under a scheme that corrects for externalities? If we accept the generalized Pareto criteria, then we have no choice but to include them. The implications of such an approach would be dramatic indeed: at the extreme, we could contemplate the misanthropic individual who claims to legitimately and honestly be made worse off by *any* transaction among any individuals at all.

If adopted, this organization of society could theoretically block all economic activity and, indeed, virtually all human activity. If any one of us objected to the way religion was practiced by a subset of society, that practice could be prohibited. Thomas Gale Moore has commented on this:

Part of the problem with the concept of freedom is over the admissible set of externalities. It could be that we include everything that anyone considers relevant. Then if I object to your way of worshipping God, it becomes relevant.[66]

The existence of property rights and the viability of markets in the rights are obviously crucial. If one objects (feels worse off) because of the exercise of a property right by another, a market transaction can settle for society the issue pertaining to the intensities of the participants' preferences. This, obviously, is the critical problem of environment action; individuals with strong preferences for environment amenities have no cheap way to express the existence or intensity of their desires in an organized market. Hence, they resort to expropriation via the political market.

Given a wealth distribution, the assignment of a property right will crucially affect the success of compensation possibilities in a world with positive transaction costs. If, for example, individual A feels worse off because of the screening of pornographic movies and an attempt is made to compensate him for the loss in welfare occasioned by said movies, he may demand an infinite sum if his predilections are so strong. On the other hand, if the right to prevent pornographic movie production and screening does not reside with the individual, the maximum amount of compensation he can offer to prospective movie producers to forestall their activity is limited to the wealth at his disposal. This is certainly a finite sum and will, in general, be less than the sum he would ask for in the earlier case.[67] Consequently, the allocation of goods will, in a world of positive transaction costs, depend on the initial distribution of wealth and property rights. Moreover, each distribution will be associated with a different Pareto optimal allocation of goods among which no choice can be made without resort to arbitrary constructs such as a social welfare function.

Although economists usually separate the efficiency issue from that of the initial wealth distribution, the suggestion that concerned individuals "buy off" others up to the limit of their wealth may be less viable with high transactions costs.

The Pareto rule is not universally accepted. Even economists refuse to accept the Pareto criteria as they attempt to invoke them. Consider the following passages:

If one person is made better off while no one else is made worse off, then there is a presumption that the society as a whole is better off.

But if economic welfare were already distributed very unequally and the person who was made better off already had a disproportionate share of the total, one could legitimately judge this to be a decrease in social welfare.[68]

One cannot escape the distributional question, unless one insists on regarding it as irrelevant. If the collective good involves aid to the needy aged, one may take a different view of the effects of the coercion than if it involves providing a civic yacht harbor.

Nor (in my view) are these difficulties with the optimal solution merely symptoms of imperfections in the taxing schema. Citizens have social values about appropriate tax policies too. Suppose we are building a public playground to be used by underprivileged children. If A is a rich misanthrope and B is a poor Samaritan, there is no compelling reason why B should carry more of the tax burden, even though he may be willing to do so.[69]

A market economy that starts with an unjust distribution of economic resources will yield an unjust distribution of goods and services, regardless of its efficiency.[70]

Although it is doubtful that everyone would regard the general Pareto criterion as a viable basis for the organization of society, let us pursue some of its implications. Here alternative Pareto optimal allocations are involved. If each individual member of society has (in the absence of buy-offs or compensation) absolute veto power over each alternative, proposed state of nature (and indeed he has if no state of nature can be adopted that he believes will subjectively leave him worse off), the set of admissible states of nature that are achievable might well be empty. There is probably no activity conducted or contemplated by an individual that would not meet with the objections of another.

Social Choice

Modern welfare economics is either silent on all reorganizations of society that receive less than unanimous support or retreats to some nonindividualistic ethical ordering known as a "social welfare function." The difficulties encountered in the attempted construction of social welfare functions are illustrated by the well-known Arrow impossibility theorem:

If we exclude the possibility of interpersonal comparisons of utility, then the only methods of passing from individual tastes to social preferences which will be satisfactory and which will be defined for a wide range of sets of individual orderings are either imposed or dictatorial.[71]

More recently, the work of A. K. Sen reveals a similar problem.[72] If individuals have the right to choose which of two alternative states of nature is to be more highly ranked in the social ordering of the alternatives, under a reasonable set of consistency conditions it appears there is no stable or well-defined social order that does not involve a dictator.

Robert Nozick, in *Anarchy, State, and Utopia*, analyzes the problem as follows: "The trouble [with the Sen result] stems from treating an individual's right to choose among alternatives as the right to determine the relative ordering of these alternatives within a social ordering."[73] Loosely speaking, if every individual has the right to have his desires prevail in every case for every state of nature (every proposed or potential activity of action by other individuals), formal inconsistencies cannot be avoided.

In view of these conclusions, it is not necessary to raise issues of static versus dynamic considerations, to explore how the government would acquire the necessary information about individuals' preferences in an environment with high transaction costs so that individuals have incentives to overstate their losses and understate their gains occasioned by the actions of others, or to even discuss the issue of compensation by the state for its regulatory actions. These issues are irrelevant given the logical implications of the definition of externalities and Pareto optimality.

Nozick suggests a possible solution to these problems:

A more appropriate view of individual rights is as follows. Individual rights are co-possible; each person may exercise his rights as he chooses. The exercise of these rights fixes some features of the world. Within the constraints of these fixed features, a choice may be made by a social choice mechanism based upon a social ordering; if there are any choices left to make! Rights do not determine a social ordering but instead set the constraints within which a social choice is to be made, by excluding certain alternatives, fixing others, and so on.... Even if all possible alternatives are ordered first, apart from anyone's rights, the situation is not changed: for then the highest ranked alternative *that is not excluded by anyone's exercise of his rights* is instituted. Rights do not determine the position of an alternative or the relative position of two alternatives in a social ordering; they *operate upon* a social ordering to constrain the choice it can yield.[74]

In an even more fundamental statement of the proposition, Nozick states:

Individuals have rights, and there are things no person or group may do to them (without violating their rights). So strong and far-reaching are these rights that they raise the question of what, if anything, the state and its officials may do. How much room do individual rights leave for the state?[75]

Side Constraints

We will continue to carry the concepts of externalities and Pareto optimality in the analysis, but will suggest that they operate in a context in which side constraints exist. Let us assume that individual members of society have a well-defined (but as yet unspecified) set of rights to conduct activities as they please. Any Pareto criteria reorganizations undertaken by the state because of externalities must not violate the side constraints. We continue to ignore the reorganization costs (transaction, information costs, etc.) that the state would incur in its activities. In other words, we assume that the state is a costless, frictionless, perfectly functioning mechanism that does not use resources in the conduct of its reorganization—the state is thus a principle rather than an entity at this stage of the discussion.

The approach of imposing and guaranteeing side constraints for individual rights is certainly not foreign to the traditions of law or economics in this country. The Bill of Rights asserts certain individual rights that may not be abrogated or infringed upon by the state or by other individuals.[76] Hence, many externalities that meet the Buchanan-Stubblebine definition are not sufficient grounds for intervention or reorganization; for example, A may sincerely believe that B would benefit from reading of the Scriptures and would be harmed by reading pornography. Similarly, B may hold the opposite view of the benefits and costs of the respective literature to A. Yet with relevant side constraints neither would be authorized to impose his preference ordering on the other individual.

Constitutional Guarantees

The drafters of the United States Constitution had a better appreciation of the role of side constraints than do contemporary statesmen. Guarantees of the exercise of religion, speech, press, and the right of assembly fit naturally into the category of individual rights whose guarantees constrain other individuals acting individually or through the state. Clearly, the drafters of the Fifth Amendment intended to protect individual rights in private property from arbitrary abuse by the government under the police power. Such protection could have been achieved by placing property in the First Amendment along with the rights to freedom of speech, association, and religion.[77] However, perhaps recognizing the difficulty in some cases of obtaining property through the market system (a case we would call extraordinarily high transactions costs today), the protection of individual property rights was placed in the Fifth (and Fourteenth) Amendment with the statement that private property shall not be "taken for public use without just compensation." In addition, the Fourteenth Amendment states that no person shall be deprived "of life, liberty, or property without due process of law."

Given recent developments in the law such as the abandonment of the substantive due process clause in the 1930s and the currently proposed emasculation of the Fifth Amendment taking clause, private property rights may be left completely unprotected in practice. Under earlier interpretation, property rights were protected by the Fifth and Fourteenth Amendments with provisions or exceptions carefully drawn. Imagine a linear continuum with absolute police power at one end and the due process protection at the other. First Amendment freedoms are located on the spectrum very close to the due process end. Consequently, the First Amendment rights are frequently regarded as virtually absolute; they can be abridged only by government through the due process clause in which the burden of proof for overriding the First Amendment rights clearly rests on the government; the government must prove its case before individual First Amendment rights can be abridged. Imagine also that private property rights are on the continuum and are close to the due process end. Because the set of circumstances under which property rights can be abridged is a larger set than that for traditional First Amendment rights, property rights are not as close to the due process end of the spectrum as are First Amendment rights. Their presumed position on this end of the spectrum is clear because of the stated protections in the Fifth and Fourteenth Amendments: just compensation and due process.

If the safeguards of just compensation and due process are eliminated, property rights are left without practical defense except insofar as they are a necessary precondition to the exercise of free speech, assembly, religion, etc. De facto, they shift from a position close to the due process end of the contimuum all the way to the end characterized by the police power. In summary, if "submissive" due process rules; if it is presumed that all legislative regulation of land is by definition correct, reasonable, and fair; and if the burden of proof rests on the individual to prove that said legislative action is unreasonable, arbitrary, and unfair; then the original due process protection for property rights is lost. If, in addition, the remaining protection for private property rights (the Fifth Amendment taking clause) is eliminated, private property rights are left unprotected. If, in the ordinary course of its business, the state regulates all land, if the legal presumption is that the state's regulation is fair and reasonable, if the burden of proof is on the property owner to show that it is not arbitrary and unreasonable, and if the state does not pay compensation for damage it does by its regulation, then private property rights have vanished.

Externalities Broadly Conceived

Thomas Gale Moore anticipates the point made here very well:

If any externality is permitted, then we can put no restrictions on the types of activities which could be taxed. Free speech, freedom of religion, and so on, can only be justified if some restrictions are placed on the admissible set of externalities.[78]

Although there may be many ways of restricting the set of admissible externalities, the strategy of defining individual rights which act as side constraints is well within our legal and political traditions.

Moore proposes that the admissible externalities be only those which physically affect an individual through his senses:

In a sense, everything that an individual is aware of must have come through his senses. Then to say that the externality must affect his senses could be interpreted to include everything. We will restrict it to those externalities which directly impinge on his senses. If he hears about someone doing something he objects to, this will not count. On the other hand, if he is forced to watch what he objects to, that is an admissible externality. Thus, for example, a fervent member of the WCTU would suffer relevant externality from being forced to witness a drunk on her front step, but would not if she hears about a man drinking in a bar....

Let us consider the relevance of this value judgment for the subject of speech. If I advocate to another individual LSD, a particular product, or free love, and the individual willingly listens, the net externalities can be considered zero unless the individual is stimulated to action *and* the action has externalities.[79]

Robert Nozick reaches a similar conclusion by another route:

The difference seems to me to reside in the difference between a face-to-face community and a nation. In a nation, one knows that there are nonconforming individuals, but one need not be directly confronted by these individuals or by the fact of their nonconformity. Even if one finds it offensive that others do not conform, even if the knowledge that there exists nonconformists rankles and makes one very unhappy, this does not constitute being harmed by the others or having one's rights violated. Whereas in a face-to-face community one cannot avoid being directly confronted with what one finds to be offensive.[80]

If the set of relevant externalities is limited to those where data are received directly through the individual's senses (e.g., seeing rather than hearing about the town drunk), it is doubtful that the criteria would be accepted in those very cases of externalities which seem to concern the environmentalists most. For example, under Moore's criteria if an environmentalist witnesses the chopping down of a redwood tree, it is a legitimate externality; if he only hears that the tree is cut down, it is not an admissible externality. Similarly, individuals who object to the slaughter of baby seals in Newfoundland would not have a legitimate claim for intervention or compensation unless they witnessed the event firsthand; newspaper accounts or film clips would presumably not give sufficient reason for qualification of this act as an externality.

The incentive structure inherent in this definition would clearly lead to a misallocation of society's resources. One can imagine interested groups organizing (as they now do) to discover and monitor potential externalities and, in order to qualify the externalities as relevant, dispatching a representative to the scene to witness and personally document the event in question. In other words, if a particular activity had to be witnessed in person through the senses in order to have that activity qualify as a relevant externality, interested individuals would quickly organize into groups in order to send a representative to witness these events. Thus, except for one-time or first-time activities, the set of externalities not witnessed firsthand or directly through the senses would shrink to the null set. In the context of Moore's example, if the drunk in the gutter is not a legitimate externality because he is not observed firsthand by the WCTU member, we can expect that, once this rule is publicized, the WCTU will systematically patrol the streets and bars in order to observe the drunk firsthand and thus qualify the event as a legitimate externality.[81]

There must certainly be alternative ways to define the set of individual rights which constrain the activities of the state.

The larger the constraint set of individual rights, the smaller the set of admissible externalities subject to state action. This approach, which may strike some as a finesse of the problem, reduces the area of controversial activities by definition. Some externalities are ignored as irrelevant; voluntary market transactions, depending on the magnitude of negotiation costs, will internalize others. When transaction costs are prohibitively high, the state may internalize the remaining relevant externalities, compensation questions aside.

Where does this leave us? In a certain sense, we have reached a familiar position that has fairly wide acceptance in the economics and the legal profession; that is, the market itself will internalize in a private property system some (many or few?) of the externalities without state interference.[82] Beyond that point, transaction costs may be so high (particularly in cases where many individuals in the course of their activities each impose a small cost on each of the remaining individuals, the net effect of which is large for any particular recipient) that the state may, on some criteria, interfere and modify the activity of the market participants. The departure from standard doctrine is the assumption of the set of individual rights which constrains the admissible set of externalities that the state can manipulate. Without the constraint set, the set of admissible externalities subject to state action is the universal set of activities. Consequently, given the diversity of tastes and preferences among the members of society, it is reasonable to conclude that in the absence of unanimity or compensation, the set of Pareto states of the world achievable by the government in its effort to correct externalities would be the empty set.

Regulation in the Public Interest

Practical political considerations neither require nor permit that we design an individual side constraint set to meet the theoretical considerations discussed in the previous sections. Others have addressed and will address the difficult, long-run task of defining a philosophical framework within which to develop legal and economic principles of social organization.

Although the preceding framework of individual side constraints has both promise and constitutional precedent, it is highly unlikely that our society will, within the foreseeable future, take the quantum jump to a system based on entirely redefined ethical and legal principles. More likely, we will continue to make marginal or incremental adjustments in the law and our institutions as we attempt to reach practical solutions to the taking issue. We will continue to muddle through—a euphemism for what is called "the living law."

Here is how Robert H. Haveman describes the current state of the economics of the public decision process:

Once the full set of inputs and outputs attributable to a public decision is isolated, the next step in benefit-cost analysis is to attach a value or price to each input and output. The price which is attached should represent the value which society places on the input or the output. If measured in dollars, the value of the inputs is the amount which would have to be paid to all of the people adversely affected by the decision, just to compensate them for the dissatisfaction which they incurred. Similarly, the value of the outputs is the amount which those people who gained from the decision would be willing to pay rather than go without the output. Once these values are placed on inputs and outputs, they become known as *costs* and *benefits*....

...In planning a program or designing a project, the criterion consistent with maximizing the value of the nation's output is the *maximum net benefits criterion*. According to this criterion, the optimum size or design of a project or program is that for which the excess of benefits over costs is as great as possible.[83]

It is important to recognize the specific concerns of those who argue for the extended use of police powers as opposed to eminent domain. The goals may be broadly characterized as environmental, but the term is too broad and encompassing to be informative in this context. Environmental concerns may relate to the abatement of a particular pollutant or may instead refer to promotion of the "natural, cultural, and aesthetic values" that the authors of the Rockefeller Brothers Fund Report promote. Contributors to the debate who are of this persuasion argue that society, through its government, cannot (or will not?) tax itself to raise the money to compensate the private owners of property that they propose to regulate. For example,

[T]he protection of critical environmental and cultural areas will require placing tough new restrictions on the use of private land. These restrictions will be little more than delaying actions if the courts do not uphold them as reasonable measures to protect the public interest, in short, as restrictions that landowners may fairly be required to bear without payment by the government. The interpretation of the takings clause is therefore a crucial matter for the future of land use planning and regulatory programs.[84]

Public Goods

When some activity or action is alleged to be in the public interest, the speaker conveys the impression that everyone will benefit and everyone will benefit equally. This condition is satisfied, at least in theory, by the public goods polar case in economic theory.[85] By assumption a given amount of a particular good or service can be consumed in total by every member of society; the consumption by one individual does not decrease the amount available for consumption by another. Traditional examples are national defense and fireworks displays. Contrast these cases to ordinary private goods where, for example, an individual drinks a bottle of wine which is then not available for consumption by another.

There are difficulties with public goods concept when the analysis is carried over to the real world. It is difficult enough to find examples of public goods for which each and every individual consumes exactly the same amount of a commodity or service. But it is even more difficult to find public goods that also satisfy the requirement that each individual consuming the public good regards it as a "good" rather than a "bad." To make the obvious point, if national defense is a public good, why do significant numbers of our fellow citizens regard it as a curse rather than a blessing? But if not everyone desires the public good, public decision-making criteria are considerably more complicated since they must take account of the fact that while some prize the good and others detest it, each regardless of his preferences *must* consume the same amount of the good. Hence, while many social critics have argued that public goods are underproduced, there is reason to believe that the opposite hypothesis may be true: public goods may be overproduced in this society to the extent that the desires of the "captive riders" are systematically ignored.

The relative ease with which arguments in favor of government decision making with regard to resource allocation have been made demonstrates the preoccupation with documenting market failures as opposed to constructing operational models of public choice. Whether the issue be monopoly or externality, the standard prescription is to turn the problem over to the government; the tacit assumption is that the government will function in an optimal fashion, serving the public interest and serving it costlessly.

The Public Interest

This is certainly a logical time in the course of the debate over the taking issue to insist that the proponents of regulation (and, for that matter, those of eminent domain) state very clearly the operational criteria that they propose the government should use. Too much is at stake—in terms of both economic and political liberty and real income—to rely on the heroic assumption that what the government does—by definition, tradition, or law—will be in the public interest. The problem of serving the public interest is not nearly as simple as some of the sages would have us believe. Consider Walter Lippmann on the subject:

Living adults share, we must believe, the same public interest. For them, however, the public interest is mixed with, and is often at odds with, their private and special interests. Put this way, we can say, I suggest, that the public interest may be presumed to be what men would choose if they saw clearly, thought rationally, acted disinterestedly and benevolently.[86]

and an opposing comment from Ayn Rand:

All "public interest" legislation (and any distribution of money taken by force from some men for the unearned benefit of others) comes down ultimately to the grant of an undefined, undefinable, non-objective, arbitrary power to some government official.

The worse aspect of it is not that such power can be used dishonestly, but that *it cannot be used honestly*. The wisest man in the world, with the purest integrity, cannot find a criterion for the just, equitable, rational application of an unjust, inequitable, irrational principle. The best that an honest official can do is to accept no material bribe for his arbitrary decision; but this does not make his decision and its consequences more just or less calamitous.

A man of clear-cut convictions is impervious to anyone's influence. But when clear-cut convictions are impossible, personal influences take over. When a man's mind is trapped in the foggy labyrinth of the non-objective, that has no exits and no solutions, he will welcome any quasi-persuasive, semi-plausible argument.[87]

The *public interest* (or the common good) is an empty phrase unless it is interpreted literally to mean an unambiguous improvement in the situation of each and every member of society or, on a weaker criterion, to leave no one any worse off. Since it is difficult to even imagine an activity that does not hurt someone, let alone uniformly increase the lot of everyone, the concept is empty—a piece of rhetoric used to persuade others through the political process.[88] In fact, public interest arguments usually mean that the good of some men takes precedence over the good of others. In certain cases the common good appears to mean the good of the majority versus the good of the minority or of the individual. Note that the argument for the public interest or the common good is usually invoked by special interests. No doubt it was argued that it was in the public interest to strip our Japanese-American citizens of their constitutional rights—property and liberty—when they were interned in prison camps early in World War II.[89] Similarly it was allegedly in the public interest to send unwilling conscripts to Southeast Asia to kill and be killed. Every despot in history, whatever the nature of his atrocity, conquest, pillage, or slaughter, has alleged that he was acting in the public interest.

The difficulty with the notion of the public interest is that it assumes that there is a desirable end state and that the government is the best judge of what that end state should be. Instead, let us focus on the role of law and institutions as enabling a procedure or process to operate. If this approach is accepted, the burden of proof rests on the state to indicate why the proposed end is desirable and to reveal the operational criteria that will be employed to identify and achieve that end. Thus if the state is to regulate land use—with or without compensation—we must know what the decision criteria are. If control over property is shifted to a public agency and that agency is vested with arbitrary authority guided simply by a mandate to serve "the public interest," the result in terms of resource allocation and distribution may be worse than that experienced in an unregulated system of private property.

The Economic Problem of Society

A recapitulation of the economic problem may be useful here: resource allocation decisions in every society must be conducted so that resources are directed toward satisfying the wants of individual members of society. Because the wants exceed the capacity to serve (given finite resources and the current state of technology) and because the various wants may be inconsistent with one another, some device must be used to assign relative valuations to the wants of individuals. In a decentralized economic system, individuals register their preferences by voluntarily bidding for goods and services with their dollars in open markets. The firms or entrepreneurs who respond to the market need not have complete information about preferences of consumers; indeed, the consumers may change their preferences dramatically over time. Since the received condition of the world is one of uncertainty, the debate over whether consumers know their preferences is not terribly enlightening. The question is how best to satisfy current preferences in a world without certainty.

In a market system the combination of competition among firms, free entry into industries, and private risk taking generates a process of trial and error that channels resources into those uses that most closely approximate the preferences exhibited by consumers; and the process channels the resources most efficiently.

Certain goods and services (e.g., some types of environmental goods) are not available in a decentralized market, and then there is no cheap way for consumers to register their preferences by voting with their dollars. The quality of the air surrounding each person is not an item that is traded in the market even though the individual may have strong preferences for a particular quality level of air and may also be willing to back up his preferences with his money. Property rights to air quality have not been devised and hence cannot be exchanged. And so the state steps in, theoretically, to correct the externality and provide a more preferred combination of goods and services.

We now come to the very crucial matter: what criteria will the state use to determine the new mix of environmental and other goods? Everyone stipulates (perhaps heroically) that the state will attempt to meet the desires of its citizens, but no one has explained how the desires of individual citizens will be transmitted to the state and under what incentive structure the state will implement these preferences.

It should be obvious to all that environmental goods and services must come at the expense of both other private goods and services and other public goods. Given the finite resources and the available technology in any one period of time, a better environment (public goods) must come at the expense of something else (private and other public goods). If individuals could register their preferences among alternative combinations, the state would have information on which to base its decisions; individuals might express their effective demand for additional environmental goods by indicating the financial sum they would be willing to pay in order to obtain a better environment or the dollar sum they would demand as compensation for an additional unit of environmental degradation. These dollar sums would reflect values on an individual basis that could be aggregated into a collective value to be assigned to alternative bundles of goods and services.

This approach has not been implemented by the various agencies of the government in charge of environmental goods. Indeed, the agencies seem to studiously avoid placing dollar values on their proposed actions. We frequently hear in popular debate the allegation that the butterflies, the brown pelicans, or clean air are "priceless" or that their value cannot be measured in terms of dollars. Rarely are we told what we must give up in the way of goods and services if we want to preserve the butterflies, pelicans, or clean air. In order to begin to understand why government bureaucracies avoid placing dollar values on the benefits or the costs of their actions, let us examine the institutional framework within which the bureaucracies carry out their activities.

A Model of Bureaucratic Behavior

Assume that the several participants in the political and economic process can be assigned to one of three distinct groups: the general public, the legislature, and the bureaus of the government. According to conventional wisdom, the public "demands" goods and services from its government; these demands are registered through a variety of means (e.g., voting, election assistance, letters, pressure groups) with the legislature and are paid for in the final analysis by taxes collected from the public rather than by fees charged to the recipients of the publicly produced goods and services. Given that the legislature faces a budget that is fixed in the current fiscal period, it responds to the will of the people by choosing a combination of final public goods and services which it believes will maximize the probability of reelection. This decision is implemented by the various budget appropriations that the legislature assigns to the several government bureaucracies which, in turn, allegedly proceed to deliver the assigned bundle of goods and services to the public.

Since the legislature has neither the time nor the information to advise and monitor, let alone run, these bureaus on a day-to-day basis, considerable autonomy is vested within the bureaus themselves. The legislature passes enabling legislation that vests broad, discretionary authority in the agency which then promulgates its own rules and procedures by fiat in the *Federal Register*. However, the incentive structure for behavior within the bureaucracy itself deserves scrutiny. Even though it is commonly alleged that bureaucrats are public servants, it is plausible to assert that the bureaucrat has a life and purpose of his own.

William A. Niskanen has advanced the hypothesis that the typical bureaucrat attempts to maximize his own utility function:

Among the several variables that may enter the bureaucrats utility function are the following: salary, prerequisites of the office, public reputation, power, patronage, output of the bureau, ease of making changes, and ease of managing the bureau. All of these variables except the last two, I contend, are a positive monotonic function of the total *budget* of the bureau during the bureaucrat's tenure in office.[90]

Niskanen asserts that the bureaucrat attempts to maximize the size of his budget subject to the condition that he cover his costs with no residual profit or loss. The legislature has a downward-sloping demand function for the output of the bureau; hence, as the output of the bureau increases, the marginal unit is worth less and less to the legislature. According to Niskanen, "A bureau offers a promised set of activities and the expected output(s) of these activities for a budget."[91]

Earl A. Thompson argues that the bureaucrat will maximize his output (instead of picking an output that maximizes his dollar budget) since the bureaucrat is constrained to remain on his rising supply curve—he does not participate in any rent or profit resulting from decisions which leave an excess of the budget over costs. Thompson also makes a valuable contribution to the discussion by sharpening the focus of the problem:

[R]eview committees [legislatures] cannot measure and evaluate all of the outputs of the bureau. In this reviewer's opinion, this difficulty of measuring and evaluating performance should be at the center of any argument contrasting public and private institutions....[92]

Let us suppose that the typical bureaucrat maximizes the output of his bureau; this assumption is consistent with the popular view that the bureaucrat is intellectually and emotionally dedicated to the mission of his agency. Clearly, the legislature's demand curve for the agency's output can be shifted upward and outward by the appropriate lobbying activities. And there is ample evidence that government agencies and bureaus do in fact lobby members of the legislature on behalf of their agencies.[93]

But the legislature's demand curve is a derived demand curve that, in some ultimate sense, represents the desires of the public; after all, politicians tell us that their actions simply mirror the wishes of their constituents. Thus, the perceived demand for environmental protection, national defense, health care, etc., by the legislature is really a manifestation of the desires of subsets of the general public for production of goods and services in these areas. The intelligent bureau chief then has two groups that he wishes to lobby and influence in the support of his goal of output maximization: the legislature and the general public. To the extent that he is successful, his efforts will increase the demand for his agency's services.

Want Creation?

Since the bureau is well aware of the ultimate demand for its services, like the private sector manufacturer of shampoo or breakfast food, it engages in advertising and public relations in order to increase the wants which it hopes will justify its request for a larger budget. Note, however, that the stated purpose of these promotional activities is the hope that they will "clarify and inform public debate."[94] That, indeed, may be the effect in part, but these efforts also serve as a vehicle for influencing public opinion in a direction which will lead to the expansion of the output, power, and budget of the sponsoring agency.

The efforts of bureaucracies to expand the demand for their output fit rather neatly into the "dependence effect" invented by John Kenneth Galbraith:

[P]roducers may proceed actively to create wants through advertising and salesmanship. Wants thus come to depend on output.

This . . . means that the process by which wants are satisfied is also the process by which wants are created. The more wants that are satisfied, the more new ones are born.[95]

This argument was effectively rebutted by F. A. von Hayek:

Though the range of choice open to the consumers is the joint result of, among other things, the efforts of all producers who vie with each other in making their respective products appear more attractive than those of their competitors, every particular consumer still has the choice between all those different offers.[96]

One can reject the Galbraith proposition that supply creates its own demand and at the same time admit that there is ample empirical evidence that producers attempt to increase the demand for their products by advertising which is both informative and persuasive. However, private sector firms that engage in "want creation" are subject to competition from rivals. No one has a monopoly on soap, breakfast food, or pain killers; so no individual firm has the luxury of having the undivided attention of the consumer group it wishes to influence. Competition among bureaus, on the other hand, is largely for appropriations.[97]

Although Galbraith might well be annoyed to have his dependence effect applied to the typical bureaucracy of the public sector—an arena that he proposed should be expanded at the expense of the private sector—the argument seems to fit quite well. Bureaucracies do attempt to advertise their product and increase the demand for it.

The crucial difference between the behavior of public sector bureaus and private sector firms is that the bureau generally distributes its product *free* to the ultimate consumer. The important expenditure categories such as environmental protection, national defense, social welfare, consumer protection, and occupational safety and health are all distributed to the ultimate consuming public with zero user charges. The respective government agencies are well aware that their outputs are not produced without cost, but they make no particular effort to convey cost information to their clientele when they advertise their products. Since a zero price will be charged for the public good, neither the consuming public nor the producing bureaucracy will have an incentive to discover and publicize the true cost of the output.

Distorted Expectations

Assume that members of special-interest groups among the public realize that the legislature has a finite budget in any given fiscal period and that this budget must be allocated among competing ends. If the citizens visualize the legislature's budget as the sum of the products of outputs times the unit prices of the outputs, these unit costs take on an important role. When members of the public, systematically misled by the agencies, believe that the costs are zero (or, at least, lower than the true costs), they will request bundles of public goods and services that they *conclude* are attainable while, in fact, the bundles would violate the budget constraint of the legislature. Voters know that constraints exist, but because they assign systematically lower prices to many of the component outputs, they demand bundles of public goods and services that the legislature cannot deliver because it faces a vector of prices whose components are all either greater than or equal to the prices perceived by the public.

Why do the voters not realize that the outputs of the bureaus are not costless and why do they not associate that knowledge with the level of their taxes? There are several answers to this question. First, although citizens know the goods are not costless, they systematically assign costs that are lower than the true costs because of the information provided to them by the bureaucracies. Who among us knows the real costs of EPA or OHSA? Second, since the citizen's taxes do not increase monotonically with the amount of public goods and services which *he* prizes, a game-strategic incentive structure is in play; imagine a group of ten people who go out to dinner and agree beforehand to divide the total check equally even though each individual can order whatever he pleases. If the dinner is a one-time affair with strangers, the rational diner will reason as follows: "If we all order a $10 dinner, I will pay $10. If I order a $20 dinner while the other nine order the $10 dinner, we will all pay $11. Thus, I will get a $20 dinner for $11." Since each diner has the same incentive, there is little doubt that the total amount of money spent on the dinner would be greater under this sharing agreement than under the arrangement where each pays his own check.

A similar phenomenon occurs when the production of "public" goods is financed out of general tax funds. Each special-interest group will lobby to maximize the activity level of its favorite public expenditure on the grounds that the cost will be shared among the larger tax-paying public. As a variation of this, a systematic distortion is introduced because the outputs of the bureaus are financed from a broad tax base while the recipients of the free output are a more narrowly defined political constituency. Thus, it will, in effect, pay me to lobby actively in favor of higher salaries for professors at the University of California, but it will not pay me to lobby against higher salaries for the state highway patrol. The net expected benefit is large in the first case and small in the second. Furthermore, if a citizen should lobby against public expedititure on goods and services that he does not value highly, he can expect as a practical matter that the reduction in this category will be offset by an increase in another expenditure category, and his taxes will not be reduced on balance.

In one of the few areas where expenditure on public goods and services is specifically tied and earmarked—the case of public education financed by local property taxes—the recent evidence at the polls suggests that individuals will oppose increases in expenditure on public goods when they are more aware of the true costs of the expenditures and also perceive the direct cost to them in taxes.

According to Jack L. Knetsch,

The absence of any (or any realistic) fair-cost sharing, particularly when this absence serves little other purpose, places a great burden on objective analysis. A disequilibrium between supply and demand is imposed by greatly underpricing the outputs of resource development projects, giving rise to a large demand relative to limited availability or supply of such projects brought about by constrained budgets. A public agency is, therefore, dependent upon a substitute mechanism and is called on to parallel the allocation objectives of the market where limited goods with numerous applications are allocated, but where demand far exceeds the supply.[98]

Systematic Overproduction of Public Goods

If the public systematically assigns a lower set of costs to the public goods, the bundle of goods delivered by the legislature under its fiscal constraint will be perceived to be too small by the general public. If the set of prices (unit costs) which the public uses in its intuitive optimization is systematically lower than the prices faced by the legislature, the public's vector of demands for goods and services always will be unsatisfied. During the next iteration of the budget process, these unsatisfied demands will manifest themselves through a variety of expressions of discontent via the political process. Since the dilemma is irreconcilable because of the different set of implied prices used by the various participants in the process and the diffuse link between taxes and benefits, the legislature cannot remove the source of the dissatisfaction by rearranging its expenditures among the various public agencies. The only course open to the legislature is to expand the size of the budget in order to be able to expand the level of outputs in the bundle of public goods and services.

The expanding budget of the legislature must be financed by taxes on the private sector or by inflation (which, of course, is also a tax). If the process continues, resources are shifted from production of private goods and services to public goods and services, although there may be some rearrangement within the public goods category. This, in turn, generates still more dissatisfaction among citizens as their real incomes in terms of private goods and services are reduced while, at the same time, they continue to be dissatisfied with the level of production of public goods and services. Once these dynamics have been set in motion, there is no cheap way for individuals to register effectively their displeasure with the mix of public and private goods which the legislature has arranged. Should the individual complain to his legislator about his taxes, the legislator will probably respond that while taxes are high, there is dramatic evidence that a number of public "needs" are still woefully unsatisfied, and the legislator can point convincingly to evidence that the public is requesting still greater expenditures on public education, defense, environmental protection, health care, and so forth.

Both the taxpayer and the legislator will be correct in their assessments of the situation. The inconsistency not perceived by them is a result of distortions of the pricing system by the incentive structure built into the bureaucratic form of public goods production, distribution, and financing. As long as bureaus advertise their services as costless, as long as they distribute their goods free, as long as the goods are financed out of general tax revenues, and as long as the legislature responds to the preferences of the public in this system, the inconsistency of expectations will persist.

The dynamics of the model lead to overproduction of public goods and services, the concomitant underproduction of private goods and services, and the perpetual dissatisfaction of the public with the output mix of public and private goods. And note, this result does not depend on the notion that the essence of political success is to persuade constituents that they "deserve more than they have."

Escape from the Budget

The bureaucrats' preoccupation with expanding the size of their output reinforces and contributes to the results discussed above. The problem raised by Thompson—the difficulty of measuring and evaluating performance of the bureau[99]—has so far defied resolution in a general way. Given that the bureaus are in competition with one another for funds in the budget process, each agency will have the incentive to circumvent the budget process in the interest of maximizing its output. Rewards to employees in a public agency are not entirely random and unconnected with performance. Rewards, in terms of salary, prestige, promotion, and power, are to some extent a function of input productivity and output performance. If the bureau can command the use of resources *outside its budget*, then its output will increase absolutely and the relative performance (the output delivered from a given financial budget) will also improve. If the output of the agency can be increased at a faster rate than the budget, the agency will receive kudos from the sponsoring legislators for their successful efforts at "cost-effectiveness."

Suppose, for example, the Defense Department had the authority to direct the managers of a private-sector machine shop to produce a given quota of machine guns or missile parts as a condition for the firm to continue to conduct its normal private-sector business. This authority would enable the Defense Department to create a dramatic increase in its output without ever having to show in its own books and budget requests the value of the resources used to produce this output. The output of the Defense Department could increase dramatically with no increase in appropriations to the department.

Such an arrangement would have enormous adverse implications for the efficient allocation of resources. The Defense Department would have no incentive whatsoever to use effectively the extra-budget resources under its command. The two crucially important functions played by price in any economic organization—metering input productivity and metering rewards—would be absent. All the information provided by prices would be ignored by design and incentive in this system.

In effect, the production quota imposed by the agency on the private-sector firms would serve as a franchise or license fee, the cost of which would be passed on in large measure to consumers of the private-sector goods produced by the firms. Although the private-sector firms would have the incentive to produce their quotas efficiently (assuming that intermediate goods in the production process were not also subject to commandeering by the agency), the relative price of private and public goods would be distorted and, consequently, so would the relative outputs of the two categories. This arrangement can be thought of as decision making without prices or, perhaps a more quotable phrase, planning without prices.

Misallocation of Resources

The advocates of government land use regulations without compensation are proposing just such an arrangement for the bureaus assigned to produce environmental goods and services. When the bureaus have the authority to produce environmental goods by fiat without a budget expenditure, misallocation of resources and overproduction of environmental goods result. If the agencies can sidestep the budgetary constraint placed on them by the legislature through the appropriation process, by using the police powers to assign and direct resources without compensation, the crucial role of prices as a metering device for efficiency is destroyed.

Moreover, on a case-by-case basis, the production of environmental goods and services may be financed by a small minority of citizens while the benefits accrue to a larger group who perceive the benefits to be free. Assume that the agency directs that a particular parcel be left as open space for the public instead of developed into a residential community, and assume that no compensation is paid to the property owner for the decrease in the capital value of the property. The agency's output will increase outside the budget process, the costs will be localized on a given property owner, the special-interest group among the general public will receive the benefits of the open space free of charge, and the agency will receive the praise of its legislative sponsors.

It might be suggested that the landowners subject to the regulatory confiscation of their property would organize to oppose the legislation, and it is conceivable that this would occur. However, the relative costs of organizing are crucial. It has been observed in the past that producers are much more likely to form effective organizations to lobby and cartelize than are consumer groups. This occurs because producers in a particular industry are relatively few in number, and are permanent rather than transitory, have strong and major financial interests in the industry, while the consumers are many in number, have a small financial interest relative to their budgets, and are in and out of the market. To change the example slightly, it is easy to understand why the employees of General Motors organized into a union and equally easy to understand why their customers have not.

Property owners, like the customers of General Motors, are a diffuse group. The costs of organizing such a group into an effective lobby for political action would be high, if not prohibitive. The active real estate market in property titles ensures that turnover in the group of property owners is high and, consequently, that the costs of organization are also relatively high.

Just as environmentalists know that everything in the physical world depends on everything else, economists have known for some time that everything in the economic world depends on everything else; this is general equilibrium theory. When the land is directed to be used as open space, society as well as the property owner who experienced the loss bears a cost. The cost to society is the opportunity cost of the residential development that might have been constructed on the open-space site. As time passes, these opportunity costs surface in other ways; as more land is devoted to open-space environment preservation by the agencies, less land is devoted to housing and so a "housing crisis" develops. The market prices and rents of existing structures increase because of both the increased costs of gaining the necessary government approvals and the diminished increments to the stock of housing.[100] As the relative price of housing rises, another government agency is called upon to solve the problem caused by the so-called failure of the private market. Clearly, this is a failure of public policy rather than of private markets. Resource allocation cannot be rational, efficient, or economical unless decisions are based on the information provided by prices. If the public sector is allowed to ignore prices in its decision making, resources are misallocated and expectations unfulfilled.

It is ironic that government regulation and the production of public goods are stimulated by the argument that market prices either are nonexistent or are poor indicators of economic value. But if prices are inaccurate in the market, why does the bureaucracy, which allegedly corrects the market failure, effectively abandon price altogether?

As a fitting conclusion for this section, consider the following statement by Armen A. Alchian:

Let me emphasize the fundamental proposition that every question of pricing is a question of property rights. We could have asked: what system of property rights shall we use? The existing system of property rights establishes the system of price determination for the exchange or allocation of scarce resources. Many apparently diverse questions come down to the same element—the structure of property rights over scarce resources. In essence, economics is the study of property rights. Without scarce resources property rights are pointless. The allocation of scarce resources in a society is the assignment of rights to uses of resources. So the question of economics, or of how prices should be determined, is the question of how property rights should be defined and exchanged, and on what terms.[101]

The property rights structure proposed by the advocates of regulation without compensation is resource allocation without regard for opportunity costs—planning without prices.

Let the People Decide

There is a growing tendency to resolve environmental issues at the ballot box. Initiatives and referenda have become increasingly common. When the political pressures both for and against an environmental proposition become intense, the absence of well-defined legal and economic decision-making criteria prompts the politicians to "let the people decide."

It is not at all clear that decisions made at the polls are consistent with the philosophical precepts discussed in earlier sections of the chapter. One man, one vote does not reflect different intensities of preference, nor does it necessarily respect or serve the rights of minorities. Consider a situation in which the local population votes on the issue of whether to allow the owner of a large parcel of land to develop that land as opposed to preserving it in open space. The situation is similar to the case of three muggers who confront A and advance the following proposition: "The four of us are going to vote (one man, one vote and majority wins) on whether to relieve you of your watch and the money in your wallet. What could be more fair? This is the democratic process working in the grand American tradition." Most citizens would object to the "democratic process" in this context since A's rights are violated by the majority.[102] Hence, we note again the importance of defining and respecting the set of individual rights that acts as a restraint on collective action—whether that action be by democratic process in the polling booth or by the regulatory action of the state under its police powers.

Even in cases where the costs of the action are not imposed directly and completely on the minority group of property owners, serious distribution effects occur.[103] Suppose the voters are given a choice of accepting or rejecting a proposition that will lead to a discrete increase in the bundle of environmental goods and services available in a given area. By definition, it is asserted that all individuals will consume the same amount of these goods and services. Further assume that the proposed environmental package costs an amount of money which would be equal to $1000 per household if the costs were apportioned equally through taxes. If the "free" environmental goods are financed through a *progressive* tax system, a wealthy family might pay an extra $1500 while a poor family would pay only $500. Now assume that the proposition passes by a 51-to-49 percent vote.

If the traditional tax and benefit incidence theory were used to measure the welfare effects of this policy, the change would appear to be very progressive. Each individual receives a better-quality environment, and the burdens of the improvements are distributed in such a way that the rich pay more and the poor less than the average.

The policy may be far from progressive, in fact. If the rich who voted for the proposition had been willing to pay $3000 rather than do without the environmental improvement and the poor preferred to spend, say, $100 on environmental improvement while they devoted the remaining $400 of their tax assessment to private goods and services, then the outcome would not be as desirable as presumed. In some sense the wealthier members of the community enjoy a $1500 bonus for being in the majority while the poor people suffer a $400 loss for belonging to the minority. True, the poor enjoy a better-quality environment, but the evidence is growing that they would prefer to use the $400 for expenditures on other goods and services. Rhetoric about everyone benefiting from a better environment aside, there is "growing evidence that environmental protection seems to be most favored by the affluent and well-educated segments of society."[104] In addition, it is far from clear that the tax system is progressive in the large. Hence, the burden on lower-income groups may be greater than indicated in the preceding example.

According to Los Angeles Mayor Thomas Bradley:

[T]o many of our nation's 20 million blacks, the conservation movement has about as much appeal as a segregated bus. . . .
    Blacks generally regard ecology as irrelevant to their most pressing needs—jobs, housing, health care, education.[105]

Nicholas P. Loverich reports the results of a voter attitude survey in the city of Denver:

The use of three distinct methods of measurement of priority preferences for government expenditure among Anglo, black and Mexican American active local voters resulted in three clear conclusions: first, however measured, there is strong evidence of a dissensus on spending priorities which separates majority and minority voters; second, *that dissensus falls along an "environmental protection" versus "social services" division*; and third, that the observed differences in priority preferences between Anglo and minority active local voters are largely independent of SES controls.[106]

Siegan has pointed out how zoning has restricted the supply of housing for the lower-income groups, raised rents, raised development costs, inhibited the construction of retail establishments within walking distance of homes and apartments, and harmed the interests of small builders.[107]

The shortcomings of the social welfare function approach discussed earlier should be sufficient to convince one that majority voting through initiative and referenda is not the answer to the environmental problem or to the regulatory and taking issues that derive from it. Minority rights *and* efficient resource use suffer badly when "the people decide."

Physical Invasion Approach to the Taking Issue

Under the physical invasion approach[108] the government compensates property owners only when it occupies or takes physical possession of or title to the property in question. If it is insisted that the socially optimal government regulation of land proceed to the point where the marginal benefits and costs are equal, this criterion fails the test. Quite apart from the problems associated with identifying the benefits of regulation—problems that are inherent in each of the approaches—costs are systematically understated or ignored. Since the vast majority of regulatory activities can be encompassed in the category of regulation without compensation, the marginal cost perceived by the regulator will be zero. The agency has no incentive to determine the value of the environmental resources in alternative private uses. For example, if the agency prohibits a housing development and mandates that the property be used for open space, the agency has no incentive to take into account either the costs to the property owner or the costs to the members of the consuming public who would have purchased and enjoyed the residential units in the housing development. Thus, in addition to the distribution effects—some individuals are hurt and others benefited—this approach will result in an overproduction of environmental goods and an underproduction of private goods.

Noxious Use Approach

The noxious use or harm-benefit approach[109] is based on the philosophy that no one has the right to use his property to the detriment or harm of his neighbors. The regulatory agency determines whether a given use is

noxious, wrongful, harmful, or prejudicial to the health, safety or morals of the public. If it is so found, then the government may validly regulate it and thereby decrease its value without payment of compensation to the owner.[110]

"It may be said that the state takes property by eminent domain because it is useful to the public, and under the police power because it is harmful."[111]

This rationale has been used in the past to eliminate brickyards,[112] breweries,[113] oleomargarine manufacturing plants,[114] fertilizer manufacturing plants,[115] brothels,[116] and sand and gravel pits.[117] In each case, the ultimate resolution is an all-or-nothing proposition—the use in question is either permitted or prohibited. Ronald Coase has suggested a different perspective for these problems:

The traditional approach has tended to obscure the nature of the choice that has to be made. The question is commonly thought of as one in which A inflicts harm on B and what has to be decided is: how should we restrain A? But this is wrong. We are dealing with a problem of a reciprocal nature. To avoid the harm to B would inflict harm on A. The real question that has to be decided is: should A be allowed to harm B or should B be allowed to harm A? The problem is to avoid the more serious harm.[118]

Coase suggests that the economist's notion of opportunity cost is very relevant in deciding these issues. Thus, the decision to prohibit the brickyard in a residential neighborhood should rest on the question of whether total output for society is greater with or without the brickyard. If this strategy is not followed, there is a clear danger that the regulatory action will do more harm than good.

It is perhaps worthy to note that the purpose of regulation under this approach is to eliminate all harmful private activities. That goal is neither realistic nor desirable. Coase[119] and Demsetz[120] argue that the ownership of factors of production should be thought of as ownership of rights to perform various activities. These activities may be harmful as well as beneficial; e.g., they may create smoke, noise, smells, and so forth. But, these harmful effects are accompanied by beneficial effects since the exercise of the property right involves the use of a factor of *production*. The decision to enjoin the use of the property right, then, should be based not on purely legal grounds but rather on the net contribution the exercise of the right will make to the value of total output.

The cost of exercising a right (of using a factor of production) is always the loss which is suffered elsewhere in consequence of the exercise of that right—the inability to cross land, to park a car, to build a house, to enjoy a view, to have peace and quiet or to breathe clean air.[121]

Given conflicting uses, Coase's analysis[122] suggests that a private property system with competitive markets will, in the absence of negotiation or transaction costs, generate an efficient allocation of resources that is independent of the liability rule or assignment of property rights. However, wealth transfer effects are present on a one-time basis. Extending this work, Demsetz[123] has argued that when information, negotiation, and transaction costs are not so high as to preclude incurring the expense, voluntary market exchanges would generally create the most appropriate allocation of resources. In the remaining cases where the cost of excluding free riders is high, Demsetz suggests regulatory activities based on cost-benefit analysis may be used.[124]

Calabresi[125] has argued that in the face of the tremendous difficulties encountered in gathering the necessary data to implement the Coase theorem, a wide variety of government interventions can be justified when based on reasonable estimates of the amounts and least-cost bearers of transaction cost. This comment must be taken seriously in view of Calabresi's comment on the Coase theorem:

[I]f one assumes rationality, no transaction costs, and no legal impediments to bargaining, *all* misallocations of resources would be fully cured in the market by bargains. Far from being surprising, this statement is tautological, at least if one accepts any of the various classic definitions of misallocation.[126]

Yet there is little evidence that government interventions are based on scientific criteria, let alone appropriate ones. Even it it were agreed that the least-cost bearer should carry the burden of regulation,[127] the existing political framework of bureaucracy still would provide incentives for resource misallocation.

Government regulation or interference with the market also has been justified by some on the ground that society has goals in addition to and competing with the maximization of total output. To my knowledge there is no way of deriving these social goals from individual preferences. Thus we have the environmentalists' flagship cases like *Mugler v. Kansas*[128] and *Powell v. Pennsylvania*[129] that meet the criteria of neither Coase nor Calabresi. Even if a particular conflict were resolved according to the maximum output criteria of Coase, one might wish to object if the regulator activity violated certain rights of individuals. For example, even if it could be established that the true preferences of individuals led to a higher value of output when oleomargarine factories are prohibited by law, we might wish to challenge the abrogation of the rights of owners of margarine factories. Again, if it could be shown that total output would be increased unambiguously by the expropriation of a particular minority, say the Jews, blacks, or Japanese Americans, would we want to accept the Coase criteria? Surely there are important individual rights that dominate the increase in total output for society, particularly when organized markets in such rights do not exist.

Diminution-in-Value Approach

The diminution-in-value approach[130] is a variation of the preceding harm-benefit approach. Instead of an all-or-nothing solution where the use is either permitted or prohibited, here the decision is based on the *extent* of the loss to the property owner. If the loss occasioned by the government's regulation is substantial enough, compensation must be paid; otherwise, not! The usual argument in favor of the criteria has been that they meet the public's notion of fairness or justice; no one individual should be called upon to bear the costs of benefits that accrue to others.[131]

An equally important advantage from the point of view of resource allocation is that the costs of government action are visible and are taken into account by the regulatory authority. In the absence of compensation, the agency has no incentive to weigh the costs of its actions. Without the inhibiting effect of required compensation the agency will act as if it had an unlimited budget for pursuing its goal of environmental protection. When the costs of its regulatory activities are perceived to be zero, the agency will rationally expand its activitiesto the point where the subjective value of an additional unit of environmental protection is equal to zero—the marginal cost perceived by the agency.

As a practical matter, the test has been robbed of much of its usefulness by the recent decision in *Just v. Marinette County*[132] where the court abandoned the approach, arguing that the regulation in question preserved the status quo as opposed to improving the current public condition. Inasmuch as the market value of the property (like all property) was based upon expected future uses of the parcel, the property owners suffered a substantial reduction in value because of the court's interpretation. If subsequent rulings follow this case as a precedent, the diminution-in-value theory may be abandoned de facto.

Enterprise-Arbitral Approach

The enterprise-arbitral distinction[133] approaches the issue from a different perspective and arbitrarily partitions government regulatory activity into two categories, one which requires compensation and one which does not. In the enterprise function the government engages in activities such as maintaining an army, roads, schools, and so forth. These activities are alleged to be in competition with the private sector and, as such, divert resources to the government sector. Consequently, compensation is required in these cases according to Professor Saks. This position is supported by the argument that there are certain risks of tyranny present in the first category of regulation, and so compensation is required in order to place a constraint on the unlimited desires of the government.[134]

But when the government adjudicates disputes among competing private property owners, it is performing its arbitral function, and no compensation is required regardless of the severity of the private loss. When the government is settling the disputes among members of the private sector, it is alleged that no tendency toward tyranny is present, and the deterrence of compensation is not needed.[135]

Surely the boundaries between the arbitral and enterprise functions are very fuzzy. Take the case of the environmental protection: to what extent is this simply a case of mediating among competing private parties and, as such, a case in which the government has no enterprise incentives or appetites? Are not subsidy elements involved? It should be very clear to proponents and opponents alike that the government's concern with land use regulation is in large measure encompassed by the enterprise function. The government is engaged in producing environmental goods through land use regulation in much the same manner as it promotes public safety through its defense and police expenditures, communication and transportation as it runs the road system, and education as it operates schools. The past record of governmental land use regulation is more than sufficient to dispel any notion that the issues are strictly in the arbitral category. Hence, under a strict interpretation of this approach, the vast majority of cases fall into the enterprise category, requiring compensation.

Spillover Approach

In another approach, *spillovers*[136] are defined to include land whose use results in a physical restriction on the uses of (1) other land, (2) the use of a common property to which citizens have equal rights, and (3) the use of property in such a way as to affect the health and well-being of other individuals or property owners. According to Sax,[137] the government would prohibit these activities without compensation whenever such spillovers occur.

Unfortunately, this approach is more a statement of the problem than a proposed solution. Granted, spillovers do occur, but they are ubiquitous in a modern society. Recall the Demsetz statement that "property rights convey the right to benefit or harm oneself or others."[138] Since virtually all activities undertaken by people involve spillovers, vesting government with the authority to prohibit all spillovers without compensation is equivalent to vesting untrammeled power to stop all activities—economic and otherwise. To assert that the state will not in fact stop *all* activities that create spillovers is to beg the question: how will the state decide which externalities or spillovers are to be eliminated and which are not? Professor Berger has recognized the shortcomings of this approach:

Thus the rule becomes such that when the government would, in the real world, be likely to act, compensation is not required, except in the case of physical invasion by the government, and there are even exceptions to that. Though this rule would undoubtedly be very convenient for government regulators, it suffers from the very same infirmities as the physical invasion test, to which it is almost identical: unfairness to owners and economic inefficiency.[139]

Concluding Remarks

Under the police power inherent in sovereignty, land use regulation by the government must be in the public interest: the regulation must promote the health, safety, morals, and general welfare of the public. Since the courts have elected to defer to the legislature on the question of when regulation is reasonably in the public interest, and since the legislature has passed the responsibility on to its agencies and their bureaucrats, the incentive structure in our present political institutions generates pressure to overregulate and undercompensate. Given the choice between implementing land use controls via regulation without compensation and taking with compensation, the bureaus rationally will choose the former course.

When government bureaus escape the discipline of the budget process, a systematic distortion in resource allocation results. In the absence of the necessity to pay for the resources it uses or directs, the bureau will oversupply environmental public goods at the expense of private goods and other public goods. Unless the agencies compensate for the resources under their command, the ultimate allocation of those resources is arbitrary and ad hoc: planning without prices. No society can perform near its potential when prices are ignored. Moreover, since prices and property rights are inextricably linked in any economic system, the abandonment of prices in the decision process has dramatic implications for change in our traditional structure of private property rights.

It is fashionable, if not original, to conclude with a call for further research. The important role played by property rights in our tradition of civil and economic liberties is in danger of being altered because of the political exigencies of the moment.[140] Hence, a promising but most difficult line of research should be explored with all possible speed, diligence, and intellect—that of defining the set of individual rights which act as a constraint on the set of admissible social actions. Until this task is accomplished, fundamental individual rights will continue to erode in the face of pressures to advance the cause célèbre of the day.

Notes

1. F. Bosselman, D. Callies, and J. Banta, The Taking Issue (Washington: Government Printing Office, 1973).

2. W. Stoebuck, *A General Theory of Eminent Domain*, 47 Wash. L. Rev. 553, 605 (1972).

3. R. Posner, Economic Analysis of Law (Boston: Little, Brown &

Co., 1972); H. Manne, The Economics of Legal Relationships (St. Paul: West Publishing Co., 1975).

4. A. Alchian, Pricing and Society (London: Institute of Economic Affairs, 1967), p. 6.

5. G. Calabresi and A. Melamed, *Property Rules, Liability Rules, and Inalienability: One View of the Cathedral*, 85 Harv. L. Rev. 1089, 1092 (1972). © Copyright 1972 by The Harvard Law Review Association.

6. Posner, *supra* note 3, at 10.

7. D. Large, *This Land Is Whose Land? Changing Concepts of Land as Property*, 1973 Wisc. L. Rev. 1039.

8. G. Hardin, *The Tragedy of the Commons*, 162 Science 1243 (1968).

9. "In matters relating to business, finance, industrial and labor conditions, health and the public welfare, great leeway is now granted the legislature, for there is no guarantee in the Constitution that the *status quo* will be preserved against regulation by government." Beauharnais v. Illinois, 343 U. S. 250, 286 (1952) (Douglas, J., dissenting). *See also* McGowan v. Maryland, 366 U. S. 420, 426 (1961) where the Court stated: "A statutory discrimination will not be set aside if any state of facts reasonably may be conceived to justify it."

10. *See* Miller v. Board of Public Works, 195 Cal. 477, 234 P. 381 (1925); Goldblatt v. Town of Hempstead, 369 U. S. 590 (1962).

11. Mid-Way Cabinet etc. Mfg. v. Co. of San Joaquin, 257 Cal App.2d 181, 186, 65 Cal. Rptr. 37 (Sup. Ct. 1967).

12. Stoebuck, *supra* note 2, at 569.

13. U.S. Const. Amend. V.

14. Stoebuck, *supra* note 2, at 555.

15. Bosselman, *supra* note 1.

16. M. B. Johnson, *Piracy on the California Coast*, 6 Reason (No. 3, July, 1974) 18; M. B. Johnson, *A Critique of the Concept of Federal Land Use Regulation*, 5 Environmental Law 573 (1975).

17. A. van Alstyne, California Inverse Condemnation Law, California Law Revision Commission (Palo Alto, Ca.: School of Law, Stanford University, 1971), p. 315, n. 13. *See also* J. Sax, *Takings and the Police Power*, 74 Yale L. J. 36 n. 5 (1964).

18. Bosselman, *supra* note 1.

19. *Supra* note 9. *See also* Mugler v. Kansas, 123 U. S. 623 (1887); Goldblatt v. Town of Hempstead, 369 U.S. 590 (1962); Euclid v. Ambler Co., 272 U.S. 365 (1926).

20. Euclid v. Ambler Co., 272 U.S. 365 (1926).

21. Karlin, *Land Use Controls: The Power to Exclude*, 5 Environmental Law 529 (1975) [hereinafter cited as Karlin, *Land Use Controls*].

22. *See, e.g.,* Yick Wo v. Hopkins, 118 U.S. 356 (1886); Chicago, M.

& St. P. Ry v. Minn., 134 U.S. 418 (1890); Allgeyer v. Louisiana, 165 U.S. 578 (1897); Buchanan v. Warley, 245 U.S. 60 (1917).

23. *See* N. Karlin, E. Horten, and L. Polster, *Zoning: Monopoly Effects and Judicial Abdication*, 4 Sw. U. L. Rev. 1 (1972). *See also* Comment, *Land Use Controls: Is There a Place for Everything?* 6 Sw. U. L. Rev. 607, 617–18 (1974).

24. Powell v. Penn., 127 U.S. 678 (1888).

25. Euclid v. Ambler Co., 272 U.S. 365 (1926).

26. *See* McGowan v. Maryland, 366 U.S. 420 (1961); Kotch v. Bd. of River Pilot Comm'rs., 330 U.S. 552 (1947).

27. Wolkowitz, "Regulatory Agencies: The Effect of Being Ineffective," unpublished manuscript at Southwestern University Law School.

28. *See* Karlin, *Land Use Controls, supra* note 21.

29. People v. Stover, 12 N.Y.2d 462, 191 N. E.2d 272, 240 N.Y.S.2d 734 (1963).

30. Village of Belle Terre v. Boraas, 416 U.S. 1 (1974).

31. Mugler v. Kansas, 123 U.S. 623 (1887).

32. Powell v. Penn., 127 U.S. 678 (1888).

33. *See* J. Sax, *Takings and the Police Power*, 74 Yale L. J. 36 (1964) [hereinafter cited as Sax, *Police Power*].

34. Penn. Coal Co. v. Mahon, 260 U.S. 393 (1922).

35. Bosselman, *supra* note 1, at 134.

36. Karlin, *Land Use Controls, supra* note 21.

37. *See* Just v. Marinette County, 56 Wis.2d 7, 201 N. W.2d 761 (1972).

38. M. Anderson, The Federal Bulldozer, (Cambridge, Ma.: M. I. T. Press, 1964).

39. Berman v. Parker, 348 U.S. 26, 33, 35, 36 (1954).

40. Bosselman, *supra* note 1. *See also* Plater, *The Takings Issue in a Natural Setting: Floodlines and Police Power*, 52 Tex. L. Rev. 201 (1974); Large, *supra* note 7; William K. Reilly (ed.) The Use of Land: A Citizen's Policy Guide to Urban Growth (New York: Crowell, 1973), pp. 145–175.

41. Sax, *Police Power, supra* note 33.

42. *Id.*

43. L. F. Moss, *Private Property Anarchists: An American Varient*, in Further Explorations in the Theory of Anarchy 1, 3, 4 (1974) (G. Tullock, ed.).

44. M. Rothbard, Man, Economy and the State (Los Angeles: Nash Publishers, 1962), p. 156.

45. L. Berger, *A Policy Analysis of the Taking Problem*, 49 N. Y. U. L. Rev. 165, 213 (1974) [hereinafter cited as Berger].

46. Perhaps such recognition is neither a necessary nor a sufficient reason for regulatory action: "Some fifteen years of theoretical and empirical research, conducted mainly by economists, have demonstrated that regulation is not positively correlated with the presence of external economies or diseconomies or with monopolistic market structure." R. Posner, *Theories of Economic Regulation*, 5 Bell J. Econ. & Mgt. 335, 336 (1974).

47. Presumably, the redistribution is intended to be from the rich to the poor. *But see* G. Stigler, *Director's Law of Public Income Redistribution*, 13 J.L. & Econ. 1 (1970); L. Chickering, *Land Use Controls and Low Income Groups,* No Land Is an Island 119 (San Francisco: Institute for Contemporary Studies, 1975).

48. *See* Karlin, *Land Use Controls, supra* note 21.

49. *Id.*

50. *See* E. Phelps, Economic Justice (Baltimore: Penguin Education, 1973), pp. 9–31, for a summary of the current state of welfare economics.

51. G. Stigler, *supra* note 47; G. Tullock, *The Charity of the Uncharitable*, 9 W. Econ. J. 379 (1971).

52. *See* J. Sax, *Takings, Private Property and Public Rights*, 81 Yale L.J. 149 (1971) [hereinafter cited as Sax, *Private Property*].

53. H. Demsetz, *Toward a Theory of Property Rights*, 57 Am. Econ. Rev. (No. 2, May 1967) 347, 348 (Proceedings Issue).

54. A.C. Pigou, The Economics of Welfare (London: Macmillan, 1932), p. 183.

55. R. Coase, *The Problem of Social Cost*, 3 J.L. & Econ. 1 (1960).

56. H. Demsetz, *Some Aspects of Property Rights*, 9 J.L. & Econ. 61 (1966).

57. E.J. Mishan, *The Relationship between Joint Products, Collective Goods, and External Effects*, 77 J. Pol. Econ. 329, 343 (1969).

58. B. Commoner, The Closing Circle (New York: Knopf, 1972), p. 23.

59. Bosselman, *supra* note 1, at 2.

60. Berger, *supra* note 45, at 165.

61. R. Ellickson, *Alternatives to Zoning: Covenants, Nuisance Rules, and Fines as Land Use Controls*, 40 U. Chi. L. Rev. 681, 688 (1973).

62. R. Haveman and J. Margolis (eds.), Public Expenditures and Policy Analysis (Chicago: Markham Publishing Co., 1970), p. 9.

63. James Buchanan and William Stubblebine, *Externality*, 29 Economica 371, 373, 374 (1962). Reprinted with permission.

64. *Id.* at 374.

65. *Id.* at 372.

66. Thomas Gale Moore, *An Economic Analysis of the Concept of Freedom*, 77 J. Pol. Econ. University of Chicago Publisher. 532, 536 (1969).

67. This result holds because of the presence of "income effects" in the general case.

68. A. Freeman, III, R. Haveman, and A. Kneese, The Economics of Environmental Policy (New York: Wiley, 1973), p. 81 and n. 1.

69. P. Steiner, *The Public Sector and the Public Interest*, in Public Expenditures..., *supra* note 62, at 38.

70. L. C. Thurow, *Economic Justice and the Economist: A Reply*, Pub. Interest (No. 33, Fall 1973) 120, 122.

71. K. Arrow, Social Choice and Individual Values, 2d ed. (New York: Wiley, 1963), p. 59, (original emphasis omitted).

72. A. K. Sen, Collective Choice and Social Welfare (San Francisco: Holden-Day, 1970). On a different line of attack:

Collectivization, insofar as this is taken to imply some coercion, would never be chosen by the rational individual .... [T]he individual will choose collectivization only because of its relatively greater efficiency in the organization of decisionmaking. ... The individual must consider the possible collectivization of all activities for which the private organization is expected to impose some inter-dependence costs on him. His final decision must rest on a comparision of these costs with those expected to be imposed on him as a result of collective organization itself.

J. Buchanan and G. Tullock, The Calculus of Consent (Ann Arbor, Mich.: University of Michigan Press, 1962), p. 90.

73. R. Nozick, Anarchy, State, and Utopia (New York: Basic Books, 1974), p. 165.

74. *Id.* at 166.

75. *Id.* at ix.

76. "Free speech, free press, free exercise of religion are placed separate and apart; they are above and beyond the police power; they are not subject to regulation in the manner of factories, slums, apartment houses, production of oil, and the like." Beauharnais v. Illinois, 343 U.S. 250, 286 (1952) (Douglas, J., dissenting).

77. *See* Karlin, *Land Use Controls, supra* note 21; Director, *The Parity of the Economic Market Place* 7 J. L. & Econ. 1 (1964); Wolkowitz, *supra* note 27.

78. Moore, *supra* note 66, at 536.

79. *Id.* at 536.

80. Nozick, *supra* note 73, at 322.

81. Granted, Moore relies on the qualifier "forced." But then the argument is moved to a different level of contention: is the WCTU member who encounters a drunk as she (he) walks an accustomed route to the store "forced" when an alternative route existed?

82. *See* Demsetz, *Some Aspects...*, *supra* note 56; Coase, *supra* note 55; Moore, *supra* note 66.

83. R. Haveman, Public Expenditures ..., *supra* note 62, at 8 (footnote omitted).

84. The Use of Land, *supra* note 40, at 145–46.

85. P. Samuelson, *Aspects of Public Expenditure Theories*, 40 Rev. Econ. & Stat. 332 (1958).

86. W. Lippmann, Essays in the Public Philosophy (Boston: Little, Brown, 1955), p. 42.

87. A. Rand, Capitalism: The Unknown Ideal 170–71 (New York: New American Library, Inc., 1962).

88. As Justice Holmes once wrote, the concept is "little more than a fiction intended to beautify what is disagreeable to the sufferers." Tyson & Bro. v. Banton, 273 U.S. 418, 446 (1927) (Holmes, J., dissenting).

89. *See* Korematsu v. United States, 323 U.S. 214, 216 (1944), where the Court stated: "Pressing public necessity may sometimes justify the existence of such restrictions. ..."

90. W. Niskanen, Bureaucracy and Representative Government (Chicago: Aldine, Atherton, 1971), p. 38.

91. *Id.* at 25 (original emphasis omitted).

92. Thompson, *Book Review*, 11 J. Econ. Lit. 950, 953 (1973).

93. *See* M. Peterson, The Regulated Consumer (Los Angeles: Nash Publishing, 1971).

94. *See* Train, *Foreward* to Bosselman, *supra* note 1.

95. J. Galbraith, The Affluent Society (New York: New American Library, 1958), pp. 124, 120, 121.

96. Hayek, *The Non-Sequitur of the "Dependence Effect,"* 27 S. Econ. J. 346, 347 (1961).

97. The regulatees, as a group, are of less concern to the regulators in the land use area. See text below.

98. J. Knetsch, *Economic Analysis in Natural Resource Programs*, in Public Expenditures ..., *supra* note 62, at 565–66.

99. Thompson, *supra* note 92.

100. *See* Johnson, *A Critique ...*, *supra* note 16.

101. Alchian, *supra* note 4, at 6.

102. To argue that a vote is legal in one case and illegal in the other begs the question.

103. *See supra* note 47.

104. R. Deacon and P. Shapiro, *Private Preference for Collective Goods Revealed through Voting on Referenda*, 65 Am. Econ. Rev. 943, 954–55 (1975).

105. T. Bradley, *Minorities and Conservation*, 57 Sierra Club Bull. (No. 4, April 1972) 21.

106. N. P. Lovrich, *Differing Priorities in an Urban Electorate: Service Preferences among Anglo, Black, and Mexican American Voters*, 55 Soc. Sci. Q. 704, 717 (1974) (emphasis added). SES refers to socioeconomic status.

107. *See* B. Siegan, *Controlling Other People's Property through Covenants, Zoning, State and Federal Regulation*, 5 Envt'l L. 385 (1975).

108. Sax, *Police Power, supra* note 33.

109. Berger, *supra* note 45.

110. *Id.* at 172.

111. E. Freund, The Police Power (Chicago: Callaghan & Co., 1904), p. 546–47.

112. Hadacheck v. Sebastian, 239 U.S. 394 (1915).

113. Mugler v. Kansas, 123 U.S. 623 (1887).

114. Powell v. Penn., 127 U.S. 678 (1888).

115. Fertilizing Co. v. Hyde Park, 97 U.S. 659 (1878).

116. L'Hote v. New Orleans, 177 U.S. 587 (1900).

117. Goldblatt v. Town of Hempstead, 369 U.S. 590 (1962).

118. Coase, *supra* note 55, at 2.

119. Coase, *supra* note 55.

120. Demsetz, *Some Aspects...*, *supra* note 56.

121. Coase, *supra* note 55, at 44.

122. Coase, *supra* note 55.

123. Demsetz, *Some Aspects...*, *supra* note 56. *See also* Ellickson, *supra* note 61.

124. *Id.*

125. G. Calabresi, *Transaction Costs, Resource Allocation and Liability Rules—A Comment*, 11 J.L. & Econ. 67 (1968).

126. *Id.* at 68.

127. *See* G. Calabresi, *supra* note 125; Berger, *supra* note 45.

128. Mugler v. Kansas, 123 U.S. 623 (1887).

129. Powell v. Penn., 127 U.S. 678 (1888).

130. Berger, *supra* note 45, at 175.

131. *See, e.g.,* Stoebuck's summary of the Lockeian argument: "[C]ompensation is designed to even the score when a given person has been required to give up property rights beyond his just share of the cost of government." Stoebuck, *supra* note 2, at 587.

132. 56 Wis.2d 7, 201 N.W.2d 761 (1972).

133. Berger, *supra* note 45, at 177; Sax, *Police Power, supra* note 33.

134. Berger, *supra* note 45, at 178.

135. *Id.*

136. Sax, *Private Property, supra* note 52; Berger, *supra* note 45, at 179.

137. Sax, *Private Property, supra* note 52.

138. Demsetz, *Toward a Theory ...*, *supra* note 53, at 347.

139. Berger, *supra* note 45, at 181.

140. "[W]hen we decide each issue solely on what appears to be its individual merits, we always over-estimate the advantages of central direction. ... If the choice between freedom and coercion is thus treated as a matter of expediency, freedom is bound to be sacrificed in almost every instance." F. Hayek, Law, Legislation and Liberty (Chicago: University of Chicago Press, 1973), p. 57.

3

Some Thoughts on the Political Economy of Land Use Regulation

Martin Anderson

Johnson, in Chapter 2, has thoroughly and comprehensively identified and explored the major issues involved in the taking issue, pointing out the basic problems and questions that are pertinent to the government's interference with the use and enjoyment of privately owned land, whether it be the outright confiscation of that land or the attenuation of its use through regulation.

He effectively points out the difficulties involved in wrestling with the theoretical intricacies of "externalities." In spite of the prodigious efforts devoted to this problem in the past, it seems quite clear that we have a long way to go before any sort of general agreement will be reached on this issue. Johnson's discussion of the inequities inherent in referendum votes on certain public policy questions was very instructive; this line of attack is a very promising one that should be more fully developed in future work.

One part of the chapter that especially intrigued me was his references to the concept of "the public interest." These seemingly innocent words, *the public interest*, have, in my opinion, been responsible for masking much of what has been happening in the public policy arena for many years. The words are rarely defined and are often used by proponents of new government programs and regulations to obscure the specific intent of what they are pursuing.

Much of Johnson's discussion makes it clear that he is aware of this. He states that "the concept of 'the public interest' (or the common good) is an empty phrase . . . a piece of rhetoric used to persuade others through the political process . . . (and) is usually invoked by special interest." I agree. Unfortunately, he also lapses into the use of the same term in other sections of his work. Perhaps this is necessary, but I should like to propose an alternative: namely that we all take a pledge to only use the term *the public interest* when, and if, it can be used precisely.

Defined precisely, *the public interest* can refer only to some action that would benefit *all* members of society, i.e., the public. As used conventionally invariably it refers to some course of action that benefits *some* members of the society at the expense of other members (while many may not be affected at all). In fact, the use of any collective terms, whether it be the public interest, the common good, mankind, etc., tends to hide the effects and consequences of government programs in general.

A necessary first step in effectively analyzing any public policy issue, including the taking issue, is to identify specifically what is being done and to whom it is being done.

In an examination of this issue some years ago I commented that:

Epistemologically speaking, only an individual can value something. It is only conceptually correct to speak of values from the viewpoint of a single person. There are no "group" values, no "collective" values, no "society" values. The concepts of group or society are abstractions which refer to collections of individual entities. Only the individual entities themselves are capable of valuing and of receiving benefits and costs....

A proposed methodology for evaluating the costs and benefits of a program which directly affects the lives of many individuals is a situation where collective concepts are inappropriate. At best it represents nonrigorous, imprecise thinking which obscures what is actually happening. A correct methodological approach to the evaluation of government programs would have to ask such questions as: (1) Who benefits and how much? (2) Who pays or gets hurt and how much? (3) If some people benefit and some incur costs, is it proper to deliberately sacrifice the interests of some people so that others may benefit?...

...there are no collective goals, no collective benefits, no collective costs. There are only individual goals, benefits, and costs. It is time to abandon fuzzy concepts which are only euphemistic devices for masking the essence of what is being done...[1]

Substantial progress might be made toward resolving some of the difficult issues inherent in public policy programs, such as the taking issue, if the advocates of government intervention were confronted with the consequences that their recommendations imply for specific individuals. At minimum, it would upgrade the quality of policy studies. Today one could select almost any study of a major public policy issue conducted by a member of the academic establishment, substitute some euphemism such as "bleep bleep" for "the public interest," and not in any way interfere with the meaningfulness of the study.

Johnson also comments on the purported purposes of government "regulation and taking," arguing that the state has intervened for three main reasons: (1) to redistribute income or wealth, (2) to prevent or eliminate monopolies, and (3) to correct spillover effects or externalities. I suspect that in some measure all these reasons have a certain degree of validity, but I also suspect that there is a more fundamental reason that lies behind all three—the special-interest group. Virtually all major pieces of current social legislation have come about because of the political pressures exerted by relatively small groups of individuals with special interests within our society.

And the state has responded, via the actions of our legislators in their eternal quest for votes, by taking actions which confer benefits upon the individuals that form these special-interest groups. The benefits are often highly focused, while the costs are just as often spread widely among the taxpayers. Of course, in other cases, such as air pollution, the opposite may be true, as Johnson contends (". . . the production of environmental goods and services will generally be financed by a small minority of citizens while the benefits accrue tò a larger group. . ."). In any event, the main point is that some groups benefit at the expense of other groups.

Understanding how some groups in our society benefit at the expense of other groups is critical to the formulation of more sensible public policies, policies that have a chance of being implemented as well as being proposed. Of course, it is unlikely that the special-interest groups that now enjoy special legislative privileges will renounce their interests when the situation is clarified for them. In fact, most members of these groups probably understand very well not only how they benefit, but who pays for the benefits.

What may well happen in the event of a more widespread understanding of the true consequences of government actions taken in the public interest is the awakening of political pressures from those individuals who begin to perceive themselves as net losers. Such a process may be discouragingly slow, but it can happen.

In the environmental area we have seen recently the emergence of the Environmental Impact Statement (EIS). The purpose of this statement is to identify and explain any significant effects that a proposed project could have on the environment. For example, in California all state agencies, boards, and commissions must, when proposing to carry out some activity that might have an effect on the environment of the state, provide a detailed statement setting forth the following:

1. The environmental impact of the proposed action
2. Any adverse environmental effects which cannot be avoided if the proposal is implemented
3. Mitigation measures proposed to minimize the impact
4. Alternatives to the proposed action
5. The relationship between local short-term uses of the environment and the maintenance and enhancement of long-term productivity
6. Any irreversible environmental changes which would be involved in the proposed action should it be implemented

Perhaps what we need now is a counterpart to the Environmental Impact Statement. Think of what might happen if every time a government agency proposed a new program it were required by law to prepare a detailed statement, called a Social Impact Statement (SIS), identifying and explaining any significant effects that the proposed program would have on *individuals*.

The Social Impact Statement might include such information as: which particular groups of people would benefit directly and to what degree, which people would be adversely affected and to what degree, and projected costs of the project and the anticipated source(s) of the money to pay for it. The accuracy and validity of such a statement probably would be debatable, but the one thing it could do is focus attention on what is at the heart of most government programs—the question of who gains and who loses.

Johnson concludes with the suggestion that we bend our efforts to "the task of defining the set of individual rights that act as a constraint on the set of admissible social actions." This is certainly a critical task, but I wonder if it is *the* critical task. In my judgment we already have a reasonably well-defined set of individual rights; essentially we know what is right and what is wrong. The problem seems to be much more one of people doing things that they know violate individual rights, than one of people acting in benign ignorance. If this is true, then we must determine how to change the course of people who act, not out of ignorance, but with a reasonably clear perception of what they are doing and to whom they are doing it.

In any public policy issue, including the taking issue, there seem to be three basic problems. First, there is the problem of clearly and accurately understanding the existing state of affairs, something which is almost universally lacking in regard to the effects of most major areas of government activity. We need to know the numbers of people who are affected either adversely or advantageously, and to what degree; we need to know who benefits and who loses; we need to know how much those who benefit gain and what costs are incurred by the losers. In the whole area of regulation, and more particularly in the regulation of land or the taking of land, we seem to have just begun to penetrate the economic and social tangles caused by decades of past government regulations—whether they be zoning (here Bernard Siegan's study is an outstanding exception, although we should not forget that it is one study of one city), eminent domain, or environmental restrictions.

Second, there is the question of what we should do in an ideal world. I stress the word *ideal* here, for we should feel under no compunction to set forth a proposed course of action that could and will account for the uncountable specifics that accompany the implementation of any policy in the real world affecting real people. Even though we may never attain the ideal world we can spin forth in our fondest dreams, there is a very real purpose that is achieved by setting it forth. For the ideal becomes the end result we aim for, it provides the guiding principles by which we can explore specific pieces of the reality that confronts us, it comforts us when we perceive how slowly the world seems to proceed toward that goal (or, in some cases, speeds away from it).

Here I think a great deal has been achieved. The many writers that Johnson has cited—such as Alchian, Posner, Stoebuck, Rothbard, Stigler, Sax, Coase, Demsetz, Buchanan, Moore, Nozick, and Johnson himself—have gone a long way in setting forth how the taking issue could be handled in a more ideal world.

Third, there is the problem that may be the most critical of all. Given that we know all we should know about the current state of affairs in regard to the operation of any particular government program, policy, or regulation (let us call this situation "alpha") and also that we agree on where we should be in an ideal world (call this situation "beta"), how do we get from alpha to beta?

This is a large void in virtually all the analyses of public policy that are available to us, and this is not confined to the taking issue, although it may be particularly appropriate here. We usually put some effort into finding out something about the current state state of things, a great deal of effort in theorizing about where we should be, and virtually no effort into figuring out "how to get there from here."

It seems that finding out more about situation alpha lies in the realm of *empirical research*, whereas intellectual effort dealing with situation beta is usually called *theoretical research*.

Perhaps what we need to do is develop a third kind of research, a sort of *strategy research*, that would probe into that void that lies between understanding what is currently happening and what we would like to have in an ideal world (to carry the Greek nomenclature one step further, let us call this void situation "chi"). In general, academicians have given relatively little thought to the question of what should be done if we know alpha and agree on the proper beta.

Take, for example, the current welfare policy. There is general agreement that the welfare situation is a mess. (In fact, I believe this conclusion about welfare is quite debatable, but nonetheless it is a fact that virtually everyone is agreed that our current welfare situation is calamitous.) In view of this, most of our intellectual effort has been devoted to devising grandiose models and plans that, in an ideal sense, would resolve all our currently perceived problems. Whether it is a negative income tax, a demogrant, or the latest version of the family assistance plan, they all focus on the end product. Very little is said about how one should go about moving ahead on such plans; little analytical thought is devoted to what might be called a *strategy of implementation*.

In effect, what happens in the consideration of a major public policy issue is this: (1) Some thought is given by the analyst to alpha. Usually he is content to accept what is generally perceived to be true about the problem. In cases where he seriously attempts to determine for himself whether the facts justify the beliefs that people hold on the issue, he often gives up when he discovers the enormity of the task confronting him.

Typically he concludes by urging the government agency that is administering the program he is investigating to accumulate and publish more reliable and meaningful statistics. (2) There is then a quantum jump to the beta level where the analyst develops a carefully thought-out plan or model that portrays an alternative to how things are now. Usually the model or plan is "simplified" by eliminating consideration of some of the annoying bits of reality that would impair the symmetry of the final solution. This, of course, can lead to very valuable theoretical tools that can produce a good deal of insight into the issue at hand. The difficulty lies in the reintroduction of the discarded elements of the problem when the model or plan is applied to the real world. (3) This task of dealing with chi is typically left to the politician. To him falls the extraordinarily difficult task of assessing the pros and cons of the new policy proposal, of trying to deal with the vague uncertainties of what the costs and benefits may be five or ten years from now, or at least by the next election. He is the one who has to determine what people will be affected, in what way, to what degree, and how they will react. In fact, when one considers the general lack of appreciation for the difficulties inherent in the implementation of any major government program, and the time and abilities that most political figures are able to devote to these difficulties, it is quite remarkable that the results and consequences of these programs are not far worse.

In the last major section Johnson categorizes and evaluates the major approaches to the taking issue. They include: (1) the physical invasion approach, (2) the noxious use or harm-benefit approach, (3) the diminution-in-value approach, (4) the enterprise-arbitral distinction approach, and (5) the spillover approach. In his discussion of these approaches I was somewhat puzzled by several of his statements. In discussing the noxious use approach he states, "...the purpose of regulation under this approach is to eliminate all harmful private activities. That goal is neither realistic nor desirable." Why is it not desirable to have as a goal the elimination of all harmful private activities? Later, while commenting on the maximum output criteria of Coase, it is stated, "...we might wish to object if the regulator activity violated certain rights of individuals." Why would we not object under these circumstances? Finally, in his discussion of the spillover approach, he asserts that "since virtually all activities undertaken by man involve spillovers, vesting government with the authority to prohibit all spillovers without compensation is equivalent to vesting untrammeled power to stop all activities—economic and otherwise." This seems to be somewhat overstated.

The one general approach that is omitted from his list, but whose elements seem inherent in part to most of the approaches, is what might be called the property rights approach to the taking issue. Virtually all questions of pollution, the taking of land, the attenuation of its use by regulation, etc., are ultimately questions of individual property rights.

I suspect that the main difficulty confronting us is not in defining what these individual property rights are or how they should be protected in principle; rather the difficulty lies in the application of some old principles to new situations. During the last two centuries there have been dramatic increases in population, explosive growth in our economy, and literally fantastic advances in technology—all of which have led to a bewildering new array of moral and legal problems to be dealt with. And I am afraid that the philosophers, political scientists, and lawyers have not kept pace with the doctors, businessmen, and scientists.

For example, virtually all pollution is nothing more or less than the disposal of privately owned garbage (excepting, of course, any garbage owned by governments). And as the technical means of certain aspects of garbage disposal become more sophisticated, it becomes more difficult to determine when an individual's rights are being violated and bow to protect those rights.

Take the case of someone who picks up a paper bag full of trash, walks over to his next-door neighbor, and drops it on the front lawn. Few of us would have any trouble discerning that the property rights of the neighbor had been violated by this man. The neighbor might call the police who, on arrival, would know clearly what to do.

On the other hand, let us assume that the person used a slightly more technically sophisticated method of garbage disposal and burned it in an incinerator. The incinerator would then puff out a large cloud of very tiny, airborne pieces of dirt which would slowly settle over the neighborhood, depending on the wind. Now the problem is much more complicated. How do you determine where the particles come from? How many particles have to fall before they become noticeable? You can prevent your neighbor from throwing a bag of trash on your lawn, but can you prevent him from building a fire?

In most problems of this type the principles involved are usually clear; it is the application of these principles to the rapidly changing world that is so difficult. In an analogous situation, we can find general agreement on the principle that people should not steal or kill; yet the determination of whether a person committed a crime can be a controversial, lengthy process.

It seems to me that the only approach to the taking issue that is valid and has a practical chance of success in the long run is one that is based on individual property rights and that uses the judicial system to protect those rights. More government regulation is not the answer, but it is necessary to fashion an institutional system that can deal with the myriad violations of individual rights which occur with increasing rapidity as our society grows and changes.

Johnson, early in Chapter 2, quoted Rothbard's solution to the air pollution problem: "The remedy is judicial action to punish and proscribe pollution damage to the person and property of others." The same principle applies to the taking issue.

Note

1. *Cost-Benefit Analysis for Government Decisions-Discussions*, (remarks by Martin Anderson), 57 Am. Econ. Rev. Proc., 101, 105–107 (May 1967). Reprinted with permission.

4

Land Use Regulation without Compensation: A Mugwumpian View

Donald G. Hagman

Introduction

I am a gun hired to splay some thoughtful bullets on Johnson's provocative chapter, Planning without Prices: A Discussion of Land Use Regulation without Compensation. Mine is not to be a main and independent essay; rather it is a commentary. At the outset, in the event that the chapter's title does not forewarn the reader, let me advise that I am middle-of-the-road. In my opinion, 100 percent of what the free market-eers say about the problem of the taking issue is half true, which is about the mark I give to the environmentalists who argue that no regulation, however harsh, should be invalidated as a taking. A 50 is a pretty high mark. My faith in my own views hovers about there, the taking issue being a complex business, at least as complex as any other that is the subject of my scholarly efforts.

Many observations in Johnson's careful analysis warrant comment. However, three, maybe five, issues will use up my time, energy, and space. The inexactitude of the count is due to my imprecision, not Johnson's. He is rather clear that the problem is threefold: first, regulation too harsh for societal good is being sustained these days; second, there should be a principle for invalidating these regulations; third, the poor are losing out. My response is fivefold. First, the problem may be too many regulations rather than too harsh regulations, which could be ameliorated by a reorganization of government based, second, in part on Johnson's notion of common property. Third, rather than invalidating harsh regulations, we might consider having government pay compensation when they are imposed. Harsh regulation, after all (and fourth), merely shifts values around; it does not destroy them. Fifth, let us not use the poor.

Too Many Governments Rather than Too Much Government

Johnson explains why governments use regulation. They use it because they can thereby increase their outputs without increasing their inputs. I wish to emphasize, however, that Johnson should not necessarily be

121

arguing against too much government; rather he should be arguing against too many special-purpose "governments."

The special-purpose "governments" are bureaus of government. Bureaus include the departments of the state government or of the large local governments—such as the highway or resources departments. Bureaus also include state agencies which operate regionally, such as the California Coastal Zone Conservation Commission. Surely to be included are the special districts, which have limited purposes. Even local governments such as cities and counties can be included as bureaus. While general-purpose, they are special in the sense that their concern is limited to those who live, invest capital in, work, shop, and relax there. A bureau of government, in Johnson's sense of an entity unable to properly allocate resources, might be defined as any unit of government which de facto is charged with acting for less than the entire public weal.[1]

To the extent that the government is general-purpose and responsible for the total weal, we trust it. We trust the governor and the state legislature because, at least in the long run, they tend not to engage in excesses. Too little environmental legislation in one decade leads to more environmental legislation in the next and a reaction against it in a third; for example, the governor and the legislature see that extreme pursuits of the environment or any particular goal is counter to the common weal. The governor and the legislature, in short, are capable of making tradeoffs across a broad spectrum. Representing all the people and concerned with their total well-being, they are even sensitive to the need to deregulate. Therefore, while the regulatory fervor of the state in relation to private enterprise ebbs and flows, as long as the legislature and the governor are elected democratically by all the people, the people are likely to get approximately the mix of socialism (state ownership and control) and capitalism that they prefer. If socialism works reasonably efficiently and democratically, as in Sweden, say, we who are relatively capitalistic should not criticize it merely because we choose less state ownership and control.

The trouble begins when the bureaus take over. A state highway department is a bureau which is concerned with building highways. So we get highways whether we have relatively higher needs for other public goods instead—mass transit, for example. A local government is a bureau because its actions externalize on neighbors who are not represented and whose weal is of no concern to the acting government. A special district externalizes both outside its boundaries and within it as it pursues its narrow goals—irrigation, sewage, and mosquito abatement—even though other public goods might be more needed within its service area. But special districts are not as dangerous as they might be if they had substantial power to regulate. Generally speaking, their regulatory powers are modest. That brings us to regional regulatory agencies such as the California Coastal Zone Conservation Commission. In such agencies all that could be wrong with bureaus is wrong. They are neither general-purpose nor statewide, and they have considerable, virtually unchecked, power to regulate. Underfunded, they are further enticed to regulate. They are independent bureaus, relatively free from legislative or gubernatorial correction. Finally, they are new, which means that there is no layer of long-time employees who, like a fourth branch of government, are deadening hands on overzealous departures from tradition. Such units are positively dangerous. As the narrowest of bureaus, the tradeoffs they make deal with a small segment of human welfare. Almost by definition they cannot serve the commonweal, and they have the regulatory power to maximize their output with minimal input, meanwhile lowering the output of the regulatees.

But we are a great, productive people. We can tolerate some of these California Coastal Zone Conservation Act commission-type organizations. What we cannot afford in several such bureaus operating on the same turf at once. When several are operating, not only is regulation oppressive, it is also conflicting, as each bureau enacts regulations which maximize its own narrow outputs. Wealth-producing institutions are so burdened by the conflicting regulations that they give up in disgust and bankruptcy. Even if we consider only the bureaus of one level of government, the problems are serious. Carried away by rhetoric, I once described the impact of federal environmental legislation as follows:

These laws are new, controversial, and incompletely defined. What they mean for land use—what developers, factories, farmers, and the government can and cannot do—is remarkably unpredictable. Uncertainty abounds. Clarification ebbs and flows: The Congress legislates; the EPA bellows or whimpers, depending on the environmental fervor of the times; the courts apply the spirit of the law once, then again the letter.

This uncertainty is compounded since these new laws were all passed in splendid disregard for one another. Their effect is a synergistic nightmare, a paralyzing mishmash. Noise regulations dictate an airport out there, but indirect source rules under the Clean Air Amendments preclude it out there—it should be closer to maximize access by mass transit. Yet as a nonpoint source of water pollution, it cannot be put in areas of low water quality. This bubbling cacophony of multitudinous edicts comes from freshman federal administrators attempting to apply new and untried laws whose land use implications were never adequately considered.

This confusion has a devastating impact upon the land market. Indeed it produces the most palpable effects of these regulations so far. Buyers and sellers are so confused by the numerous and conflicting signals that they don't know where to jump. Markets that seem likely to be heavily impacted by these regulations may dry up. Sellers refuse to sell at a discount, hoping perhaps that the regulators will go away. Buyers, on the other hand, are not about to pay full development prices for land that may be undevelopable. Values just lie there quivering; supply and demand are unable to meet.[2]

The solution to the problem of too many special-purpose governments is not to eliminate all bureaus and just have the legislature and the governor run everything. Obviously that is a preposterous proposal. Some specialization in subfunctions of government is necessary in our complex society. But before the ideal governmental arrangement is suggested, consider another of Johnson's points.

Common Property

He distinguishes between private property, common property, and state ownership. Acknowledging that "little attention" has been given to the middle alternative, but concluding that "a change to common property will be dominated in virtually every relevant characteristic by a private property system," Johnson rushes on to worry about the state.

Perhaps one should pause for a moment to consider common property, not in Hardin's sense of the "commons," with its associated "tragedy" of destruction by overutilization, but of common property which is created by contract. Since it is created by contract, one could concede it to be dominated by a private property system, yet be different from private property, from a "commons," and from state ownership.

Two aspects of the private property aspects of common property appeal to me. First, as a middle ground, it comports with my inclination to seek consensus solutions that recognize the merit of the concerns of both extremes, in this case the extremes being those of the free marketeers and the governmentalists. Second, it is a red flag to an academic to hear of an underresearched viable alternative. The application for a grant to study common property is practically written in my mind's eye.

As an example of private contracts to create common property, one might begin with a small condominium, where both private and common property rights are carefully delineated by contract and a condominium association administers the common property and rights. The scale of that concept can grow, through planned unit developments to new towns with the common rights and property administered by a governing body, with the new towns association even employing a staff. Growing out of contract, this association is a kind of private government and, largely to reduce transactions costs, this private government sometimes becomes a full-fledged local government, with powers derived by sharing in the sovereignty of the state as well as emerging by contract. Yet the difference in the corporate character of an entity that changes from a new towns association to a local government may not be very apparent in terms of the services provided or the rules imposed.

To the extent that it can be thought of as having evolved out of contract, it is not likely that the new town government will engage in some of the evil practices Johnson attributes to the "bureaus" of government. There are two reasons that the evils are remote. First, the local government is general-purpose. It includes all the concerns of the denizens of the area considered to be of relevance to their commonweal. Therefore, common goods are kept in balance with private goods. And the local government is forced to make the tradeoffs so that one common good, e.g., parks, does not outstrip needs relative to another desired common good, e.g., a community power supply. The second reason has to do with scale. Even in a large new town association cum local government, the government can still be thought of as "us," as "we the people"—it does not acquire a separate identity as "the government." "The government" is some larger local government, or the state in the sense of the state of California or the United States of America, entities which really do seem separate.

That is not to say that local government does not need to be carefully watched. Any government, however local, can be misused if the area governed is composed of both propertied and nonpropertied. If either group can capture the government, de facto it will tend to rewrite the terms of the contract on the cheap by the exercise of governmental power. And a local government must be watched to be sure that it does not externalize too badly on others who are not part of the contract.

Who can play this watchdog function? Here is a role for the state, in the sense of the state of California or the United States of America. The role is to set rules to preclude unfair advantage being taken of the local propertied by the nonpropertied or vice versa, and to preclude undue externalization.

To sum up, these two sections—regulatory restraint and, more broadly, government that serves the commonweal—are most likely to emerge from relatively smaller-scale general-purpose governments. Denizens of a particular socioeconomic, geographic, environmental turf should be allowed to contract with one another for the amount of common property (public goods) they wish to provide, to secure the reduction of transactions costs by clothing the contract with a local, general-purpose government, and, in exchange for local government, to have the state set basic rules of conduct for intralocal and interlocal government action.[3]

Compensable Regulations

As Johnson suggests, much of the "debate is over where to draw the line" between the police power and eminent domain. That statement is short-hand. It needs some amplification.

If regulation is regarded as reasonable, a court will uphold it as valid. If regulation is regarded as too harsh, a court will invalidate the regulation. The reason often given for the invalidation is that "private property [cannot] be taken for a public use without just compensation," a statement which, of course, is the language found in the national and all (at least by implication) state constitutions. Harsh regulation equals a taking of property, the courts reason, and since the regulating government offered no compensation, the court holds the regulation invalid.

When one thinks about it, invalidation is a massive display of judicial power in absolutist disregard for separation-of-power principles. A legislature, representative of the people, passed the law and the executive executed it, but the courts in effect have a veto power that cannot be overridden. The propriety of courts having such a veto power has not always existed. It certainly did not come from our common-law tradition, and it does not exist today in many countries with a common-law tradition. In fact, it was not established in America until 1803 in that landmark case, *Marbury v. Madison*.[4]

While the power of courts to invalidate harsh regulation is now well established, that does not mean they will. Many are not now using their stamp of invalidity with nearly the rigor of yesteryear. Coupled with increasingly harsh regulation emanating from legislative halls in recent years, this refusal of the courts to veto has led to considerable distress among the propertied interests.

Note that the statement of the matter thus far focuses on the line between a valid and invalid regulation. That is not necessarily the same as two other lines which might be considered—the line between eminent domain and the police power, and the line between compensation and no compensation. These lines tend to be the same; so if the government exercises the power of eminent domain, then compensation is paid. If the government validly exercises the police power, then compensation is not paid. There is a further consequence to the classification: If the exercise of governmental power is on the eminent domain side of the line, compensation is paid at 100 cents on the dollar for property taken. If the action is recognized as the exercise of the police power, no cents are paid for the dollar in value "taken."

If 100 cents on the dollar is paid, that is almost as advantageous to propertied interests as invalidation. Either full payment for the loss is received or the government decides to remove the regulation because the public benefit is not compelling enough to warrant payment. In order to secure a compensatory remedy, of course, the challenge to the distressed property owner is to establish that the governmental action amounted to eminent domain. Contrary to arguing that the governmental action is invalid, the property owner insists that the action is valid and that the court should classify the action as eminent domain and require the government to pay. Lawyers know such as a statement of an action in inverse condemnation. Courts that are loath to "veto" legislative acts might be more easily persuaded to classify acts as eminent domain since classification constitutes far less judicial activism than does invalidation. And it is surely more in compliance with the constitutional command for a court to hold "if taken, then compensation" than it is to decide "if taken, then invalidation." It could turn out, then, that in cases where courts would traditionally have invalidated, they would now require payment of compensation at 100 cents on the dollar. This new remedy, although involving less judicial activism, is actually a better remedy from the property owner's viewpoint because it will more likely dissuade government from passing harsh regulations in the first place. Previously the risk was only a slap on the hand, invalidation; in inverse condemnation the government risks having to pay for its harsh action. A giant leap to maximize output by harsh regulation means that the bureau must come up with the input. Courts are beginning to accept this new remedy.[5] Property owners have found a new strength. But governmental-environmental forces are fighting back. Since their arguments are not without merit, perhaps a compromise is in order.

Everyone will admit that some regulation is valid. Everyone will admit that whether government acts by exercising the police power or the power of eminent domain, it can only act in either case in the public interest. Everyone will admit that the line between the police power and eminent domain cannot be precisely defined. Let us consider fuzzing the line between eminent domain and the police power and insert the notion of partial compensation between full and no compensation.

Justice Douglas, the great obfuscater, has fuzzed the eminent domain–police power line for us. In a case involving eminent domain action, he said:

We deal ... with ... the police power [which is broadly construed]. This principle admits of no exception merely because the power of eminent domain is involved. ... Once the object is within the authority of Congress, the right to realize it through the exercise of eminent domain is clear. For the power of eminent domain is merely the means to the end.[6]

But that dictum leaves the full and no-compensation line intact. To fuzz that line, one must draw on Graham Waite's seminal piece, *Government*

Power and Private Property.[7]

Waite's point can best be made by using an example. Suppose that farmer Jones has a 500-acre farm worth $1000 per acre, for a total of $500,000. Of the $1,000, $500 represents its value due to potential urban uses, and $500 is its value as a farm. If the state highway department now comes along and takes a 1-acre corner of the farm for a freeway, Jones would be paid 100 cents on the dollar—$1000 under traditional eminent domain rules. His remaining property would be worth $499,000. If, on the other hand, the state had regulated Jones's property, limiting it to agricultural use in perpetuity, $250,000 would be "taken," leaving Jones with property worth $250,000. Despite the magnitude of the loss in the second case, a present-day court might well uphold the action as valid. Yet, if both actions are taken in the public interest and if the just compensation clause is basically a fairness rule,[8] would it not be fairer to pay less or no compensation in the first case and some compensation in the second? Admittedly, to call the one acre taken not a taking involves some imagination. Perhaps it would help to conceive of the taking as a tax. Every property owner is subject to a tax of having a small portion of his property devoted to public use. Is the idea any more farfetched than to hold that the $250,000 in the example has not been taken?

Since not paying the farmer his $1000 might take getting used to, consider regulation with compensation. This idea does not have a long history in America. Some[9] think it began in 1953 with a *Harvard Law Review* note[10] which criticized the idea. The late great Jacob Beuscher, the founder of law school courses in planning law,[11] was its most prestigious foe.[12]

Bosselman liked the idea and called it the third alternative in zoning litigation.[13] Costonis calls it the accommodation power, lying between the police and eminent domain power, and suggests that the compensatory payment could take a variety of noncash forms such as in transferable development rights.[14] I call it compensable regulation.

My main entry in the regulation with compensation sweepstakes is in a larger paper called *Compensable Regulation: Lessons from Our Peers.*[15] It traces the intellectual discussion of the idea[16] in America, beginning with the 1953 *Harvard Law Review* note. A companion piece, *Planning and Regulatory "Acquisition,"*[17] refers to some nineteenth-century legislative acts involving compensable regulation which were upheld by the courts. Perhaps the most famous of these acts is that of Massachusetts which paid compensation to landowners around a public park whose heights were limited in order to promote the beauty of the public park.[18] These legislative provisions for compensable regulation largely passed from the scene as land use regulation without compensation came to be upheld as valid.

There was a brief legislative appearance of the idea again in the late 1960s and early 1970s when there was a desire to prevent virtually all uses of land in ecologically sensitive coastal areas.[19] But as the courts began to uphold harsh legislation without payment of compensation, legislatures decided to regulate without compensation. Compensable regulation has its longest-standing embodiment in the Highway Beautification Act of 1965, with its requirement for payment of compensation for signs which state regulations require must be removed along the interstate highway system.[20] The act is most interesting because, while signs have less protection from harsh regulation than almost any other use of property— ranking virtually as nuisances[21] so that courts rarely invalidate harsh regulations being applied to signs—the Highway Beautification Act now provides 100 cents on the dollar compensation in the event of required sign removal. Perhaps the lesson is that the sign lobby is strong. Perhaps, on the other hand, the regulators-without-compensation school might learn from the experience. Too harsh regulation of even the least-protected property risks a counter overreaction of full compensation.

The "Lessons from Our Peers" part of my title in the larger paper also traces the history and present use of compensable regulation in Australia, Canada, England, and New Zealand, as well as in the United States. Curiously, while we think of England as being the most socialistic of these countries, the landowner has more protection from overzealous regulation there than in any of the other countries.[22] The English statutes provide for a right in the landowner to require purchase when regulation is too harsh[23] and require payment of compensation when planning permissions are revoked.[24] That England has come to such an accommodation might be attributable to the fact that courts cannot invalidate there. Therefore, the statutes reflect a compromise—but something that is done because it is right rather than because it is constitutionally required.

The statutes in Australia, Canada, and New Zealand are not as favorable. New Zealand is probably the next most protective of property interests, Australia next, and Canada very American in approach. Indeed, Canadian landowners may have less protection than those in America because the statutes give little protection. And the courts in Canada as well as in the other countries cannot invalidate merely because regulation is too harsh.

The *Compensable Regulation* paper also reviews judicial as distinguished from legislative attempts to develop compensable regulation in the United States. Obviously, it is an easier and a quite different thing for a court to uphold legislatively provided compensable regulation than it is for a court to create it out of the just compensation clause. But that judicial remedy is well established when the regulation looks forward to an acquisition.[25] It is so well established by now that it is hardly even interesting as a matter of principle. Indeed, it is because I so sharply distinguish the "acquisition" cases and the compensable regulation cases that the two subjects are covered in separate chapters in the larger project.

So far as I can determine, there are only three reported cases where courts have acknowledged the right of a landowner to sue in inverse condemnation for *mere* (nonacquisitory) regulation. All are recent. In the order *decided*, they are *Brown v. Tahoe Regional Planning Agency*,[26] *HFH, Inc. v. Superior Court of Los Angeles County*,[27] and *Charles v. Diamond*.[28] None constitutes terribly strong precedents. The judge who decided *Brown* later decided[29] that harsh regulations could not even be invalidated let alone be the basis for recovery of compensation. The *HFH* case has been heard by the California Supreme Court, which will likely hold that there is no remedy in inverse condemnation. The New York case still must wind its way to higher courts if it is to have a significant impact.

Still, it is a beginning, and anticipating further development of the concept, the *Compensable Regulation* paper details some of the options of such a concept. One of the most important is that compensation need not be 100 cents on the dollar. For example, it could be as low as the difference in rental value of property regulated in an invalid as distinguished from a valid manner for the term of the invalid regulation. For example, say property is regulated for agricultural use and has a value of $10,000 in that use with a rental value of $1000 per year. Assume further that the most severe regulation that would be valid is to have that property regulated for single-family residential use. The value would then be $50,000 with a rental value of $5000 per year. The difference in rental values is $4000 per year. If a regulation was invalidly applied for a year, the risk to the governmental fisc is $4000, not $50,000 as under a 100 cents on the dollar formula. Such a risk may be a tolerable one so as to avoid the concerns of opponents of compensable regulation that governments would be paralyzed from regulating at all due to fear of calamitous financial exposure. The American Law Institute, in a Model Land Development Code,[30] has basically accepted such an approach.

The American Law Institute (ALI) approach, however, may itself be unconstitutional because the difference between the market use of property and the least use that can be validly regulated is regarded as a property interest taken. For example, assume that the property described above had a highest and best use for multiple family for which market value was $100,000 and rental value $10,000. Under the ALI proposal, the government would acquire the development right (an easement, a property right) for all use above the agricultural use, which would be worth $90,000 ($9000 per year) but would be paying only the difference between the too harsh regulation in agricultural use ($10,000 market, $1000 per year) and the valid residential regulation ($50,000 market, $5000 per year). In short, the government would be *acquiring* an interest worth $90,000 ($9000 a year) for $50,000 ($5000 a year).

Because of the rule that government cannot regulate in a way so as to permit it to acquire property interests on the cheap, I venture that the ALI provision is unconstitutional.[31] However, it could be made constitutional if the payment were regarded as for damages rather than for the acquisition of an interest.

But these are subtleties; a full exploration of these can be found in *Compensable Regulations: Lessons from Our Peers*.

Opportunity Costs and Shifting Value

Free marketeers might find the compensable regulation concept attractive. But some caution is in order. If government does begin to compensate more generously when it imposes regulations in the public interest at the expense of a few regulatees, government has to fund these payments. Someone might point out to government that when it regulates in the public interest, some private property owners lose, but others gain. It might then occur to government that the gains, the benefits (the windfalls, as I call them), should be recaptured in order to fund wipeout mitigation. It is intellectually difficult, and may be morally indefensible, to be for wipeout mitigation through compensable regulation and yet be against windfall recapture.

The notion that wipeouts are offset by windfalls may be missed in part by Johnson, who indicates that "when ... land is directed to be used as open space ... the cost to society is the opportunity cost of the residential development that might have been constructed on the open-space site." I do not think so, being in general agreement with the most prestigious study of the windfalls-for-wipeouts problem yet conducted. Under the heading *Shifting Value*, the Uthwatt Report states as follows:

The public control of the use of land ... necessarily has the effect of shifting land values; in other words, it increases the value of some land and decreases the value of other land, but it does not destroy land values. Neither the total demand for development nor its average annual rate is materially affected, if at all, by planning ordinances. If, for instance, part of the land on the fringe of a town is taken out of the market for building purposes by the prohibition of development upon it, the potential building value is merely shifted to other land and aggregate values are not substantially affected.[32]

The fact that regulation shunts demand from one place to another may result in opportunity costs on the regulated place, but it does not do so in gross.

Of course, if enormous areas relative to developable areas are regulated for nondevelopment, the shift cannot occur. So Johnson is correct in being concerned with the regulation for nondevelopment of too much land. My perception is, however, that the regulation of too much land for nondevelopment is not the major problem.

The major social costs come not from the regulation itself, but from conflicting, irrational, erratic regulation. It is, therefore, conflicting, erratic regulation rather than regulation itself that should be of most societal concern.

To those overall social costs one must add the costs to government of regulation which, as Johnson points out, are not free. We must also add the costs to the private sector of working under a pervasive but berserk nonsystem of controls. A cynical but increasingly true statement is that these nonsystems are resulting in a high-cost method of securing undesirable land use allocation.

Therefore, it is all of us rather than a particular private property owner that should be our primary concern. We can take care of the individual owner by paying compensation. We cannot take care of "us" that way. It is necessary for the benefit of all to do one of two things. We can stop regulating and let the market take over. Alternatively, we can regulate better. I am not persuaded that the former alternative is the best. I think that planning and regulating can provide a framework for putting things in order and thus be wealth-creative. But I also think, along with the free marketeers, that the noses of government must be rubbed in the true costs of conflicting, erratic regulation. If those full costs had to be considered by government, we could then have a fair test of the quality-of-life–creating merits of free marketeerism versus regulation. Better regulation takes reorganization of governments along the lines suggested in the second and third sections, for the present regulatory overburden stems primarily from many special-purpose bureaus, each trying to maximize their own outputs at the expense of individual well-being and commonweal.

The Poverty Issue

Johnson touches on the poor in two places in Chapter 2. In the first place, he alleges, land use controls are not supposed to be used to redistribute wealth; and, to the extent that they do, the redistribution has been from the poor to the rich. In the second place, he observes, the poor have not been the beneficiaries of the environmental movement as compared with the opportunity costs of the poor.

Redistribution of Wealth

I am terribly egalitarian; I believe the rich should be poorer and the poor richer. My intellect can be excited by a project such as windfalls for wipeouts, but in order to engage my heart, the distribution has to be from rich to poor rather than from rich to rich, as in the case with windfalls for wipeouts. In order to have a windfall or to suffer a wipeout, one must be a property owner. To own property, as economist Mason Gaffney reminds us in his essays on the property tax, is to be rich.

Johnson is absolutely right. Land use controls are not supposed to redistribute wealth directly. They are not like a progressive income tax, which is designed to tax the rich more so as to provide more social benefits to the poor. The purpose of land use regulations, rather, is to control and maintain orderly development. Since that is its purpose, the traditional governmental planner draws pretty plans and zoning maps, usually in total disregard of economic consequences to the affected property owners.

There are, however, a few financial matters that concern land use planners employed by government. One of the purposes of zoning, as contained in the Standard State Zoning Enabling Act, which is the model for zoning enabling acts in many states, is "conserving the value of buildings."[33] That purpose might be read more broadly as preserving total value of *all real property* within a community—it should not be allowed to go down.[34] Second, it could mean that the government is concerned about maintaining its property tax base through land use control.[35]

A growth-oriented community exemplifies the first point. In many such communities, not only were property values not to go down, there was thought to be a God-given right that zoning should make them go up. That is why, as one realtor's sign proclaimed, "one good real estate investment is worth a lifetime of labor." Another, quoting Theodore Roosevelt, states that "Buying real estate is not only the best way, the quickest way and the safest way but the only way to become wealthy."

For all their environmental insensitivities, the communities eager for growth were giving the poor a shot at the wealth (while of course the landowners and developers were getting theirs). Rezoning was available for the asking—so available that the supply of developable land often outstripped the demand, lowering costs so that the poor could afford the small house in a suburb which, in any case, was a lot better than the slum. Concomitant to rezoning on demand was community subsidy of infrastructure. Often controlled by the land developers, the suburban cities would provide the streets, the sewers, the water, and so forth, which made development possible. While much of this subsidy probably was stolen by the landowners in the form of higher land prices, some probably turned up in the form of lower housing costs.

Tax base maintenance, the second aspect of property value preservation, did redistribute incomes—but from poor to rich. The case is most dramatically made in New Jersey where so-called fiscal zoning became an art form. Fiscal zoning is the use of zoning to exclude low-income persons who cost more in municipal services than they produce in property taxes. Fiscal zoning is also used to attract the rateables, e.g., research facilities, with their landscaped lawns and highly paid Ph.D. employees. The use of fiscal zoning was rampant in New Jersey for a simple reason: local property taxes were higher there than anywhere in the nation. And compliant New Jersey courts went along with the towns, sustaining zoning which excluded the poor through housing cost—raising large lot zoning, prohibitions on mobile homes, minimum house sizes, and the like.[36] The poor were thereby denied their place in the suburban sun. Growth was still welcome, but it was only the research facilities and the Ph.D's who were welcome.

Of course, exclusionary land use control is not motivated solely by a desire to preserve property values of the tax base. There is an unofficial reason. Individuals discriminate on racial and wealth grounds. But discrimination by private means costs money. For example, if I want to be assured that the poor and the minorities do not live near me, I can purchase enough land so that my nearest neighbor is out of sight and out of mind. Alternatively, I can discriminate by getting together with my white, middle-to-upper-class neighbors. We decide to clothe ourselves with a local government dress. That gives us zoning power which we can use to discriminate on the cheap. By imposing high minimums of development, we can force up the cost of development and thereby keep the poor out. By keeping the poor out, of course, we can also keep out minorities, or at least prevent a token from becoming a critical mass.

That's the way it was—planners drawing their beautiful plans without regard to windfalls and wipeouts because of the assumption that rezoning on demand would lead only to windfalls. Growth was welcome and subsidized, except where immigration of the poor and minorities was likely and property tax burdens were high, in which case the rezoning and subsidy could be expected only for "nice" growth.

Comes the environmental movement. Everyone who has their place in the suburbs now decides that growth is not so good after all. Even the not-so-poor are no longer welcome. Even "nice" growth is no longer so welcome. Land use controls become even more exclusionary. Like the OPEC nations, the suburbs had a good thing. People demanded space just as the economy demands oil, so the suburbs raised the price. The infrastructure subsidy was removed. The price of admission now is not only that one is forced by exclusionary controls to purchase more land than he might want, but he must pay all the infrastructure charges associated with the new development *and*, if the market will bear it, there is a buy-in fee for the existing infrastructure *plus*, in really desirable, savvy communities, the admission charge includes a little profit for the existing community.[37] The rich are willing and able to pay these costs; the poor must go away empty.

Thus far in this section the focus is on growth or no growth, tax base, and neighbors cum governments as actors in the zoning game. Those actors do not necessarily act in the overall public interest, but at least it is a government acting. There are other actors in the zoning game. These include the land speculators and realtors who play the zoning game for their profit. Zoning regulations may be theoretically passed to "protect and promote the health, safety, morals, and general welfare of the public," as Johnson states—they get changed to promote the private welfare of the landowners and land merchants. Any public benefit is incidental.

I have not significantly footnoted this section, not because I wouldn't know where to start, but because I wouldn't know where to end.[38] My repetition of the exclusionary land use control story, which hopefully is familiar to everyone reading this book, is to demonstrate that land use controls are indirectly and officially used to redistribute wealth and that private parties, playing the land use control game, have used them to maximize their private wealth. I have also demonstrated that these controls redistribute wealth from poor to rich.

Perhaps since it is inevitable that these controls will redistribute wealth, my only point is that they should be used for that purpose, but to distribute from rich to poor. How that might be done is not the subject of this chapter, but of others.[39] Here I only wish to dispel the notion that redistribution of wealth is an improper function of land use controls.

Environmentalists versus the Poor

Johnson's second point alludes to the lack of benefits enjoyed by the poor from the environmental movement. He is, of course, absolutely right. The title to this subsection is in fact drawn from a paper I wrote on January 7, 1970, seven days after the National Environmental Policy Act became the law of the land. That paper was an attempt to persuade the then still strong Office of Economic Opportunity (OEO) that it had better start defining poverty problems as environmental problems (e.g., rat bites in the slums as a problem of garbage, i.e., solid waste pollution). It was also a plea for more funds for the National Health and Environmental Law Program (NHELP), an OEO legal services back-up center at UCLA which was chartered as capable of representing poverty interests in the new environmental movement but was not funded to do so.

The paper opined that if one did an overlay of where the worst air, water, noise, solid waste, etc., pollution problems were, that overlay would coincide with where the poor live and work. The point is simply illustrated—the rich never live downwind from the rendering plant. Therefore, the quality of the environmental life of the poor will improve more than that of the rich to the extent air, water, noise, and solid waste pollution is removed. But Johnson is nevertheless right: some persons cannot afford a high-quality environmental life because they do not yet even have a high-quantity life-enough to eat, employment, basic medical care, etc.

Thus, the pitch to OEO was that the poor needed representation to ensure that environmental resources were not stolen out of resources available to poverty programs and that environmental improvement was not financed by regressive taxes. OEO was not interested. OEO was one of Johnson's bureaus—pushing hard on poverty, OEO could not see the reality of the changing world. And where is OEO today? It is no more, just as I predicted.[40] But the Environmental Protection Agency is still going rather strong.

Environmentalists practically admit their programs are not pro-poor. Rather, they are pro-environment—the poor are someone else's concern. After all, the poor will always be with us, they say; a desirable environment can be permanently lost. Like militarists, even many poverty warriors, who I always thought were interested in the poor, entered the war on environmental degradation—they were interested only in being where the action was. The poor had had their chance.

But the environmentalists resent the free marketeer, Chicago school type throwing stones at them. There is little intellectual affection between the two groups at best because of the environmentalists' penchant for regulating; but on the poverty issue, the environmentalists' resentment is more emotional. Environmentalists dislike the masquerade which suggests that scratch a capitalist, free marketeer, Chicago schooler, landowner, or speculator, and you will find a heart bleeding for the poor. The environmentalists do not believe it; neither do I.

Conclusion

Words, words, words—there are many in this paper. Yet finishing it leaves the writer with a sense of disquietude. There is so much to be said; the problem is so complex. It would be nice if one could be "religious" about regulation and truly believe it right that regulation be eliminated. It would be easier if one could assert a simple rule at the other extreme—all regulation is valid. Mugwumpian views are harder. But on our way to a solution of the problem, it does seem important to recall that harsh regulations might be made more acceptable not only from the regulatees' but from society's point of view if some compensation is paid. That reform, plus the reorganization of the regulators (so that some of the incentive-killing aspects of regulation due to overbreadth, conflict, and erraticism are eliminated) might be a step in the right direction. The direction will be more just if the property owners and the takers of that property recall that there is a substantial group of Americans who are unconcerned over the controversy because they have nothing to take. Providing them with more property must be our first concern.

Notes

1. Even a state such as California is a bureau within the terms of the definition vis-à-vis the public in other states and nations. And the United States or any nation is a bureau in world terms.

2. D. Hagman and D. Misczynski, *The Quiet Federalization of Land Use Controls: Disquietude in the Land Markets*, The Real Estate Appraiser, Sept.-Oct. 1974, 5 at 7. Copyright 1974, Society of Real Estate Appraisers, Chicago. Reprinted with permission.

3. State (i.e., state and federal government) would still be significant because local governments need an institution for reducing transactions costs among themselves. And externalities and spillovers could be such, for example, as to require redistribution of wealth between rich and poor communities.

4. 1 Cranch 137 (1803).

5. M. Berger, *To Regulate, or Not to Regulate—Is That the Question*? 8 Loy. L. A. L. Rev. 253 (1975), is the most recent article on the matter. Perhaps drawing on my amicus brief for HFH in HFH, Ltd. v. Superior Court for the County of Los Angeles, 15 Cal. 3d 508, 125 Cal. Rptr. 365, 542 P.2d 237, he lists most of the literature as follows at note 234.

J. Delafons, Land Use Controls in the United States, 2d ed. (Cambridge, Ma.: M.I.T. Press, 1969); L. Badler, *Municipal Zoning Liability in Damages—A New Cause of Action*, 5 Urban Law. 25 (1973); L. Berger, *A Policy Analysis of the Taking Problem*, 49 N.Y.U.L. Rev. 165 (1974); F. Bosselman, *The Third Alternative in Zoning Litigation*, 17 Zoning Digest 73 (1965); D. Carmichael, *Transferable Development Rights as a Basis for Land Use Control*, 2 Fla. St. U.L. Rev. 35 (1974); J. Costonis, *Development-Rights Transfer: A Proposal for Financing Landmarks Preservation*, 1 Real Estate L. J. 163 (1972); J. Costonis, *Development Rights Transfer: An Exploratory Essay*, 83 Yale L.J. 75 (1973); J. Costonis, *The Chicago Plan: Incentive Zoning and the Preservation of Urban Landmarks*, 85 Harv. L. Rev. 574 (1972); A. Dunham, *From Rural Enclosure to Re-Enclosure of Urban Land*, 35 N.Y.U.L. Rev. 1238 (1960); D. Hagman, *A New Deal: Trading Windfalls for Wipeouts*, Planning, Sept. 1974, at 9; J. Krasnowiecki & J. Paul, *The Preservation of Open Space in Metropolitan Areas*, 110 U. Pa. L. Rev. 179 (1961); J. Krasnowiecki & A.

Strong, *Compensable Regulations for Open Space: A Means of Controlling Urban Growth*, 29 J. Am. Inst. Planners 87 (1963); J. Rose, *From the Legislatures: Proposed Development Rights Legislation Can Change the Name of the Land Investment Game*, 1 Real Estate L.J. 276 (1973), J. Rose, *A Proposal for the Separation and Marketability of Development Rights as a Technique to Preserve Open Space*, 2 Real Estate L.J. 635 (1974); S. Sussna, *New Tools For Open Space Preservation*, 2 Urban Law. 87 (1970); G. Waite, *Governmental Power and Private Property*, 16 Cath. U.L. Rev. 283 (1967); Comment, *An Evaluation of the Rights and Remedies of a New York Landowner For Losses Due To Government Action—With a Proposal for Reform*, 33 Albany L. Rev. 537 (1969); Comment, *Compensable Regulations: Outline of a New Land Use Planning Tool*, 10 Williamette L.J. 451 (1974); Note, *Development Rights Transfer in New York City*, 82 Yale L.J. 338 (1972).

He also cites F. Michelman, *infra*, note 8 and A. Van Alstyne, *Taking or Damaging by Police Power: The Search for Inverse Condemnation Criteria*, 44 S. Cal. L. Rev. 1 (1970). Another recent article is J. Magavern, *The Evolution and Extension of the New York Law of Inverse Condemnation*, 24 Buff. L. Rev. 273 (1975).

6. Berman v. Parker, 348 U.S. 26, 32–33 (1954).

7. 16 Cath. U.L. Rev. 283 (1967).

8. F. Michelman, *Property, Utility, and Fairness: Comments on the Ethical Foundations of "Just Compensation" Law*, 80 Harv. L. Rev. 1165 (1967).

9. J. Cabaniss, *Inverse Condemnation in Texas—Exploring the Serbonian Bog*, 44 Texas L. Rev. 1584, n. 107 (1966).

10. 66 Harv. L. Rev. 1134 (1953).

11. D. Hagman, *The Teaching of Land-Use Controls and Planning Law in American Law Schools*, 1972 ASPO Land Use Controls Ann. 61 (1973).

12. Jacob Beuscher, *Some Tentative Notes on the Integration of Police Power and Eminent Domain by the Courts: So-Called Inverse or Reverse Condemnation*, 1968 Urban L. Ann. 1.

13. F. Bosselman, *The Third Alternative in Zoning Litigation* (pts. 1, 2) 17 Zoning Digest 73, 112 (1965).

14. J. Costonis, *Possible Futures for Compensation Law in Land Use Controversies: of "Fair Compensation" and the Accommodation Power* (forthcoming).

15. The paper is chapter 17 in D. Hagman (ed.), *Windfalls for Wipeouts? Betterment Recapture and Worsenment Mitigation in CANZEUS* (forthcoming). CANZEUS is the mythical society of Canada, Australia, New Zealand, England, and the United States.

16. See references at note 5, *supra*.

17. In D. Hagman (ed.), *Windfalls for Wipeouts? Bettermant Recapture and Worsenment Mitigation in CANZEUS* ch. 16 (forthcoming).

18. Held valid in Attorney General v. Williams, 174 Mass. 476, 55 N.E. 77 (1899).

19. Mass. Coastal Wetlands Act of 1965, 130 Mass. Gen. Laws Ann. § 105 (Supp. 1971); R.I. Gen. Laws Ann. § 2-1-16 (Supp. 1973).

20. 23 U.S.C. § 131(g).

21. Since "[T]he Legislature has provided . . . that [certain advertising displays] . . . 'are public nuisances' . . . [i]t was within the police power of the state [to terminate them]." People ex rel. Dept. Pub. Wks. v. The Golden Rule Ass'n, 49 Cal. App.3d 733, 777, Cal. Rptr. 596, 598 (1975).

22. Since England has no constitution yet has substantial property owner protection, the absence of just compensation and due process clauses does not necessarily leave private property unprotected, as Johnson may be suggesting.

23. Town and Country Planning Act, 1971, c. 78, § 180.

24. *Id.* § 164. These provisions are also discussed in D. Hagman and S. Pepe, *English Planning Law: A Summary of Recent Developments*, 11 Harv. J. Legislation 557 (1974) and D. Hagman, Urban Planning and Land Development Control Law (St. Paul: West Publishing, 1971), ch. 21 (1975).

25. Scrutton v. Sacramento, 275 Cal. App.2d 412, 79 Cal. Rptr. 872 (1969) is a leading regulatory "acquisition" case. Scrutton wanted to subdivide his property, but the county kept preventing it through regulation because it had in mind acquiring it for an airport. When the county abandoned its project, Scrutton sued in inverse condemnation and recovered.

26. 385 F. Supp. 1128 (D. Nev. 1973).

27. 116 Cal. Rptr. 436 (1974).

28. 47 App. Div. 426, 366 N.Y.S.2d 921 (1975).

29. Western International Hotels v. Tahoe Regional Planning Agency, 387 F. Supp. 429 (D. Nev. 1975).

30. Proposed Official Draft § 9-112(3) (April 15, 1975).

31. It might not be constitutional if Waite's thesis explained *supra* at note 7 is accepted.

32. Expert Committee on Compensation and Betterment (Uthwatt Committee), Final Report 15, Cmd. 6386 (1942).

33. § 3 (Rev. ed. 1926) (emphasis added).

34. Some statutes and ordinances so provide. For example, Mich. Stats. Ann. § 5.2931 (1958) provide that "Such regulations [zoning] shall be made with reasonable consideration [to] . . . the conservation of prop-

erty values. . . ." The Lakewood, New Jersey, Zoning Ordinance, November 14, 1957, article 1, indicates that "The purpose of this Ordinance is to . . . conserve and stabilize the value of property. . . ." The Salem, Oregon, Planning Ordinance, No. 4578, October 29, 1953, indicates zoning is "to stabilize and conserve the value of property." The Vallejo, California, Proposed Zoning Ordinance, § 4(a) (1960), indicated zoning was "to conserve the value of property."

35. Smith-Hurd Ill. Ann. Stats. § 11–13–1 (1962) provided for zoning "to the end that . . . the taxable value of land and buildings throughout the municipality may be conserved. . . ."

36. Southern Burlington County NAACP v. Township of Mount Laurel, 67 N.J. 151, 336 A.2d 713 (1975) discusses these cases and constitutes a massive reversal of approach. New Jersey municipalities are now required to take affirmative action to be inclusionary.

37. J. Redding and F. Jacobson, "Impact Taxes: From Infra to Extrastructure," in Windfalls for Wipeouts? Betterment Recapture and Worsenment Mitigation in CANZEUS, ch. 12 (D. Hagman, ed., forthcoming); R. Ellickson, "Suburban Controls on Urban Growth: An Economic and Legal Analysis," paper presented at the UCLA Law and Economics Workshop, February 5, 1975.

38. Exclusionary land use controls are discussed, and a bibliography can be found in D. Hagman, "Public Control of California Land Development," *California Zoning Practice* (Berkeley, Cal.: Continuing Education of the Bar, Supp. 1975), §§ 5.73–5.74, and periodic updates. For a national focus see D. Hagman, *Public Planning and Control of Urban and Land Development* (St. Paul: West Publishing, 1973), ch.18, and D. Hagman, *Urban Planning and Land Development Control Law* (St. Paul: West Publishing, 1971), ch. 18.

39. An exceptional, tongue-in-cheek proposal is D. Hagman, *The Managed Growth Trickle-up Theory*, Land Use Law & Zoning Digest, No. 1, at 7 (1975).

40. My story is told at greater length in D. Hagman, *NEPA's Progeny Inhabit the States—Were the Genes Defective?* 1974 Urban L. Ann. 3.

5 A Political Economist Views the Taking Issue

Otto A. Davis

Introduction

The taking issue is a complicated phenomenon which involves a combination of economic, political, legal, and ethical issues. While I am not an expert in all the disciplines involved here, this fact shall not constrain my commentary. Indeed, on issues of this sort the lack of expertise is seldom a handicap in the formation of a strong opinion. But while I can speak as an expert on the economic side of the problem, I must admit that I feel somewhat similar to a friend of mine who commented while serving on an advisory committee to a study group on one of our national problems: "I'm a complete novice on this problem so I can express an opinion and lose my entire reputation in the area and I will not have lost a thing."[1] Such is the situation with my views on the legal and perhaps even ethical aspects of this issue.

Basically, the problem which we are considering here involves the definition of property rights. Although it is a tradition in economics to take property rights as given and not subject to change, different definitions lead to alternative outcomes, and the tools of economic analysis can help us identify these different outcomes. The law is obviously involved here because the legal "rules of the game" define property rights. Two aspects, at least, of politics come into play here. First, the issue is basically a political problem in which the desires of one interest group are opposed by the interests of another. Second, politics is also involved at a more fundamental level because, in the constitutional sense, we cannot avoid the issue of whether our present decision-making machinery—general assemblies guided by the rule of the simple majority—should be allowed to make this kind of a decision. Ethical issues come into play because all these problems involve our preferences about what kind of a society we prefer to live in.

Since these problems are all intertwined and interwoven, we shall not make a complete effort to unravel them. Nevertheless, it will be useful to at least partially separate the economic from the political aspects of the issue.

141

Some Political Issues

The founders of our republic clearly recognized that they were framing the rules of government for a dynamic society.[2] Many of the founders themselves were learned men who thought deeply and wrote profoundly about the virtues and dangers associated with a democratic form of decision making. They were well aware of the fact that a majority of the citizenry, just as a small group of powerful persons or a monarch, can be despotic and dictatorial. Accordingly, in the framing of the Constitution, and especially in its amendments, they set forth a series of rights—areas of life deemed too important to be left to the whim of majority rule— which need not be given for all time but which can be changed only through the operation of the complicated machinery of constitutional amendment. This machinery was deliberately designed to be complex and fragmented so the momentary passion associated with a popular issue might have less of a chance of being influential in affecting legislation that might impinge upon those rights.

Of course, before any issue can be granted the protection of the Constitution and removed from the realm of day-to-day politics, the judicial system of our courts must decide whether it falls in a category intended for such protection. The two relevant amendments and the associated court cases appear, at least from the point of view of a mere political economist, to have been admirably discussed by Johnson, and it would not be fruitful for me to attempt to improve upon his treatment. On the other hand, I cannot help but comment on, and sometimes argue with, some of the underlying philosophical points as well as the analysis.

The great political philosophers, who were writing before and immediately after the Constitution was framed, were worried that a despotic majority might replace the sometimes arbitrary and dictatorial rule of the kings.[3] Some events in our own history illustrate that this fear was not unfounded—after all, if the North had not won the Civil War, slavery might have lasted into the twentieth century, and we did move our West Coast oriental population inland during World War II—but the typical way that interest-group politics has worked in this country was not foreseen by our founders. At least a casual reading of the operation of our political system leads one to believe that typical governmental excesses involve situations in which a relatively small number of individuals stand to gain a great deal by some particular action or program while the costs are spread across the great majority of our citizenry. The so-called pork barrel projects are largely of this nature. Laws that limit our intercoastal maritime trade to American flag vessels and the requirement that certain parts of our foreign trade be shipped in American flag vessels serve to limit competition and thus serve the interest of certain portions of both management and labor. Our maritime program, which subsidizes the construction and operation of a certain portion of our own vessels, serves the interests of the same unions whose bargaining power is strengthened through the program. Agricultural price support programs have benefited a certain portion of our farmers at the expense of the consuming public and the American taxpayer. Other agricultural programs, under the guise of rural development, have invested public monies for largely private benefits. Examples range from the construction of fish ponds to a large part of our reforestation programs. Administration after administration has now given lip service in an effort to try to end the education program which gives aid to the so-called impacted school districts. This program serves to channel public funds into rich communities such as those around Washington, D.C. The Davis-Bacon Act requires that construction projects which receive federal aid or other such contract assistance employ workers who are paid the "prevailing local wage." This provision of the act serves the interest of our construction unions since the term *prevailing local wage* has been interpreted as meaning the union scale and this prevents undercutting and underbidding by nonorganized workers and companies. All these are examples of instances in which the benefits are concentrated but the costs are spread widely since they can often be "passed along" to the general public.

This rather commonly observed mode of operation of the political process in our modern democracy may be caused by the concentration of benefits. This concentration makes it easier for, and gives an incentive to, those possibly affected by the law to lobby for their own interests and programs while those who bear the costs have no special or important reason to provide an equal counterforce. The basic point is simplicity itself. The concentration of benefits provides an incentive for organizing a political lobby, and the relatively smaller size makes it easier to organize for this type of activity. Since the costs are spread, no one person suffers very much so that the incentive for organization on the other side is relatively small. At the same time, given the relatively large number of citizens that are involved, the difficulty of organizing an active lobby is considerable. In a system which depends for its effectiveness upon prevailing political powers, this situation gives rise to governmental excesses of a kind not fully appreciated by either our founding fathers or the classical political philosophers. Of course, the underlying reason for the pervasiveness of the situation involves the costliness of the transmission of information. Those directly affected have incentive to inform themselves and to act. All those who are affected only through the tax system have little incentive to learn about and to act against these excesses of governmental policy and programs. After all, the real incidence of the benefits of these programs is often difficult to discover, even by experts, and they are often hidden in confusing rhetoric pointed in quite a different direction.

The taking issue is an example of a political phenomenon that gives an illusion of not fitting into this traditional mold. If, for instance, one takes the example of the California coast land where planners and environmentalists, as well as part of the public, appear to favor the enactment of laws which would place restrictions upon the owners of coastal property and limit their ability to develop their property without compensation for the loss of this right, then the costs would appear to be concentrated while the benefits might appear to be widespread. If the above argument about the excesses of democracy is correct, then one would confidently predict that all efforts to enact the law redefining and restricting property rights would be easily defeated. Yet, at least some observers predict that such a law will be enacted within the next few years.

A definitive answer to this situation or paradox is probably impossible at this time. However, it is possible to question some of the widely accepted assumptions in the rhetoric. In so doing this case, too, will tend to assume a close resemblence to the more typical pattern. Who are the beneficiaries of the law limiting the development of our coastal areas? The rhetoric would have us believe it is "all the people." This rhetoric may depart drastically from reality. After all, it is reasonable to presume that some portion of the population will never visit the coast. Another portion, not necessarily mutually exclusive with the above, may not be admirers of nature and may prefer developed to nondeveloped areas. Can these people be gainers?

A more hard-nosed view of the situation leads to the conclusion that there are at least two identifiable groups of gainers from the passage of such a law. The first is a group publicly identified as being politically active in favor of this law. These are the environmentalists who have a strong desire to preserve nature as it is so that they and future generations who hold preferences similar to their own can enjoy observing and studying relatively undeveloped scenic beauty. The second group, who are certainly not identified in the public mind as being in favor of such a law, are those who own coastal properties which have already been developed. While a law which limits further development would not make these owners monopolists, it would certainly give them a less competitive market in the future. Since the demand for the services of this kind of property is hardly likely to diminish, present owners would certainly stand to capture a handsome capital gain from the passage of the law.

How large are these two groups? While accurate figures are not easily available, few people argue that the owners of developed coastal properties are anywhere near a majority of the California population. We probably could agree to a guess that they are likely to be a small portion of that population. Further, despite the widespread publicity obtained by the Sierra Club and other environmental and conservationist groups, it is doubtful that their membership is large when measured against the number of registered voters in California. Hence, when one looks more closely, this issue appears to be one in which an intense minority stands to gain by the passage of the statute. The difference between this and a typical case outlined above is that the costs also appear to be distributed among a small minority of persons—the owners of undeveloped coastal properties. In this way this case differs somewhat from the traditional one.

On the other hand, if the courts should decide that compensation is required, then this example appears to fall true to the traditional category since the taxpayers are required to produce the compensation. Hence, we would have another example where benefits are concentrated but the costs are widespread. For this reason, I am not optimistic that the traditional definition of property rights will remain in effect beyond the next few years.

The Philosophic Welfare Economic Excuse for Governmental Intervention

A significant subset of economists have long been interested in providing a normative, intellectual basis for the existence of governmental activity, both in regard to the actual production of goods and services and for the regulation of the market system. Johnson has provided a summary of some of these works. While I have no quarrel with much of what he said, and even find myself in occasional agreement with him, some points deserve further elaboration. In all that follows, however, it will be interesting to keep the above discussion in mind since, at least as I see it, actions of legislatures and courts seldom have what I regard as a desirable reference to the appropriate kind of economic and philosophical analysis.

At least from one point of view, much of economics can be conceptualized as an analysis of how society "should" be organized. At least since the time of Adam Smith, the moral philosopher who is usually regarded as the founder of economics, there has been an active discussion in the literature about the optimality properties of a market mechanism in a society characterized by the private ownership of the means of production.[4] Smith argued that "like an invisible hand," the market mechanism would lead such a society, composed of individuals interested in pursuing their own selfish interests, to find a position which was best for the entire society. In his scheme of things, very few activities were left to the government, and the private economy was to provide most of the goods and services desired by the citizenry.

Of course, the provision of a widely acceptable definition of the social optimum is not easy, and there has been much theoretical and philosophical discussion of this issue. Following Bentham, the utilitarian philosophers define the social optimum to be that position of society in which the aggregate of utility is maximal.[5] This definition, which rests upon interpersonal comparisons of utility, now has been replaced largely by another philosophic tradition. Interpersonal comparisons were thought to be difficult to make not only as a matter of practice but also as a matter of principle. Hence, most economists now insist that their theories should not be based upon interpersonal comparisons of utility.[6]

Most modern welfare economics is based upon an acceptance of the ethical notion of Pareto optimality or efficiency. The basic idea is simplicity itself. Without admitting interpersonal comparisons, we simply call a position inefficient or non-Pareto optimal if it is possible to make one or more persons better off without worsening any of the others. In other words, a position is Pareto optimal if and only if it is not possible to make someone better off without simultaneously making someone else worse off. It is important to point out that this criterion of efficiency or Pareto optimality need not lead to unambiguous choices among given sets of alternatives or to unambiguous orderings of alternatives since, theoretically speaking, there exists at least an infinity of positions which are Pareto optimal. On the other hand, there is wide acceptance of the argument that one should insist, within the limits of practicality, that all solutions be efficient since, by definition, a non-Pareto optimal solution means that someone can be made better off without making someone else worse off. The qualifying phrase *within the limits of practicality* is used here to denote the fact that although these theoretical possibilities of improving at least one person's position without inflicting harm on anyone else must be admitted whenever the situation is not Pareto optimal, the practical means of actually accomplishing such improvement may not be at all obvious to the frail minds of humans.

This rather abstract notion of Pareto optimality might be neither useful nor terribly interesting were it not for some of the developments of modern welfare economics. The most important of these developments can be considered as one of the most central theorems of economics.[7] It can be stated informally as follows: given certain assumptions about the technology, the availability of information, the characteristics of goods and services, and the absence of monopoly power, there exists a set of market prices such that profit-maximizing firms and utility-maximizing consumers which respond to those prices automatically cause the economic system to attain a Pareto optimum position. This argument makes explicit and refines the old assertion of Adam Smith. The theorem is, further, a powerful argument for the organization of our society so that exchange takes place through the mechanism of competitive markets. If the assumptions of the theorem were universally satisfied, then the government could limit itself largely to programs aimed at the attainment of the desirable distribution of income and be rather certain that the vehicle of competition would cause the system to attain efficiency.

There is little, if any, need to review the entire set of assumptions which appear to be required for the results of the theorem to obtain. Indeed, economists have long been searching for a minimal set of assumptions which will be sufficient for markets to attain Pareto optimality. It is doubtful that the end of the search is anywhere in sight. Accordingly, it is appropriate to review here only those which appear to cause the greater part of the difficulty in the real world. After a brief review, we will then concentrate our discussion upon those which might have some relevance for the taking issue.

Consider first the assumption about technology. The basic idea here is that all firms have convex production possibilities sets, which means that there should not be increasing returns to scale. Of course, it is widely recognized that there can be increasing returns over a range as long as that range is not significant in terms of industry output. While this assumption is critical to the discussion of the operation of a market system in many areas of economic policy, it certainly cannot be the issue here. We might add further that as far as we know, no one has raised this issue as an excuse for the public regulation of the uses of land and other such properties.

A second assumption concerns the availability of information. Producers are assumed to have knowledge of available technology, and consumers are supposed to know whether particular goods and services are available as well as be familiar with their characteristics. Both producers and consumers are presumed to know the relevant set of prices. This assumption could possibly be an issue, and we shall develop an argument below to show why it probably is irrelevant for the question at hand.

A third condition worth noting is the absence of monopoly power. It is the competitive market that, under certain circumstances, is supposed to be the key to attaining Pareto optimality. In some societies which are isolated and underdeveloped and somewhat feudal in nature, the presence of monopoly power can constitute the major economic argument for regulation and reform (and maybe revolution). In the United States, however, as Johnson notes, the ownership of land is highly fragmented. Only the very poorest of our citizens are unlikely to be landowners. Most of the remainder of our citizenry will, some time in their lives, own at least a small plot of land. Indeed, in the exercise of the power of eminent domain for the purpose of urban renewal, the diversity of ownership, which causes difficulty in assembling large parcels, has often been cited as the economic reason and justification of the exercise of that power in the conduct of that program. We simply cannot have it both ways; so, at least in my view, the argument set forth by Johnson is compelling, and monopoly power is largely absent and is certainly not a problem in the operation of the market with respect to the uses of land.

A final condition concerns the characteristics of the goods and services produced by the economic system. First, not only are there supposed to be no "public" goods—that is, goods such as radio waves or television signals which are noted for the fact that when one listener or viewer "uses" them by reception, the quantity available for use by other persons is not diminished—but the production and consumption of other goods and services (called "private" goods) is not supposed to directly affect decision units who are not doing the producing or consuming. In other words, there is supposed to be an absence of what in technical language goes under the name of "nonpecuniary externalities." In both the planning and the economics literature this condition is the one usually cited as the reason why we must have land use planning and zoning. Accordingly, in the discussion below we shall examine this issue in considerable detail.

All the above assume that markets do or can be made to exist. Although the nonexistence of markets and difficulties in bringing them into being are problems for certain areas of economic activity, I think that few people would deny the existence and operation of the market for land and its uses in the United States.

In the section below we shall deal with the dual issues of information and externality. We shall see that these are often intimately interwoven and that while there has been much talk and discussion, there has been little empirical effort to shed some light on these problems.

Perspectives on the Problems of Information and Externality

The past half-century has witnessed a marked decrease in the reliance upon the market for the allocation of land and associated properties, and a corresponding increase in the utilization of social controls such as land use planning and zoning. In light of the above discussion, it should be interesting to examine the economic rationale for this decreased role of markets and the changing conception of property rights.

It is almost commonplace to observe the many statements which define perfect markets are applicable to the market for land and property. Since the ownership of property is widely dispersed in the United States, there are relatively large numbers of independent buyers and sellers, none of whom control the market. On the other hand, the product is far from homogeneous. In addition, new participants often enter the market only a few times during their lifetimes, so that unlike the situation for common consumer items which are characterized by repeat sales, information about property is not quite as easily available through mere experience. On the other hand, there are institutions which are designed to provide information, so it may be worthwhile to briefly examine some of these.

Goods which are not homogeneous, especially when they are seldom purchased, generally pose informational requirements upon the markets that are at least different by degree, rather than kind, from other goods and services. As a result, additional institutional aids are sometimes developed. These institutional developments are clearly evident in terms of the market for land and property.

Although many products rely upon advertisements to generate both attention and information, few markets rely upon advertisements in quite the same way as the property market. In that market, individual parcels, rather than an entire brand line of items are often advertised. In addition, the advertisements are an invitation to explore and to learn more about the properties being advertised to a much greater degree than are advertisements for product lines which are often aimed at immediately inducing a purchase. These differences, however, are hardly fundamental to the operation of the market.

The property market also has companies (commonly known as real estate agencies) whose purpose is to bring together the buyer and seller. While these companies do not operate like the typical retail store which purchases products for sale to the public, this distinction does not appear fundamental to the operation of the market. After all, the real estate agents learn about and pass on to prospective buyers information about properties which are for sale. It is true, of course, that the information may not be unbiased, and it is sometimes said that certain agents tend to give one message to a seller and another to prospective buyers. On the other hand, information about products is seldom perfect in any market, and the degree of approximation to the ideal does not seem greatly different here from what it is in other situations.

In addition to the real estate agents, this market also affords specialized persons (called appraisers) who for a fee can provide independent and more or less objective information and professional judgments about properties. Few other markets afford such specialized information services. In this sense, the property market should have better information than most.

It is also true that the nonhomogeneity of the product and the special definitions of property rights, such as the distinction between mineral rights and other uses of the property, afford special difficulties. In Pennsylvania and certain other states where there is a great deal of coal mining, for example, there is no legal liability associated with subsidence even when it might cause major problems for developed properties. Hence, the buyer has to beware. On the other hand, information is available both through private firms and consultants and from governmental services which are provided free of charge.

In view of the above, it seems appropriate to conclude that, although the property market is certainly nonhomogeneous, there is an adequate approximation to the assumption that individuals on the buying and selling sides know what is available. Hence, informational problems do not appear to be the reason for the regulation of the market.

Probably more important for our present purposes, there appears in the literature the acceptance of the fact that the property markets suffer from and are characterized by interdependence. Externalities are said to abound. Indeed, introspective evidence as well as informal discussions with those persons in the act of selecting housing lends support to the view that "neighborhood effects" indeed exert important influences in the market. The mere acceptance of the existence of zoning ordinances and land use planning tends to indicate that society has accepted the view. Consider the following statement of Haig:

It so happens that unless social control is exercised, unless zoning is fully and skillfully applied, it is entirely possible for an individual to make for himself a dollar of profit but at the same time cause a loss of many dollars to his neighbors and to the community as a whole, so that the social result is a net loss. A glue factory on the corner of Park Avenue and 50th Street might show a net profit, considered by itself and ignoring the losses of its neighbors. The truth is that an individual simply by buying title to a single lot should not be given the right to use it as he chooses, whenever by merely buying the lot he does not meet his full site costs. Zoning finds an economic justification in that it is a useful device for insuring an approximately just distribution of costs, forcing the individual to bear his own expenses.[8]

The same comment could be applied to the economic justification of land use planning. Our society appears to have accepted the existence of externalities and extreme interdependence in the property market. Consider, for example, the following statement of Dunham:

Much of the enabling legislation for zoning recognized this distinction between an external cost and an external benefit. Such legislation speaks of "securing" or "preserving," "avoiding" or "preventing" certain enumerated evils as the purpose of which zoning is permitted.[9]

Both zoning and land use planning are based upon the acceptance of the notion that external diseconomies exert important influences in the property markets.

This widespread acceptance of the existence of external diseconomies appears justified in the way that members of our society talk about and discuss the property markets. After all, many of us have been involved in the purchase of a residence, and all of us, whether owner or renter, have been involved in the selection of a place in which to reside. This introspective evidence will be sufficient to convince most of us that neighborhood effects are important. Do not all of us talk about the neighborhood in justifying our residential decision? Do not things external to our individual residences exert important influences upon our enjoyment of the services provided by these properties? I wager that most of us would answer these questions affirmatively. Yet, there remains the issue of whether an affirmative answer implies that external effects are important influences in the actual operation of the markets.

Two issues emerge at this point. First, if we grant the argument that the external diseconomies are important to the operation of property markets, does the acceptance of this alleged fact imply that the market should be regulated? Second, is there any objective evidence which might tend to confirm or deny our own casual and impressionistic arguments about the importance of external diseconomies in the property markets?

Despite all the thousands and thousands of hours of effort which are devoted annually in this country to land use planning and zoning, there appear to be only two studies which have explored the empirical issue of determining the extent of the external effects which can be found in the property markets.[10] Both studies utilize data from Pittsburgh and were aimed at determining whether the external effects implied by the zoning ordinance were empirically detectable in actual transactions of residential properties. Although the data base for the two studies was far from perfect, the numbers that were available were reliable, and the authors made efforts to control for other considerations. Both studies reported that an objective empirical analysis could not support the assertion that the urban property market is characterized by extreme interdependence. Indeed, the authors of both studies concluded that on the basis of the available evidence, modern zoning is far too detailed and the kinds of externalities implied by the zoning ordinance do not appear to exert important influences in the market.

How can the two bodies of evidence—one of which is subjective and impressionistic and the other of which is objective and empirical—be reconciled? We argue that the two bodies of evidence need not be contradictory and that a lack of understanding of the functioning of the property market has caused inappropriate implications to be drawn from the subjective evidence.

It may be true, as Haig suggested, that a glue factory located on the corner of Park Avenue and 50th Street in New York might impose costs upon its neighbors. However, a second part of the question is seldom considered. Why would a glue factory want to locate on the corner of Park Avenue and 50th Street? It seems obvious that even in the absence of zoning and land use planning restrictions, other sites would offer a more favorable comparative advantage to the glue factory.

While the point is elementary, it may be worthwhile to spend some time on it since it seems to have been so little understood. When a property is placed on the market, we can generally assume that the seller is searching for the highest price which his property will command. Similarly, prospective purchasers can safely be assumed to be searching for some property which satisfies their needs and requirements and which, other things being equal, is available at the lowest possible price. Hence, there is a great deal of sorting and self-selection which goes on within the market. If a buyer of a residential property dislikes and objects to nearby service stations, for example, then he would be much less likely to purchase the residence with the service station next door as would a prospective purchaser who liked the idea of the convenience of having a service station nearby. Consequently, there is a process of natural selection which occurs during the search, and this process tends to reduce the interdependence within the market.

As long as we have different tastes among the prospective purchasers, the mere fact that the buyer and the seller are both seeking the best possible individual deal acts to minimize the negative neighborhood effects in the market. Buyers finding certain uses or features undesirable in a neighborhood simply search for alternative dwellings: and those finding the same uses and features desirable (or the least desirable) tend to be better prospects for location in the given neighborhood. Thus in all situations where there are not pervasive similarities of taste, a natural process of self-selection tends to reduce the interdependence in the market.

This process of natural selection probably explains why the empirical studies fail to isolate the external diseconomies which were thought to be so prevalent in the urban property market. Viewing the available evidence, the authors of both of the empirical studies suggested that their results implied that more, rather than less, reliance should be given to the market as a system for allocating urban properties. After all, one can argue that the process of natural selection means that the major theorem of welfare economics is applicable to this market, so that it may be capable of producing results which are at least an approximation of a Pareto optimal allocation. At a very minimum, these two empirical studies should serve as a warning and suggest that a closer look should be taken at the basic justification for land use planning and zoning.

Of course, it is quite possible that those who are concerned with controlling growth and containing development of the California coast and the sizes of certain towns are referring to something other than the kinds of externalities under discussion here. If such is the case, then it would seem that we should make explicit the nature of the external effects being considered. Let us take the development of the coastal area as an example. If development is allowed in the coastal area, there will be many market transactions. With the passage of time, and if there is further growth of the population of California, one would expect developers to consider alternative sites for development, to assemble some of these, and to develop them. We might note the obvious here. Even what is miscalled unplanned development is usually planned. After all, the developer has to ask how to arrange his site and what to put on it since he must count upon either the future sale of his property or its services for his revenue. We must assume, of course, that the participants in the market consider themselves better off for their participation, or otherwise they should not be there. What possible external effects (other than those discussed above) might be great enough to cancel out such benefits?

There are some environmental issues. Consider first those effects that directly impinge upon man. One of the interesting phenomena associated with large-scale development is the fact that as the developer draws up his plans and subdivides his tract, he must consider the possibility of positive or negative neighborhood effects if he is to maximize his revenues. Hence, at this stage, the externalities are effectively internalized and certainly capable of being accommodated by the market. Of course, there is always the possibility of the problems with external effects around the boundary lines of the development. Presumably, these are legitimate concerns for planning and zoning.

Development does have implications for the quality of our water and our air. Needless to say, these are issues which are not easily accommodated by the market system since no one has found a way to devise property rights for these two materials. Further, while both land use planning and zoning can lessen the impact of development upon the determination of the quality of our air and our water, the effect in this regard should be relatively minor, given the fact that we now have important national programs aimed at producing solutions to both these problems.

Associated with the problems of air and water is the often neglected notion that we share our planet with other forms of life. Further, since neither plants nor animals can possess property in our legal system, it may be quite legitimate to ask about the effects of development upon these nonhuman forms of life. Even so, it may be appropriate to point out that our concern is largely motivated by the fact that these forms of life are often useful to humans or are valued by us for aesthetic or intellectual reasons.

A major concern here is the impact of development upon the creatures of the land and the sea. In the past we have often witnessed excesses. There are endangered species. We almost wiped out the elephant seals and other forms of sea life. These excesses, however, were little related to development as we know it today. The seals were there for the taking, and under our form of law there was no form of ownership and hence no private incentive either for farming them as cattle or for preserving their future. This lack of a definition of property rights (even on a national level!) is a great source of danger for and a threat to our ocean fish populations today. The problem is the basic deficiency in the way we have been able to define property rights, since ownership is the traditional way in which incentives have been provided in our society. It has little to do with the taking issue.

Similar remarks apply to the preservation of plant life. We humans have often found it useful to preserve other forms of life, and our record has become increasingly good in the past few years.

There is also the issue of how such life should be preserved. I think that few of us who have admired the magnificent groves of the native California cypress at Point Lobos or have driven through and walked among the redwoods along the Avenue of the Giants and in other places would argue with the notion that these wonders of nature should be preserved for the enjoyment of our future populations. But this is the very point where, it seems to me, the taking issue may be placed in proper perspective. Why should a few have to pay for the preservation of these wonders of nature when their enjoyment, which may not be widespread among the entire population, is certainly more widespread than that few themselves? At this point the issue appropriately takes on the cloak of ethical judgment and cannot be separated from our conception of justice. This is probably the kind of issue which motivated our ancestors to place a special emphasis upon the protection of individuals from the arbitrary whim of the state.

Lest too much be given away by those of us who have a strong admiration for the allocative functioning of the free market, it may be important to point out to those of us who have enjoyed walking among and observing the elephant seals under the protection of the state parks system at Ana Nuevo that the sea lions in their special cave on the Oregon coast are afforded similar protection through the motivation inherent in our private enterprise system. The point is that there are many alternative ways to arrange for the preservation and protection of nature's wonders and to provide for an appropriate sharing of the resources of our planet among the various forms of life on it. The market system itself is one such arrangement, and we know that, under appropriate circumstances and when the proper conditions are satisfied, it can produce Pareto optimal allocations. Property markets appear approximately to satisfy these circumstances and thus appear to be a more appropriate allocator of these resources than commonly thought if one judges appropriateness by the enabling legislation for our system of zoning and land use planning.

Finally, one can note that there is nothing inconsistent with the advocacy of increased reliance upon the market as a decision-making device for the allocation of property resources and upon the advocacy that the state be one of the actors in the market, so that our system of public parks and public ownership of seashores might be extended. If one looks at the issue in this way, then there is a natural tendency to feel that compensation should be provided if the state acts to alter the structure of property rights in those situations where it appears that the market is an appropriate mechanism for the allocation of resources.

Normative and Ethical Criteria for Political Action

Although its foundations in welfare economics are not as firmly established as one might like, the economic tools of benefit-cost analysis are often viewed as providing a normative basis for at least some classes of political decisions. At the most basic level, economists often draw distinctions between programs which are aimed primarily toward provision of an "ethically desirable" distribution of income in the society and those which are basically allocative or productive in their nature. For this latter class, there has been a growing movement in economics which insists that policy and programs be judged by the criteria of benefit-cost analysis. While at the most basic level the ethical acceptance of the effeciency criteria is required by this argument, many find this judgment an easy one to accept. The simple proposition that efficiency should be insisted upon and that we should strive for Pareto optimality in our allocative policy is difficult not to accept.

The economic argument is simplicity itself. Only policies which have benefits that are greater than the cost should be candidates for adoption. Aside from the problems of the measurement of both benefits and costs, which are disconcertingly difficult in many situations, the basic principles seem simple enough, and these include the proposition that all the costs be counted. In regard to the taking issue, this principle certainly implies that the cost imposed on the present owners of property through restrictions which might be placed upon the use of their property are costs of the program and should be counted when measured against the possible benefits.

Of course, there is no requirement which says that a legislature or any other form of decision making in a democracy must follow the rules of the discipline of economics. Ethical and moral judgments are necessary parts of decision making. If these two are included, then it seems to me that there is an even stronger argument for the requirement of the paying of compensation when one drastically alters property rights by constraining what can be done with properties. After all, the states collect property taxes which are supposed to be related to the market values of properties in a more or less consistent way, and these values are certainly affected by changes in the rules concerning what can be done with the properties.

Notes

1. This remark has been attributed to Prof. Robert Dorfman of Harvard University.

2. *See, for example*, the Modern Library edition of the Federalist Papers which includes an introduction by Prof. E. M. Earle; Alexander Hamilton, John Jay, and James Madison, The Federalist (New York: Random House, 1941).

3. One of the best collections in the Modern Library publication: E. A. Burtt (ed.), The English Philosophers from Bacon to Mill (New York: Random House, 1939).

4. Smith's book is still worth reading. See the Modern Library edition. Adam Smith, The Wealth of Nations (New York: Random House, 1937).

5. *See, for example*, Elie Halevy, The Growth of Philosophic Radicalism (London: Faber & Faber, Ltd., 1928).

6. See the summary discussion in chapter 8 of Samuelson's treatise: Paul A. Samuelson, Foundations of Economic Analysis (Cambridge, Ma.: Harvard University Press, 1947).

7. The theorem has been stated and proved in many forms and in many places. One of the more brilliant and not very technical summaries of this literature is given by Kenneth J. Arrow, "Political and Economic Evaluation of Social Effects and Externalities," which is chapter 1 of Michael D. Intriligator (ed.), Frontiers of Quantitative Economics (Amsterdam: Nath-Holland, 1971). *See also* the two comments on Arrow's paper by Otto A. Davis and Peter A. Diamond which appear in the same volume. *See also* the expository paper of Otto A. Davis and Morton I. Kamien, "Externalities, Information and Alternative Collective Action," which is chapter 3 of Robert A. Haveman and Julius Margolis (eds.), Public Expenditures and Policy Analysis (Chicago: Markham, 1970). Some parts of the discussion in this section are summarized from a similar section in the latter paper.

157

8. Robert M. Haig, *Toward an Understanding of the Metropolis: The Assignment of Activities to Areas in Urban Regions*, (pts. 1, 2) Q. J. Econ. 40 (1926): 179, 402. Reprinted with permission.

9. Allison Dunham, *City Planning: An Analysis of the Content of the Master Plan*, J. L. & Econ., 1 (1958): 170.

10. John P. Crecine, Otto A. Davis, and John E. Jackson, *Urban Property Markets: Some Empirical Results and Their Implications for Municipal Zoning*, J. L. & Econ., 10 (1967): 79. Frederich H. Rueter, *Externalities in Urban Property Markets: An Empirical Test of the Zoning Ordinance of Pittsburgh*, 14 J. L. & Econ., 313 (1973).

6

A Correlative Rights Approach to the Taking Issue

A. Dan Tarlock

Public regulation of land use choices to promote environmental quality threatens to strain to the breaking point the traditional distinction between noncompensable exercises of the police power and compensable expropriations pursuant to exercises of the right of eminent domain. A core principle of the environmental movement is that private choices must be subordinated to public choices.[1] Environmentalists argue that the social costs of private choice are too great because in the long run the most efficient use of many resources, which will be converted to more intensive uses under a system of private choice, is not to develop them or radically limit their development in the name of ecosystem stability and amenity enhancement. As the concept of environmental quality increasingly becomes broadly defined, it encompasses most of the major societal reasons for regulating private choice.[2] Environmentalists have thus correctly identified federal and state constitutional prohibitions against the taking of property as the major barrier to the implementation of an environmental land use policy.[3] The basic objective of this policy can be fairly characterized as the reduction of the amount of land available for commercial, industrial, and residential development. This is to be done by withdrawing land from development, by channeling growth into narrow corridors to preserve other undeveloped areas, or by limiting severely the allowable densities and use mixes of new developments.[4]

The justifications advanced for the regulation of land use choices for environmental reasons are not consistent with our traditions of private choice. When zoning was first proposed in the 1920s, it was thought that it would be necessary to strain the due process clause to its outer limits in order to sustain zoning.[5] Nonetheless, zoning was sustained by the Supreme Court in *Ambler Realty Co. v. Village of Euclid.*[6] The opinion is extremely ambiguous for it adopts at various times both narrow and broad justifications for the regulation of land use choice. If it is read carefully, however, the opinion grounds the exercise of the police power primarily on a community's need to prevent nuisances in advance of their occurrence.[7] This rationale, in contradistinction to the newer forms of environmental land use controls, is consistent with an individualistic model of private property.

In recent years it has become fashionable to criticize the narrow justification of land use controls because it does not give communities adequate authority to implement a wide variety of social and economic objectives. The Supreme Court's most recent statement on zoning provides some ground for believing that it has embraced an expansive view of the permissible extent of land use regulation.[8] Yet the question remains, Why should this be so?

Historically, land use controls have been used for two important, but ultimately modest, objectives. Uses that threaten to impose substantial costs on surrounding uses have been directed to areas where these costs will be minimized. A similar objective has been the protection of reasonable consumer expectations through subdivision regulation. Purchasers of a home in a subdivision, for example, can reasonably expect that their house and supporting facilities will perform satisfactorily. At a minimum utilities should be in place, drainage should be satisfactory, and streets should provide coordinated access to other parts of the city. Presumably individual purchasers could expressly bargain with the developer over these items, but because the development is often planned and built before a house is purchased, it has been thought proper for a city to regulate subdivision development to ensure fulfillment of these reasonable expectations.[9] Nuisance prevention and consumer protection can be defended on both efficiency and fairness grounds. They both involve situations where transaction costs prevent the organization of private bargaining units, and thus some form of collective intervention is desirable. It is also possible to approach subdivision regulation as a problem of unequal bargaining power between developer and purchaser as a result of the developer's superior information. But, information disclosure has not been required except in the case of interstate land sales. Nonetheless conventional subdivision regulation can still stand on efficiency grounds. Lifewise nuisance prevention can be defended on efficiency grounds although, as Siegan and others have shown, there is less need for zoning than has traditionally been thought, for the free market will produce roughly the same allocation as uses.

Still, as Ellickson has shown, the imposition of liability is often an efficient and fair assignment of property rights. The person who initiates a use which substantially interferes with the enjoyment of property rights claimed on the basis of prior occupation of an area by those wishing to be free from the interference is efficient because, at a minimum, the costs of an activity are placed on the person likely to know the extent of the losses his activity will impose on others, and who can most cheaply organize to prevent the losses.[10] Arguably, the imposition of liability of existing landowners with effective subsequent bargaining might be the most efficient solution, but protection of preexisting users has much to recommend it on efficiency grounds, and it accords with our utilitarian-based justifications of property—those who have invested resources are protected so that they will not be discouraged from subsequent investment. In short, the property rights assignment is fair because the injured property owner is made whole for the initiator of the activity's theft of preexisting property rights.[11]

This analysis is, of course, highly simplified and open to challenge. For example, the logic of the Coase theorem rejects the concept that one activity causes injury to another or steals a vested right. By this logic, the justification for allowing a prior user in an area to make an appropriation of the amenity level of the area so that subsequent entrants can be characterized as thieves is no longer valid. Nonetheless, these qualifications do not undermine wholly the argument that objectives of conventional land use controls are consistent with our tradition of individualistic theories of private property while the newer forms of environmental regulation are not.

Thoughtful exponents of an expanded state role in the promotion of environmental quality have been sensitive to this tension between old and new justifications for regualtion. They have attempted to justify the newer forms of regulation as modest, incremental extensions of previously sanctioned regulation. Environmental land use regulations are justified in the name of efficiency promotion. Externalities are alleged to be pervasive, and thus collective action is necessary—or so it is argued, using sophisticated concepts such as option demand—because the community does in fact value the land for less rather than more intensive uses. The reason these preferences are not recognized is because the organization of a market to register them is too costly. Closer to the truth, these justifications too often are used to justify government intervention which forces landowners to dedicate their land to the production of "goods" for society. Some forms of environmental regulations, of course, do seek to prevent imposition of bads on surrounding landowners. Drainage and erosion prevention regulations fall in this category. However, increasingly regulations which seek to preserve open space and the existing "character" of an area ask a landowner to restrain from profitable uses of land on the ground that the value society attributes to this use is greater than the value society would attribute to the more intense use that the landowner prefers.

Commentators have long been concerned about the drift toward public control of land use choice. They have realized that at the root of the question is the need for a line between permissible and impermissible state functions, but they have not been successful in drawing a line that courts and, more generally society, will accept. In short, the liberal welfare state must be justified. Early efforts to state a principle which would allow courts to distinguish between takings and valid exercises of the police power did so logically on the basis of the objective of the regulation. Dunham proposed a distinction between the government acting to prevent a landowner from harming surrounding landowners and the government compelling a landowner to maintain or initiate a use to benefit others others.[12] Compensation was required only in the later case. Building on this approach, Sax drew a distinction between the government acting to resolve conflicts between surrounding landowners and the government acting in an enterprise capacity to increase its resource base.[13] Defining property as only what is left after the government finishes arbitrating between surrounding landowners, he concluded that compensation should be restricted to instances where the government is acting in an enterprise capacity because only here is there a risk of arbitrary action which justified the need for countermajoritarian checks. As Michelman has shown, both the Dunham and Sax distinctions do not hold as long as efficiency is the claimed justification for the government action.[14] Nonetheless, these theories are important, for even though they do not define all the instances where compensation should be required, they suggest an efficiency-based justification for assigning property rights to the first person to claim them. In many cases compensation would be required in the same circumstances that Dunham and Sax require it. Moreover, as Ellickson has argued, such an assignment of property right corresponds to normal societal expectations; thus a consensus exists for collective intervention to enforce these claims when imperfections prevent their vindication by the market.

In Chapter 2 Johnson carries forward Hayek's powerful exposition of the costs of departing from a society based on principles of individualism protected through the rule of law in favor of one where development opportunities are based on planning.[15] I agree in principle with his thesis that the absence of a system of strong property rights increases the risk that collective choices undertaken in the name of efficiency will, in fact, turn out to be inefficient and have perverse redistributional effects. But, as a lawyer, I must conclude that his defense of property is ultimately not persuasive. Johnson starts from the orthodox welfare economics premise that in order for markets to exist and operate efficiently, there must be a method of pricing resources, and the recognition of private property provides the necessary means. This is only an argument that resource allocation choices should be based on information about the opportunity costs of a given allocation, however. There is no a priori reason why this information must be furnished through a private property system. It is true that the jurisprudential theories, flowing from Lord Coke and Blackstone, which underlie an individualistic conception of property also form the moral basis of welfare economics. Initially, however, it is useful to separate justifications based on the neoclassical economics and the natural law–natural rights theories of Coke and Blackstone which form the basis for the protection of private property under the Fifth Amendment.

The question Johnson poses to a lawyer is whether our legal system, and here I mean state and federal constitutions, requires resource allocation information to come through recognition of private property rights and that most allocations choices be made of a bargaining model, voluntary or coerced. As a lawyer, I would answer that the Constitution does impose constraints on the implementation of collective choices, but in more complicated and subtle ways than Johnson posits. Both he and the sources he justifiably attacks oversimplify complex constitutional issues to a degree that is unacceptable to thoughtful lawyers. Concepts of natural law and natural rights played an important part in the formation of the Constitution, but they no longer have the rigidity they once did. Planning Without Prices ignores too much twentieth-century jurisprudence to stand as a strong economic-legal defense of private property.

The major conclusion that I draw from Chapter 2 is that the problem of the initial assignment of property rights is one for lawyers alone. Economists have very little, if anything, to contribute to its solution. This is because the current property rights literature consists either of explanations of the functional utility of private property or, more recently, of explanations of how private property systems developed.[16] This scholarship is important and has been justifiably of great interest to lawyers. Unfortunately, the existing literature does not help us answer hard questions about property rights assignment because it is simply not concerned with the problems with which lawyers must deal.

The current tension between private property and government regulation arises out of need to assign property rights in common property resources that have not been previously seen as common. Land use controversies now center around questions of growth control or restriction. The issues are whether land should be developed at all, and if it should be, at what densities. Take two paradigm problems: (1) Ten overlying minicipalities share a common groundwater acquifer. Each pumps large amounts for fear that if they do not, others will. If pumping continues at the present rate, the pool will be exhausted before adequate alternative supplies are available. (2) A community decides that it has sustained enough growth and passes an ordinance which, in effect, either prohibits or drastically limits the number of residential units that can be constructed in the future.

The first problem is the standard common pool example. Welfare economics would argue that a state of common ownership should be replaced with the assignment of individual shares so withdrawals from the pool can be timed and then maximized. But why is not the second problem equally the standard common pool example? The existing residents have decided that the current amenity level of the area is being degraded too rapidly because it is currently in common ownership. To prevent further degradation, e.g., overuse, property rights are assigned to the existing residents. Both assignments find their justification, at least in theory, in the promotion of efficiency. However, I suspect that while most economists, including Johnson, would recommend the assignment of property rights in the first case, they would not recommend the assignment that I have proposed in the second. They simply have not adequately addressed themselves to the question of initial rights assignment. The Coase theorem tells us that under a very restrictive set of conditions the initial assignment is irrelevant to ultimate short- and long-run allocative efficiency. But the lawyer must work with the problem of transaction costs and with nonefficiency promotion constraints.[17] The modern case for the recognition of property rights is that the state should protect crystallized expectations because it is both fair and efficient to do so. Once protection of expectations becomes the basis of maintenance of a system of private property, the problem is to choose which of many competing expectations should be protected. Protection of expectations is a simple and powerful principle; but it is not a simple and powerful rule, unlike many axioms of welfare economics, that can be directly applied to solve specific resource use conflicts. Questions of prior notice that an expectation will not be recognized and priority of claim, to name two, become crucial, and these are variables that have never been analyzed by economists.

The balance of this chapter first traces the decline of natural law and natural rights theories and their displacement by the sociological theories of property which have laid the foundation for the assertion that private rights must be balanced against social interests. The chapter then suggests a tentative approach to the problem of the initial assignment of property rights.

Johnson's analysis can best be appreciated by an examination of the position that it contradicts. In 1971 the Council on Environmental Quality issued a report entitled "The Taking Issue: A Study of the Constitutional Limits of Governmental Authority to Regulate the Use of Privately-Owned Land without Paying Compensation."[18] This report crystalizes the twentieth-century position that assertions of private resource control must yield to state control. It is likely to influence greatly the thinking of contemporary lawyers, regulators, and courts. In the best traditions of American pragmatism, the report concludes that the "American fable or myth that a man can use his land any way he pleases regardless of his neighbors'' must be replaced by a functional doctrine which permits the state to sustain amenity-based regulations by submitting Brandeis briefs on the benefits of the regulation. The myth, the report argues, ''is inhibiting the sort of reasonable regulatory action that is needed to protect the environment *while respecting the position of individual landowners''* (italics mine). Specifically the authors recommend that Justice Holmes's opinion in *Pennsylvania Coal v. Mahon*[19] be overruled and that the Court revert to Justice Harlan's analysis in *Mugler v. Kansas Kansas*.[20] Holmes reasoned that there was no difference between a police power regulation and action which took a fee (or lesser interest) title and physically appropriated property. The difference, he concluded, between a valid and invalid regulation was only a matter of the degree of impact on the value of the property. The core of the rejection by *The Taking Issue* of Holmes's analysis is as follows:

Overruling the *Pennsylvania Coal* decision would not mean the end of judicial review. If the Brandeis proposition that regulation is different in kind from taking is accepted, the full panoply of due process protections remains, but the focus is shifted to the purpose and effect of the regulation, where the emphasis really belongs.

The Task Force on Land Use and Urban Growth recently considered taking issue at length and concluded that the Supreme Court should reexamine its precedents that focus on the diminution of property values affected by regulations and seek to balance public benefit against land value loss in every case. We are aware of the sensitivity of this matter, and of the important issues of civil liberty associated with ownership of property. But it is worth remembering that when U.S. constitutional doctrine on the taking issue was formulated during the late Nineteenth and early Twentieth Centuries, land was regarded as unlimited and its use not ordinarily of concern to society. Circumstances are different today. Now there is growing recognition of the need to see that urbanization proceeds in an orderly and non-destructive fashion and that our limited natural and cultural resources are conserved. It is time that the U.S. Supreme Court re-examine its earlier precedents that seem to require a balancing of public benefit against land value loss in every case and declare that when the protection of natural, cultural, or aesthetic resources or the assurance of orderly development are involved, a mere loss in land value will never be justification for invalidating the regulation of land use. Such a reexamination is particularly appropriate considering the consensus that is forming on the need for a national land-use policy. Although fifty years have passed, it is not too late to recognize that Justice Brandeis was right.

It has been fashionable to deprecate Harlan's ''simplistic'' approach in *Mugler,* but his theory is consistent with the intent of the founding fathers; when the government physically appropriated your property—that was a taking. A return to this simple and unsophisticated principle would go a long way toward upholding the type of environmental protection currently needed.[21]

The Taking Issue builds on a contemporaneous analysis by Sax of the University of Michigan. In *Takings, Private Property and Public Rights*[22] Sax argues, using an ingenious mix of resource allocation theory and ecology, that government intervention in the situations Johnson discusses is proper to protect and vindicate prior existing public rights. He does address the two problems Johnson and others see as crucial: (1) What protection does an individual have against majoritarian expropriation? and (2) How do we know that shifting resources from the private sector is efficient? However, his answers to these questions, which are reassuring to environmentalists, simply assume away the problems Chapter 2 raises:

Another problem raised by government action affecting property rights ... is the risk of excessive zeal. Simply stated, this is the problem of controlling the government's economic self-interest in resolving problems with the smallest possible outlay of tax funds. To the extent that government is vindicating extant public rights, as described above, its desire in general to avoid compensation is not problematic. The essence of a public rights, or public trust, approach to the question of takings, should make clear that the government *should* vindicate the rights of taxpayers as a group as well as the rights of individual property owners. The issue of excessive zeal thus becomes the question of how well a balance is struck between diffusely-held claims and traditional property interests. While the role of courts in scrutinizing that balance will be minor, the judiciary may intervene at the extremes to hold a resolution of competing claims to be so misguided as to be beyond the bounds of the police power.

As a practical matter, the problem is less troublesome than might at first appear. The "public interest," even if abstractly viewed as somehow being superior to "private interests," will not routinely prevail over traditional private rights. There will be political checks on the decision-making process employed to resolve conflicting claims on the common resource base. In many cases there will be substantial numbers on both sides of an issue, demanding a principled determination from the decision-making body. An industrial interest which stands to lose from a particular property restriction will doubtless make its views known at least as clearly as those asserting diffuse claims. Given that diffuse claims are likely to be the novel and formerly unrepresented ones, and that those with a concentrated interest at stake can be expected to make their views known, it is not unreasonable to leave conflict resolution to the legislature.

It is always possible for a property owner to claim that a legislative benefit analysis is wrong, but because such decisions inevitably involve substantial elements of legislative judgment and value preference, this hardly seems an appropriate area for constitutional decision-making. It would involve courts in a reexamination of legislative social welfare choices. Judicial intervention of this kind, therefore, ought to be limited to those cases in which the court is satisfied that the legislative determination is sufficiently distorted as to constitute an abuse of the police power; that the legislature has subordinated a judgment about maximization of social benefits to advancement of private gain.[23]

The conclusions of *The Taking Issue* and Sax are the logical product of twentieth-century jurisprudence. The idea that property was based on natural rights or natural law has been replaced with the principles that private choice must be subordinated to the needs of society, and society has interests apart from those of the individuals affected by regulation. The evolution of the idea that the interests of society, if strong enough, could outweigh substantial losses by individual property claimants was a long process, but two central figures stand out. They are Roscoe Pound, Dean of the Harvard Law School, and Francis Philbrick, of the University of Pennsylvania. Dean Pound, ever a cautious scholar, nonetheless, pioneered the idea of sociological jurisprudence. He carefully traced the origins of modern notions of property and placed them in their historical context. He did this to criticize judicial decisions involving substantive due process to prevent legislative innovation, and in the process he did much to undermine conventional justifications for property. For example, he drew from then recent judicial decisions tempering the law of capture applied to natural resources with notions of correlative rights to show the gradual adaptation of the law to what he considered the demands of modern society: "More and more the tendency is to hold that what the law should secure is satisfaction of the owner's reasonable wants with respect to the property—that those that are consistent with the like wants of his neighbor and the *interests of society*" (italics mine).[24] Pound never disregarded the positive contributions of the eighteenth and ninteenth centuries, but many influential students of Pound came to minimize them. When the New Deal brought the assaults on these precepts to a head, students of property urged a return to feudal notions of property which, despite the Magna Charta, were based on the notion that property was owned by the sovereign and each person held property not as a matter of right but because of the fulfillment of duties to the crown. It was argued that we gave up too much when we replaced the feudal system with concepts of individualism. Philbrick's influential article "Changing Conception in Property Law" expanded Pound's analysis and laid much of the intellectual foundation for the idea that the recognition of claims of property is a function of their consistency with overriding state objectives. "[I]n the case of feudalism," he wrote, "it is regrettable that there could not have been preserved the idea that all property was held subject to the performance of duties—not a few of them public."[25]

A pervasive concept in modern jurisprudence is that conflicts can be solved by laying out the relevant interests on each side and then balancing them to see which is heavier. Lawyers have always wondered how this can be done except by starting with a preference for one result. The lesson of welfare economics, as developed by Johnson, is that the idea of balancing should be replaced by the principle that the interest of society means nothing more than the sum of the interests of the winners and losers of any collective action. From this premise it can be argued that the risk of arbitrariness inherent in planning by bureaucracies suggests that the burden on an aggrieved landowner is to show that government action is arbitrary. A few courts are shifting the burden of justification, but the presumption of validity still has great force. As I said earlier, the argument developed by Johnson is ultimately not an argument for recognition of private property; it is only an argument for more accurate social accounting of some kind. Although private property can be strongly defended on efficiency grounds, the strongest argument for it is the nonefficiency argument that the recognition of private property claims is fair, as Johnson seems to concede in the latter part of Chapter 2. Recognition is fair, theories of natural law aside, because the government has induced patterns of investment based on the expectation that the investment will be protected against expropriations. Subsequent expropriations negate the very essence of the rule of law, for decisions are made not on rules announced in advance but on post hoc rationalizations.[26]

If the recognition of property rights is based on the protection of expectations, the question becomes, Which expectations? The lawyer is likely to answer those which are reasonable, but more precise criteria are needed to differentiate between protected and nonprotected expectations. Deciding what expectations should be protected when property rights must be assigned in "new" common property resources is difficult. Simple theories of prior appropriation as a basis for claim recognition are inadequate because strong counterexpectations exist. One starting point is to posit the situations where it is fair not to reward a landholder with the full ability to implement a land use choice because he is on notice that competing expectations will be recognized. The development of the common law teaches that the most difficult problems of property rights assignment are those in which there will be competing claims to the same resource, and thus the initial assignment must contain some clear restrictions on the right to initiate use. The Anglo-American law of property has evolved from the English writs which protected the possession of land against competing claimants. After security of possession was established, the law turned to the problem of defining property rights claims in terms of use. The common law of property has been quite innovative (a fact that is insufficiently appreciated by many modern lawyers) in assigning property rights in situations where two or more users make competing use demands. It has sought to assign rights so that the maximum number of users can make an efficient use of the property. For example, the law of lateral and subjacent support recognizes that a person has a right to exploit property as long as the natural pressure on surrounding land is maintained. This is an early example of the assignment of rights to promote correlative rights among competing users. To push this analysis forward, the distinction between intervention to assignment property rights consistent with the recognition of correlative rights, and the assignment of property rights to benefit more diffuse classes of society is, in my opinion, the basis for the distinction between compensable and noncompensable public regulation.

Combining Johnson's argument that efficiency calculations require compensation to established property rights in order for the opportunity costs of social choices to be determined with an expectation-based rationale[27] would reverse the recent trend of analysis exemplified by *The Taking Issue* and Sax's article. To conclude with an easy example, a prime case for reversal is *Just v. Marinette County*.[28] Wisconsin prohibits shoreland fills and the Justs, filled wetlands within 1000 feet above the normal high-water mark of a lake (a long established line demarcating private and public rights with respect to navigable waters). The county successfully required the removal of the fill. In holding that there was no taking, the court was candid that the citizens of Wisconsin were beginning to appreciate "that swamps and wetlands serve a vital role in nature, are part of the balance of nature and are essential to the purity of water in our lakes and streams." On this basis it concluded:

The Justs argue their property has been severely depreciated in value. But this depreciation of value is not based on the use of the land in its natural state but on what the land would be worth if it could be filled and used for the location of a dwelling. While loss of value is to be considered in determining whether a restriction is a constructive taking, value based upon changing the character of the land at the expense of harm to public rights is not an essential factor or controlling.

We are not unmindful of the warning in Pennsylvania Coal Co. v. Mahon (1922), 260 U.S. 393, 416, 43 S. Ct. 158, 160, 67 L.Ed. 322: "... We are in danger of forgetting that a strong public desire to improve the public condition is not enough to warrant achieving the desire by a shorter cut than the constitutional way of paying for the change."

This observation refers to the improvement of the public condition, the securing of a benefit not presently enjoyed and to which the public is not entitled. The shoreland zoning ordinance preserves nature, the environment, and natural resources as they were created and to which the people have a present right. The ordinance does not create or improve the public condition but only preserves nature from the despoilage and harm resulting from the unrestricted activities of humans.

Just seems a clear case of sacrificing one individual for a community gain by, as Johnson demonstrates, a flawed process. The result can be justified as an extension of the traditional correlative rights justification for restricting one person to allow others to benefit equally from a resource. The public simply steps into the shoes of surrounding landowners. This analogy, however, stretches the logic of correlative rights too far. The recognition of public rights is a post hoc conclusion which masks a substantial redistribution decision. However, many types of land use regulation which are alleged to be an interference with property present harder cases. Ellickson has applied an expectation-based theory to protect prior residents against the subsequent entry of nonpreferred uses. His basic argument is that prior users in an area can appropriate the amenity level of an area so that subsequent and nonconforming uses violate previously established correlative rights. This theory works in developed areas but not in less-developed areas. Theories which justify the collective establishment of correlative rights in less-developed areas (the battleground of environmental rights) are needed. Only after this is done will we begin to have a valid basis to distinguish between compensable and noncompensable regulation.

Notes

1. *See* Meyers, *An Introduction to Environmental Thought: Some Sources and Some Criticisms,* 50 Ind. L.J. 426, 451 (1975).

2. This view is being increasingly challenged. For an argument that provision of adequate housing opportunities should be the most important land use objective, *see* B. H. Siegan, *Controlling Other People's Property through Covenants, Zoning, State and Federal Regulation,* 5 Envt'l. L. 385 (1975). Siegan persuasively argues that less land use regulation will provide more housing and conserve land for other necessary uses such as the production of food by allowing the market to operate to mass densities. In recent years low-density zoning increasingly has been challenged as exclusionary, but few courts have perceived that any regulation will increase the cost of land development. The cause of decreased housing opportunities, to the extent that regulatory barriers are a causal factor, is regulation per se, not simply low-density zoning. However, the New Jersey Supreme Court's extraordinary decision in South Burlington County N.A.A.C.P. v. Township of Mt. Laurel, 67 N.J. 151, 336 A.2d 713 (1975), which imposes an affirmative obligation on local communities to accommodate a fair share of the regional demand for low- and moderate-income housing, comes close to holding that this duty can only be implemented by cutting back the permissible extent of land use regulation to nuisance prevention.

3. Caldwell, *Rights of Ownership or Rights of Use?—The Need for a New Conceptual Basis for Land Use Policy,* 15 W. & Mary L. Rev. 759 (1974), proposes that "rights of land ownership" be replaced with socially conferred "rights of use." Large, *This Land Is Whose Land: Changing Concepts of Land as Property,* 1973 Wis. L. Rev. 1039 arrives at the same conclusion following the ecologist Aldo Leopold's argument that an individual should only hold land as a trustee for future generations. *See also* Donaldson, *Regulation of Conduct in Relation to Land—The Need to Purge Natural Law Constraints from the Fourteenth Amendment,* 16 W. & Mary L. Rev. 187 (1974). Only Caldwell addresses himself to the information problems raised by Johnson when public planning is substi-

tuted for a decentralized system of property rights. He argues that "[U]se of Citizen boards of review and open planning sessions, as well as provision for input from science and the design arts, could result in more socially and ecologically responsible land use decisions than might be expected under existing technicalities of land use law." Caldwell *supra* at 773.

4. *See* Randall W. Scott (ed.) Management and Control of Growth, 3 vols, (Washington: Urban Land Institute, 1975), for a comprehensive collection of papers on the issue.

5. *See* S. Toll, Zoned American (New York: Grossman Publishers, 1969).

6. 272 U.S. 365 (1926).

7. Justice Sutherland started from the principle that in resolving questions of the limits of the police power "the maxim *sic utere tuo ut a lienum non laedes,* which lies at the foundation of so much of the common law of nuisances, ordinarily will furnish a fairly helpful clew." Later in the opinion the segregation of apartment houses from single-family residences as well as duplexes was sustained because multiple-family dwellings "come very near to being nuisances." This analysis adopts, at least in part, the argument of Alfred Bettman in the amicus brief that the police power gives cities broad authority to apply planning expertise to promote the general welfare.

8. Village of Bette Terre v. Boraas, 416 U.S. 1 (1973). *Boraas* upheld the power of a city to define family as four or more unrelated individuals, and thus bar a group of five students from living in a rented house in a single-family zone. Justice Douglas wrote expansively about the power of a city to create a quiet and homogeneous community, but the facts are so narrow that it is difficult to determine what its long-term impact will be. However, the ninth circuit upheld the Petaluma growth restriction plan on the basis of *Boraas*. Construction Industry v. Petaluma, 522 F.2d 897 (9th Cir. 1975).

9. *See* R. Yearwood, Land Subdivision Regulation: Policy and Legal Considerations for Urban Planning (New York: Praeger Publishers, 1971), pp. 60–61.

10. Ellickson, *Alternatives to Zoning: Covenants, Nuisance Rules, and Fines and Land Use Controls,* 40 U. Chi. L. Rev. 681 (1973).

11. Michelman, *Property, Utility and Fairness: Comments on the Ethical Foundations of Just Compensation Law,* 80 Harv. L. Rev. 1165 (1967).

12. Dunham, *A Legal and Economic Basis for City Planning,* 58 Colum. L. Rev. 650 (1958).

13. Sax, *Takings and the Police Power,* 74 Yale L.J. 36 (1964).

14. Michelman, *supra.* Note 11 at 1199–1201.

15. F. Hayek, The Road to Serfdom (Chicago: University of Chicago Press, 1944).

16. *See* Alchain and Demsetz, *The Property Rights Paradigm,* 33 J. Econ. Hist. 16 (1973) and Anderson and Hill, *The Evolution of Property Rights: A Study of the American West,* 18 J. L. & Econ. 163 (1975).

17. Most economic and legal scholarship stemming from Coase's seminal article, *The Problem of Social Cost,* 3 J. L. & Econ. 1 (1960), has been logically concerned with the problem of minimizing the adverse impact of one use on another. The search is for rules of property rights assignment which will induce the most efficient form of behavior modification. The best analysis is Calabresi and Malamed, *Property Rules, Liability Rules, and Inalienability: One View of the Cathedral,* 85 Harv. L. Rev. 1089 (1972). This analysis is of limited utility for the problems addressed in Planning Without Prices because government regulations of land use choices, unlike classic pollution problems, is not concerned with inducing behavior modification on the part of a property holder. The behavior modification desired is on the part of the state, and this requires the application of consistent rules of property rights assignments. Bargaining with the state is confined to those with political and economic influence. It is doubtful that we wish to legitimate postassignment bargaining as a means of achieving resource use efficiency.

18. F. Bosselman, et al., *The Taking Issue* (Washington: Government Printing Office, 1973).

19. 360 U.S. 393 (1922).

20. 123 U.S. 623 (1887).

21. The Taking Issue at 253 and 255.

22. 81 Yale L.J. 149 (1971).

23. *Id.* at 171 and 176. Reprinted by permission of The Yale Law Journal Company and Fred B. Rothman Company.

24. R. Pound, The Spirit of the Common Law (Francestown, N.H.: Marshall Jones, 1921), p. 186. *See also* R. Pound, An Introduction to the Philosophy of Law (New Haven: Yale University Press, 1922). In recent years it has been fashionable to reject much of Pound's analysis, which was based on an organic view of society, on the grounds that his vision was too static. *See* D. Wigdor, Roscoe Pound, (Westport, Conn: Greenwood Press, 1974). Perhaps the 1970s is a good time to reevaluate this criticism.

25. Philbrick, *Changing Conceptions of Property Law,* 86 Pa. L. Rev. 691, 708 (1938). Philbrick's ideas were a synthesis of the late nineteenth- and early twentieth-century reaction to the Maschaster school of liberal, laissez-faire economics. The modern, as opposed to medieval, idea that private property is a sociolegal institution and thus is simply a historic concept which must evolve in response to changed social conditions can

be traced to the nineteenth-century German political economists who influenced the founders of the modern school of public interest regulation such as Richard T. Ely. *See* G. Deitz, In Defense of Property 93–127 (Baltimore, Md.: Johns Hopkins Press (1963) for a brief discussion of the evolution of this idea from nineteenth-century Germany to the New Deal.

26. *See* Justice Stewart's concurring opinion in Hughes v. State of Washington, 389 U.S. 290 (1967).

27. This theory is sketched in Berger, *A Policy Analysis of the Taking Problem,* 49 N.Y.U. L. Rev. 165 (1974).

28. 56 Wis.2d 7, 201 N.W.2d 761 (1972).

7

Response to the Discussants of "Planning Without Prices"

M. Bruce Johnson

Anderson and I are in broad agreement on matters of substance if not emphasis. Certainly we concur that the phrase *public interest* is vacuous as it is commonly used. If, as alleged, I misused the term myself, my fall from consistency would be detected only by an observer with antennae as sensitive as Anderson's.

The three proposed contemporary justifications for regulation (i.e., redistribution, monopolies, and spillovers) were not meant to preclude consideration of a more fundamental force, the special-interest group. Probing still further, one might postulate that special-interest groups are motivated by their desires to redistribute income and wealth from others to themselves. The expected rewards of such an activity obviously have increased apace with the expansion of government regulation.

I also agree with Anderson's statement (in Chapter 3) that special-interest groups now enjoying special legislative privileges will be unlikely to renounce their interests once the economics of the situation is clarified for them. For example, airline executives no doubt understand well the implications of current deregulation proposals; yet they champion the cause of the CAB, and they caution against deregulation with ominous forecasts of chaos, confusion, and deteriorated service.

But, if the beneficiaries of special government favors are fully aware of the consequences of such legislation and regulation, what is the purpose of Anderson's proposal for social impact statements? These studies would be at least as costly as the environmental impact statements now frequently required. In addition, my own professional experience as a participant author of environmental impact studies has convinced me that the information provided therein—however scientific and sophisticated—is largely ignored in the political decision-making process that now governs land use decisions. At best, social impact statements would serve as devices that could neutralize the excessive zeal of environmentalists. At worst, additional impact statement requirements would force the economic system to a point still further inside the production possibility curve as more and more resources were dissipated in negotiation costs.

Several specific criticisms by Anderson deserve at least a brief response for clarification. Perhaps I did not express myself clearly enough when I stated that "... the purpose of regulation (under the noxious use approach) is to eliminate all harmful private activities. That goal is neither realistic nor desirable." Anderson asks, "Why is it not desirable to have as a goal elimination of all harmful private activities?" My reply: by common definition, all private activities—production and consumption—generate good as well as bad. Single-minded elimination of all harmful effects eliminates the benefits as well. Under widely accepted criteria, regulation of harmful activities should proceed to the point where marginal benefits and harms are equalized—not necessarily to the point of zero harm.

Anderson suggests there is widespread and growing agreement as to what government should do on the compensation question. Perhaps he is overly optimistic. The crucial issue is what government does and is threatening to do in the area of land use regulation. Hence, I support Anderson's closing statement that a valid solution to the taking issue "is one that is based on individual property rights and that uses the judicial system to protect those rights."

Hagman offers a fivefold commentary on Chapter 2, and, in turn, I respond to his five propositions as follows: no, maybe, yes, no, and nonsense!

Hagman's first proposition (Chapter 4) is that land use regulation may be too harsh and unsystematic because there are too many government agencies, not because there is too much government regulation. This interpretation has considerable precedent in historical discussions of regulation. Confronted with a long, almost unbroken sequence of failures for regulation, the optimists see the remedy as better regulation and better regulators. Unfortunately for this view, the evidence produced by students of regulation over the past several decades suggests that while better regulation is the goal, more regulation is the achievement in virtually every case.

There is an opposing interpretation of the regulatory bramble within which we find ourselves; it can be argued that the economy is able to function as well as it does only because the regulation by various government bureaus is unsystematic, uncoordinated, and full of loopholes. Hagman's proposal to rationalize all regulation under a single, efficient, monopoly agency is a very frightening prospect. Hagman places his trust in the governor and the state legislature, but not all of us are willing to join him. In sum, there is a strong argument against too much government rather than against too many special-purpose governments. If the latter have different rules or enforce them differently, individuals have some freedom of choice; indeed, there may be a semblence of competition among the governments.

In his second response, Hagman deals with the issue of common property and suggests that private contracts or deed covenants can be used to internalize externalities in lieu of government action. So far, so good, as we recall the important work of Siegan. However, the suggestion that such arrangements can be generalized from a condominium association to towns and cities requires more discussion than time and space permit. Instead, let me address Hagman's assertion that the evils of town governments are remote because local government is general-purpose and is thought of as "we the people" rather than "the government." Heroic theory aside, the evidence can be interpreted otherwise. As mighty and impersonal as the federal government is, it rarely contrives to damage an individual as opposed to depersonalized members of a broadly defined class. Local government, on the other hand, is precisely the unit that downzones an individual's land, bans boats or campers in the driveway, prohibits the sublet of rooms, threatens to regulate garage sales, institutes rent controls, posts the streets against parking, and declares moratoria on residential construction. Contrary to Hagman's assertion that local, general-purpose government reduces transactions costs (relative to which base case he does not say), I suggest they serve to assign the major burden of those costs on particular minorities—an example of which he has convincingly described in his discussion of the exclusionary effects of zoning in his later remarks.

Compensable regulation, Hagman's third response, is the central issue of this book. Details aside, there is much on which we can agree because the issues have been sharpened by his remarks. Yet, I puzzle over the interpretation Hagman places on a taking versus a regulation, even as I defer to his expertise in law and legal history. It is as if each case to be considered had to be assigned to one of two exclusive categories: either a regulation that required no compensation or a taking that required full compensation. It is difficult for an economist to imagine that a third alternative—compensable regulation—has not been considered and adopted. The central theme of Chapter 2 was not that regulation should be invalidated but rather that regulating agencies should pay compensation for reasons quite incidental to the law—reasons related to economic incentives, information, and optimal resource allocation. If that is "compensable regulation," we agree.

However, I strongly disagree with Hagman's assertions that wipeouts are exactly offset by windfalls, that regulation merely shifts demand from one site to another without adding cost to the system. The Uthwatt Report (1942) quoted by Hagman includes the following statement: ". . . wisely imposed planning control does not diminish the total sum of land value, but merely redistributes them by increasing the value of some land and decreasing the value of other land." Are we thus to conclude that the validity of the theorem depends on the adverb *wisely*? How does one define a wisely imposed planning control? If one observed an aggregate decrease in land values, would one conclude that the planning control had been unwise? How can the circularity be avoided? Unfortunately, the

Uthwatt Report does not address this question, nor does it present empirical evidence to support its assertions.

Land use markets generate land use patterns that are far from arbitrary allocations; market forces tend to direct resources to their wealth-maximizing uses. The imposition of land use controls—however wise—directs or forces development to second-best (or worse) locations. Otherwise, why were the alternative sites not chosen voluntarily in the first place? But this is academic; in an increasing number of American communities, development is directed out of existence rather than to alternative sites.

Hagman's comments on the poverty issue are confusing and, at the same time, quite personal. He confesses a lexical ordering: "providing them [the poor] with more property must be our first concern." That is as clear a normative statement as I have ever confronted in a discussion motivated by positive analysis. Clearly, there are better ways to assist the poor than through land use controls. Indeed, Hagman argues persuasively that past land use control has hurt—not helped—the poor. He also stipulates that the environmentalists' proposals do not serve the poor well. Such was my point in Chapter 2.

Davis's summary and elaboration (Chapter 5) of one of the themes of Chapter 2—the concentration of benefits and diffusion of costs in our political democracy—suggest that the theory may be at odds with the facts of the taking issue:

If the above argument about the excesses of democracy is correct, then one would confidently predict that all efforts to enact the law redefining and restricting property rights would easily be defeated. Yet, at least some observers predict that such a law will be enacted within the next few years.

But the "capture theory," of which the current application is a special case, relies more on the intensity of a stable, concentrated financial interest than it does on numbers in the respective groups. To repeat, unlike the permanent, concentrated interest of special producer groups (physicians, lawyers, plumbers, barbers) versus the diffuse interests of the taxpayer-consumer, membership in the group of owners of undeveloped property is transitory in the main. Thus, the property owner can be characterized as a free rider relative to the private property system; the personal costs of fighting for the retention of private property and free, competitive markets in undeveloped land are, under reasonable expectations, greater than the expected personal benefits. Even larger landowners will direct their efforts to narrow, practical concerns peculiar to their own holdings. No one has the economic incentive to lobby for free markets in land per se.

Perhaps because our system does not have a permanent, professionally licensed and disciplined group of developers, the wealth-maximization hypothesis of special-interest political behavior does not predict well in the land use case. The relative ease of entry (and exit) in the industry—desirable characteristics we associate with an effectively competitive industry—makes organization and lobbying prohibitively expensive for property owners. Thus, necessary conditions for the validation of the special-interest capture theory are absent.

Moreover, it is patently obvious that membership in the anti-private property rights group has swelled because of the failure of most to appreciate either the manner in which a market system works or that the group will indirectly, itself, pay some of the costs of environmental goods via higher prices. Note again: environmental enhancement is widely advertised as free or virtually free. If any costs are involved, the popular suggestion is that they come out of the profits of the developer.

If Hagman, an active participant in the field, believes land use regulation has no opportunity costs, how sophisticated can we expect the average citizen to be? Typically, this citizen holds no undeveloped land and believes regulation has no cost—at least to him personally. Thus, he sees personal benefits—open space and perhaps a capital gain on his own home—but no costs. Unfortunately, the majority of citizens are uninterested in the efficiency issues of the problem; the popular concern is over equity alone: should a relative few lose their property via regulation? The answer seems to be yes. Hence, I have argued that legally mandated compensation for land use regulation is the only practical way to reintroduce efficiency in the dynamics of the political economy process.

Davis's discussion of the availability of information in real estate markets is a very useful addition to these proceedings. I have no quarrel with either his line of attack or his conclusions. Indeed, these remarks prompt me to pose related questions: What can we say about the information availability and information requirements of efficient land use allocation under central authority? Davis summarized the issue well for a market system:

Producers are assumed to have knowledge of available technology, and consumers are supposed to know whether particular goods and services are available, as well as their characteristics. Both producers and consumers are presumed to know the relevant set of prices.

If this necessary condition for efficiency is, in the main, satisfied by contemporary real estate markets, will it necessarily be satisfied when those markets are replaced by the central authority of the government? Surely those independent but interrelated agents who now have economic incentive to generate and exchange the appropriate information on real estate will no longer have the incentive to do so under land use allocation by central authority. I have argued in Chapter 2—perhaps at excessive length—that the central authority has no incentive to generate this information. Unless the central authority is constrained to pay for the resources it appropriates and directs, it will have no incentive to generate or use this information.

The danger, of course, is that the central authority will, in the absence of the pertinent information discussed above, substitute its own preferences for those of the consumers it is alleged to represent. Therein lies the issue: without the information generated by the decentralized market mechanism, the disposition of land to alternative uses (or nonuses) corresponds to the subjective preferences of the planners rather than those of the participants in the market.

Davis concludes this point by noting, "Informational problems do not appear to be the reason for the regulation of the market." To that I would add a corollary: regulation of the market appears to be the reason for increasingly serious informational problems.

Also I would like to comment on the view that zoning and land use planning are cures for interdependencies. As Davis reported, the diversity of taste among consumers appears to have minimized the interdependencies through a competitive self-selection process. Yet, zoning and land use planning persist and expand. It is possible, of course, that such zoning and planning constraints are not really binding at all but are promulgated by the land use planning bureaucracy, itself an entrenched and powerful special-interest group. Controls may impede or delay the operation of economic forces in land use markets but may not, given variances and political pressures, affect the outcome except to the extent that society has experienced a dead-weight loss in time and resources.

But beyond this point, I would speculate that property owners do sort themselves out among alternative mixes of interdependencies as they search for and purchase appropriate parcels of land. However, once the choice is made, there appears to be a strong economic incentive to preserve the status quo in existence at the time of purchase. A parcel of land is a capital asset, and its current market price reflects expectations as to future values. Hence, the incentive to protect—and enhance—one's own property values by controlling, through the political process, other peoples' properties. The research on interdependencies that Davis cites may be correct; the externalities may be empirically trivial. But will they remain empirically trivial if regulation without compensation replaces the market process?

Tarlock's provocative comments (Chapter 6) highlight the fundamental differences in the approach of the lawyer and the economist. Judicial procedure seems to generate marginal changes based on Brandeis briefs, special cases, and ad hoc interpretations. Economic analysis, on the other hand, follows from the search for abstract, theoretical principles at the expense of empirical relevance and detail for day-to-day and case-by-case applications.

For example, the argument that regulation is justified because it "protects reasonable consumer expectations" is hardly persuasive; without principles that define the reasonableness and, indeed, the expectations themselves, the approach is surely arbitrary and empty in the sense that the outcome of a given dispute cannot be forecast reliably.

Tarlock's distinction between traditional land use regulation (which he says is consistent with notions of private property) and the new environmentally motivated regulation (which he says is not) is puzzling. Referring to the former case, he says:

Nuisance prevention and consumer protection can be defended on both efficiency and fairness grounds. They both involve situations where transaction costs prevent the organization of private bargaining units, and, thus, some form of collective intervention is desirable. It is also possible to approach subdivision regulation as a problem of unequal bargaining power between developer and purchaser as a result of the developer's superior information.

First, like most economists, I must plead that a precise definition of the fairness eludes me. Hence, I defer to the expertise of the lawyer-philosopher on criteria for defining and judging fairness. But it does not seem to be entirely accurate to assert that transaction costs prevent the organization of private bargaining units. More precisely, transaction costs—when high—discourage the organization of such coalitions. This raises the issue of the extent to which high transaction costs are endemic to the legal structure as opposed to the technological environment. Surely recent developments in the law have raised the relative costs of organizing private bargaining units. Thus, increased collective action, allegedly justified by high transaction costs, itself leads to still higher transaction costs and less private bargaining activity.

Tarlock's alternative justification of regulation—unequal bargaining power—has little to recommend it. To be analytically useful, a concept must be defined formally in order to have testable, empirical implications. Before one can pronounce the bargaining power to be unequal between developer and purchaser, one must specify the relevant dimensions of bargaining power. Presumably Tarlock does not define income or wealth as the relevant dimension of bargaining power since, in the absence of an equal distribution of income and wealth, all private transactions would qualify for collective regulation and determination. From the context of his remarks, I assume bargaining power refers to access to or possession of information. But this notion is equally useless; in order to recognize unequal bargaining power, one must establish a norm of equal bargaining power as a reference. Suppose it is agreed that equal bargaining power between buyer and seller exists if and only if both parties have possession of exactly the same type and amount of information. Under this interpretation, the purchaser of an automobile has unequal bargaining power unless he possesses (and, presumably, understands) every bit of data pertaining to the engineering specifications and characteristics of the automobile—the chemical properties of the plastics of the horn button, the friction coefficients of the tires, the heat transfer characteristics of the radiator, the molecular composition of the drive shaft, and so on. Obviously, most of the information possessed by the producer is irrelevant to the deliberation and decision of the purchaser. To change the example slightly, the average consumer seems to be able to operate an automobile without intimate knowledge of the principles of the internal combustion engine, the carburetor, or the transmission. Since the consumer finds information costly to process and since consumers have different tastes for information, the quest for a definition of equal information (equal bargaining power) is not fruitful.

The notion that reasonable expectations of existing property owners should be protected via regulation is a static concept that suffers from the usual faults of that approach. Tarlock says: "... protection of preexisting users has much to recommend it on efficiency grounds, and it accords with our utilitarian-based justifications of property; those who have invested resources are protected so that they will not be discouraged from subsequent investment." Consider the incentive structure that this schema promotes: if it is known that the investment of a first-in-time or preexisting user will be protected against the vicissitudes of the market, individuals will have the incentive to be first in line to establish their "property rights." Thus, the legal structure will promote a rush to development in order to establish property rights before the land use patterns are frozen. One might question whether this is consistent with the antidevelopment objectives of those proposing the schema.

Dynamic considerations are relevant as well. How will any system that freezes land use patterns by way of guaranteeing the expectations of preexisting users respond to changes in taste and technology? The opportunity costs of the old "justification" for regulation are real, and they may be very high. Perhaps the magnitude of these costs will be appreciated when the preexisting users discover that their expectations for reasonable environmental amenities and reasonable housing costs are inconsistent.

Tarlock also suggests that the initial assignment of property rights is the crucial issue and one to which economists have little to contribute. To the extent that the assignment of initial rights must meet some Kantian ideal, economists and lawyers alike must defer to the philosophers. Economic analyses of property rights do employ a positive rather than a normative approach, and correctly so. To repeat a main theme of Chapter 2, prices reflect opportunity costs in any society, and the configuration of prices is determined by the property rights system used. I did not argue that private property is a necessary condition for efficient resource allocation, although I conjecture it is a sufficient condition. Rather, I challenge the opponents of private property to reveal the collective choice model that will indicate how information pertaining to prices, opportunity costs, consumer taste, and technology will be generated in the regime they propose. Indeed, there may be no a priori reason why this information must be furnished through a private property system; but we do have an established and persuasive paradigm indicating that much, if not all, of the information will appear in a market system. The challenge to the collectivists is: What incentives exist to generate and use the relevant information under a system of central decision making? Whether my model of the economic incentive structure in a bureaucracy is correct or not, the fundamental challenge to the collectivists is not answered by a retreat to empty rhetorical statements about the public interest, community need, or pressing social problems.

Tarlock mentions two common pool problems and suggests that economists would recommend the assignment of property rights in the first but not in the second example. He describes the second case as follows: "The existing residents have decided that the current amenity level of the area is being degraded too rapidly because it is currently in common ownership. To prevent further degradation, e.g. overuse, property rights are assigned to the existing residents." Several comments are in order. It would appear that the so-called assignment of property rights would violate the reasonable expectations of preexisting users to the extent that preexisting owners of undeveloped land in the community now have their reasonable expectations for development denied. Surely owners of undeveloped land need not construct an improvement in order to qualify for legal protection. Furthermore, the assignment to (read expropriation by) the existing residents will serve efficiency no more than the assignment of said rights to prospective residents of the community. The constituencies involved in antidevelopment legislation for local communities are always narrowly defined. Competing claims among the narrowly defined constituency will also pose problems that belie the unanimity implied by the use of the phrase *community desires*. The *Just* case is an outstanding example. Were not the reasonable expectations of the Justs overridden by the state and the court?

The decision in *Just v. Marinette County* is innocent of economic analysis. The court obviously confused the value of all swamps and wetlands with the value of preserving or developing a particular parcel at the margin. The court's assertion that the value of property should be based on the use of land in its natural state is almost comical. The decision underscores the extreme rigidity inherent in the status quo, reasonable-expectation interpretation. The court apparently has no appreciation for the opportunity costs of the resources frozen under this approach. The case serves well as an example of the distorted incentives under which public authorities operate when they plan without prices.

Indexes

Name Index

Subject Index

About the Contributors

Martin Anderson, economist, is Senior Fellow at the Hoover Institution on War, Revolution and Peace (Stanford University) in California. He has been a research fellow at the Joint Center for Urban Studies at The Massachusetts Institute of Technology and Harvard University and taught at Columbia University. He received the Ph.D. from M.I.T. Dr. Anderson has served as adviser to the President of the United States and been a member of many government and private commissions.

Otto A. Davis is dean and professor of political economy at the School of Urban and Public Affairs, Carnegie-Mellon University, Pittsburgh. He was formerly associate dean and previously was on the faculty of the Graduate School of Industrial Administration of Carnegie-Mellon. He obtained his undergraduate degree at Wofford College and earned the M.A. and Ph.D. in economics at the University of Virginia. Dr. Davis served as president of the Public Choice Society from 1970 to 1972.

Donald G. Hagman, professor of law at U.C.L.A., teaches, lectures and writes about planning, environmental, local government and state and local tax law. His books include a law school casebook and a hornbook. He has designed and coordinated several research projects including HUD financed "Windfalls and Wipeouts", and serves on various local governmental committees and real estate publication boards.

M. Bruce Johnson is research professor of economics and associate director for research at the Law and Economics Center, University of Miami School of Law and has taught economics at the University of Washington, U.C. Santa Barbara and U.C.L.A. He received the M.A. and Ph.D. in economics from Northwestern University in Chicago. His extensive writings on land use have been published in professional and trade journals, and from January to June 1973, he was a member of the South Regional California Coastal Commission.

A. Dan Tarlock is professor of law at Indiana University, Bloomington, specializing in administrative, property, land use and natural resources law. He was educated at Stanford University where he holds the A.B. and L.L.B. He has taught at the Universities of Kentucky, Pennsylvania, and Southern California. He has authored numerous law review articles and two law school casebooks and is at work on a set of land use materials and a federally sponsored study of the allocation of property rights in geothermal energy.

About the Editor

Bernard H. Siegan is Distinguished Professor of Law at the University of San Diego School of Law. He writes a weekly syndicated newspaper column and has authored *Land Use Without Zoning* and *Other People's Property* (both published by D. C. Heath & Co.), along with a multitude of articles and monographs on zoning, land use and urban planning, which have appeared in professional journals and other publications. Professor Siegan received the J.D. degree from the University of Chicago School of Law and was in private practice for many years.